THE BIGGER PICTURE

THE BIGGER PICTURE

Explanations from the Company of Heaven

PATRICIA COTA-ROBLES

Printed in the United States of America

First Printing, 2019

ISBN-13: 978-1-939116-89-5 print edition
ISBN-13: 978-1-939116-90-1 eBook edition

Waterside Productions
2055 Oxford Ave
Cardiff, CA 92007
www.waterside.com

TABLE OF CONTENTS

Introduction New Beginnings xi

Weekly Vlogs xix

Preface. xxi

(Vlog 1) The First Step 1

(Vlog 2) How to Transmute Negativity into Light. 6

(Vlog 3) Healing Our Painful Polarization 11

(Vlog 4) How Did We Create Such a
        Patriarchal Society? 15

(Vlog 5) The Return of the Divine Feminine 21

(Vlog 6) Reconnecting With Your Higher Self 26

(Vlog 7) Should I Invoke the Light on Behalf
        of My Loved Ones? 30

(Vlog 8) Invoking the Violet Flame 34

(Vlog 9) Downloading the Patterns of
        Perfection for the New Earth 38

(Vlog 10) Are You Empowering Your
        Pain and Suffering? 42

(Vlog 11) The Positive Effects of the
        Law of the Circle. 48

(Vlog 12) Reversing the Negative Effects of
        the Law of the Circle 54

(Vlog 13) When Will We See Progress? 59

(Vlog 14) Transcending Your Human Ego 65

(Vlog 15) What is Your Purpose on Earth? 71

(Vlog 16) Why is This Such a Critical Time on Earth? . 76

(Vlog 17) A Contingency Plan for Earth. 82

(Vlog 18) Some Clarity About This Time
            and the Term "New Age" 88

(Vlog 19) How Did We Create Such Divisive
            World Religions?. 94

(Vlog 20) The Avatars of the Piscean Age
            Jesus and Mary Magdalene 98

(Vlog 21) The True Purpose of Jesus'
            Crucifixion and Resurrection 104

(Vlog 22) How Did Jesus' and Mary
            Magdalene's Message Become so
            Misconstrued? 110

(Vlog 23) The Next Phase of the Divine Plan 117

(Vlog 24) Abundance and Eternal Peace
            are Part of Our Covenant with God 124

(Vlog 25) Transmuting Poverty Consciousness 130

(Vlog 26) Reclaiming Our Covenant with God 134

(Vlog 27) The Key to Financial Freedom 138

(Vlog 28) Cocreating Abundance 144

(Vlog 29) Loving All Life Free 149

(Vlog 30) You Are Powerful Beyond Your Knowing. . .154

(Vlog 31) You Are Here to Make a Difference. 160

(Vlog 32) The Power of the Spoken Word. 164

(Vlog 33) Ways to Empower Your Lightwork 168

(Vlog 34) Manifesting Change and
            Your New Life Path 172

(Vlog 35) Be a Peace Commanding Presence. 177

(Vlog 36) Expanding the Divinity in
            Your Heart Flame 182

(Vlog 37) The Next Step in Expanding
            Your Heart Flame 187

(Vlog 38) Our Lightwork is Making a Difference. . . .191

(Vlog 39) I Am Ascending Into My I am Presence 196

(Vlog 40) We Are Being Called to a Higher Service . . .201

(Vlog 41) Remembering Our Heart Commitment 206

(Vlog 42) What is Transfiguring Divine Love? 212

(Vlog 43) Invoking the Newly Empowered
        Flame of Transfiguring Divine Love 217

(Vlog 44) Empowering Our Planetary Grid
        of Divine Love 222

(Vlog 45) A Quantum Shift Toward
        Christ Consciousness 227

(Vlog 46) Who Are Our Asleep and
        Recalcitrant Sisters and Brothers? 233

(Vlog 47) Ascending Off of the Wheel of Karma. . . .239

(Vlog 48) Who Are the Millennials
        and the Children? 244

(Vlog 49) What Awakening the Millennials and
        the Children Will Mean for All of Us. . . .248

(Vlog 50) Activating the Consciousness Codes
        of the Millennials and the Children 253

(Vlog 51) If the Millennials and the Children
        Are Karma Free Why Are So Many
        of Them Suffering? 259

(Vlog 52) Transforming Our Earthly Bodies 266

(Vlog 53) Our Responsibility in Transforming
        Our Earthly Bodies 272

(Vlog 54) Awakening Our Dormant
        Elemental Vortices. 278

(Vlog 55) The Resurrection Flame a
        Gift from on High 285

(Vlog 56) Ressurecting the Immaculate
        Concept of Our Divine Missions 291

(Vlog 57) Clarity About Our
        Physical Transformation 296

(Vlog 58) Activating New Strands of Dna 301

(Vlog 59) Our Body Elemental is Initiated
        Into the 5th Dimension 306

(Vlog 60) The Mystical Month of May 312

(Vlog 61) Mother Mary and the Mystical
        Month of May 316

(Vlog 62) A Blessing for Humanity
        from Mother Mary. 323

(Vlog 63) Healing Our Contaminated
        Bodies With the Violet Flame. 327

(Vlog 64) Journey Into Mother Mary's Temple
        of the Immaculate Heart 333

(Vlog 65) Integrating Our Recalibrated Heart Flame .339

(Vlog 66) Purifying Humanity and Mother Earth . . .344

(Vlog 67) A Quantum Shift During
        the June Solstice 350

(Vlog 68) The 12 Aspects of Deity Associated
        With the New Earth 356

(Vlog 69) Answers About Humanity's
        Physical Transformation 362

(Vlog 70) Preparation for This Cosmic Moment 368

(Vlog 71) The Next Phase of Our
        Physical Transformation 374

(Vlog 72) Activating Our 5th-Dimensional
        Solar Spine and Twelve Solar Chakras . . .379

(Vlog 73) Activating Our 5th-Dimensional
        Crystalline Solar Light Bodies 388

(Vlog 74) Final Critical Steps of Preparation 395

(Vlog 75) Be Here Now! 402

(Vlog 76) Infinite Gratitude from Our
        Father-Mother God and the Company
        of Heaven 413

(Vlog 77) Empowering the Patterns of
        Perfection for the New Earth 417
(Vlog 78) Victory is Ours! 422
(Vlog 79) Cleansing the Psychic Astral Realm 429
(Vlog 80) Remembering the Oneness of All Life 434
(Vlog 81) An Unprecedented Healing from
        Mother Mary and Pallas Athena 439
(Vlog 82) A Rare Opportunity for the
        Recalcitrant Souls 444
(Vlog 83) Activation of the Consciousness Codes
        Within the Millennials and the Children . 447

About the Author Patricia Cota-Robles 453

INTRODUCTION
NEW BEGINNINGS

Hi Precious Heart, I am Patricia Cota-Robles and I want to thank you for volunteering to be born during this auspicious time on Planet Earth. You may not realize this but you are powerful beyond your knowing. You have come to Earth to assist with an essential facet of God's Divine Plan and the time for you to begin fulfilling your purpose and reason for being is NOW.

Whether or not you are aware of it on a conscious level, you have been preparing for lifetimes to be the Open Door for the Light of God during this critical phase of Humanity's Ascension process. You already have within the Divinity of your Heart Flame everything you need to know in order to God Victoriously accomplish whatever it is you have volunteered to do. All that is remaining is for you to tap into that sacred knowledge, so that you will remember the *BIGGER PICTURE* of who you are and why you are here. That is precisely why our Father-Mother God and the Company of Heaven have revealed the vitally important information I am sharing in this book titled "*The Bigger Picture.*"

To initiate within your Heart Flame the process of remembering the bigger picture of who you are and why you are here, our Father-Mother God asked me to begin by sharing with you a quote. The Divine Intention of this quote is to awaken within you a profound TRUTH:

The Truth About YOU
A Quote from our Father-Mother God

"You are a precious and Beloved Child of God. Your unique Golden Thread of Life confirms your Divinity and reveals the reality that you are an essential part of Earth's Ascension in the Light. This knowing will renew your faith in yourself and will remind you that you are a priceless Human Being. Once this realization truly registers in your heart and your conscious mind you will never again say, 'What good could I possibly achieve? What value am I? What difference will one soul make?' You will recognize those words to be a sacrilege.

"We are your Father-Mother God. We created you and we have chosen to express some beautiful manifestation of Life through you. You are destined to fulfill a portion of the glorious Divine Plan unfolding on Planet Earth. Now is the time for you to release the unique perfume and music of your Being to bless all Life. The purity of your individual fragrance and keynote is unlike any other ever released by the evolving Sons and Daughters of God. Something sacred is hidden within your Being that has never been known by another. It is an exquisite expression of Life which your I AM Presence alone can externalize. It is time for you to accept this Divine Truth. It is time for you to stand revealed as your mighty I AM Presence grown to full stature.

And so it is."

The Divinity within your Heart Flame which is your I AM Presence, has magnetized the information in this book into your sphere of awareness. It may seem as though you were drawn to *The Bigger Picture* by chance, but that is not the case. Your I AM Presence drew your attention to this book, so that you will have greater clarity and understanding about the events that are surfacing in your life and on the planet. Your I AM Presence wants you to have this sacred knowledge so that you will remember the Divine Plan that you have volunteered to fulfill on Earth. Then you will know that you have the ability to transmute into Light the negative things that are happening in your life and around the world. You will also realize, beyond a shadow of a doubt, that you have the ability to cocreate the patterns of Divine Love, Oneness and Reverence for ALL Life that are destined to manifest on the New Earth.

The negativity surfacing on Earth at this time is a result of the human miscreations that Humanity either deliberately or inadvertently created through thoughts, words, feelings and actions that were not based in Love. This negativity may have been created in this lifetime or in the myriad other lifetimes we have had on this planet, but that is irrelevant. All that matters is that those challenging thoughtforms and conditions be transmuted back into Light. This will clear the way for the tangible manifestation of the patterns of Divine Love, Oneness and Reverence for ALL Life associated with the 5th-Dimensional New Earth.

The Beings of Light in the Realms of Illumined Truth

The enlightening information in this book is being given to Humanity by our Father-Mother God and the Beings of Light in the Realms of Illumined Truth. These are our sisters and brothers, Sons and Daughters of God just like you and me, but these Beings of Light have evolved to a much higher level of consciousness. They are like college professors compared to you and me who are more like kindergarten students in the overall scheme of things. These Beings are selfless Messengers of our Father-Mother God. They have come through the veil to meet us halfway due to the urgency of the hour. They are communicating with Humanity through open heart and mind telepathic communication.

We were always supposed to have access to this assistance and this guidance from On High. However, when we fell into the dense and discordant frequencies of separation and duality aeons ago, we lost our way and the ability to communicate with our I AM Presence. Once that occurred, we could no longer reach up in consciousness or receive guidance from the Realms of Illumined Truth. Since that fateful time, we have been *"weeping and wailing through our valley of tears"* struggling through trial and error to find our way back to our I AM Presence and the Beings of Light.

We have been striving in vain to accomplish our Divine Plans for millennia, but now everything has changed. At long last, Humanity is awakening. People everywhere are beginning to open their hearts and minds as they listen for *"the still small voice"* of their I AM Presence. The Beings of Light are standing in readiness awaiting our invitation to guide us through this critical phase of Humanity's Ascension process. These precious Ones are available to assist every single person. All we have to do to receive their guidance is lift up in consciousness and reconnect with our I AM Presence and the Realms of Illumined Truth.

These Beings of Light, whom I often refer to as the Company of Heaven, have the ability to help us successfully reverse the adverse effects of our fall from Grace so that we can accomplish our Divine Plans. As I introduce you to our

Heavenly Sisters and Brothers, please open your heart and feel the Infinite Gratitude and Divine Love they are breathing into your Heart Flame in appreciation for the opportunity to connect with you now on a conscious level through your I AM Presence.

The Company of Heaven consists first and foremost of the all-encompassing Presence of our omniscient, omnipotent, omnipresent Father-Mother God, the Cosmic I AM, All That Is. This is the Divine Presence from which every atomic and subatomic particle and wave of Life throughout the whole of Creation was birthed. It is within the Divine Matrix of our Father-Mother God's Infinite Body that all Life lives, moves, breathes and has its being.

All of the rest of the Company of Heaven are Sons and Daughters of our Father-Mother God just like you and me. The only difference is that they have completed their lessons of becoming cocreators with our Father-Mother God. They are now serving in the Higher Realms of Light assisting the Sons and Daughters of God on Earth and in other systems of worlds to complete our lessons of becoming cocreators with our God Parents.

The Beings of Light within the Company of Heaven are known through all Creation by various titles depending on their level of evolution and their service to Life. They are known as: Solar Logos, Cosmic Beings, Galactic Beings, Elohim, Directors of the Elements, Crowns, Thrones, Principalities, Archangels, Seraphim, Cherubim, and all graded Orders of Angels. They are Ascended Masters, the Galactic Federation of Light, the Elemental Kingdom and the I AM Presence of every Son and Daughter of God.

During this critical moment in Earth's Ascension process, all of these Beings of Light are awaiting Humanity's heart call and our invitation for them to assist us any way they can. They are only allowed to intervene in our lives in ways that are perfectly aligned with our Divine Plans and that reflect the highest good for all concerned. The Company of Heaven will not interfere with our free will. We must invite them and give them permission to help us. Then, with the cooperation of our I AM Presence, they will guide us unerringly to the most viable solutions and the most effective actions necessary to accomplish our goals.

The information that is being given to Humanity at this time by the Beings of Light in the Realms of Illumined Truth is designed to enhance what we already know. It is not intended to dispute our present belief systems or to tell us that what we believe is wrong. We have all been guided by our I AM Presence through the lessons and learning experiences we needed in order to bring us to this point in our evolutionary process. Now it is time for all of us to take the next step.

The Divine Intent of this sacred knowledge is to give us greater clarity and understanding so that we will be able to lift our heads above the surfacing chaos and see the BIGGER PICTURE. All of the information that I am sharing in this book is from the Beings of Light in the Realms of Illumined Truth. Even having said that, I do not ever want you to accept something as Truth just because someone told you it is true. I would like for you to read this book as food for thought. Then take the information into the Divinity of your Heart Flame and ask your I AM Presence to reveal to you the Truth contained within the pages of this book. Listen to your inner guidance and you will learn how you can utilize this information to help you fulfill your Divine Plan.

Anything that does not resonate as Truth for you just let it go. If I am sharing something that is important for you to know in order for you to fulfill your Divine Plan, but it does not resonate as Truth for you just yet, be patient. You can be sure that your I AM Presence will keep presenting that information to you in gentle and loving ways over and over again until it resonates as Truth in your heart.

This is a new beginning, and the information in this book has come to you from On High. It was written through the unified efforts of Heaven and Earth and will pave the way for a new level of awakening within the heart and mind of anyone who is open to receiving this sacred knowledge.

I AM deeply honored to share this information with you. Together, we will fulfill our Divine Plans. In Oneness and with Divine Love and Reverence for ALL Life we will assist Mother Earth and ALL Life evolving upon her into the full embrace of the New Earth.

God Bless you, for your willingness to BE the "*Open Door that no one can shut.*" The Light of God that is now flowing into the Mental and Emotional Strata of Earth is blessing all Life on this planet through your Heart Flame. As you contemplate that Truth remember...

"*The Light of God is ALWYS Victorious and YOU are that Light.*" And so it is.

WEEKLY VLOGS

For each of the 83 sharings in this book THE BIGGER PICTURE there is a short video posted on our website www.eraofpeace.org under the title Weekly Vlogs.

PREFACE

The Company of Heaven is reiterating that ALL of the activities of Light that have been given to Humanity through our Weekly Vlogs, our Free Seminars, our Monthly Newsletters and this book, The Bigger Picture, have been encoded in the *Eternal Moment of NOW*. This means these powerful opportunities from the Heavenly Realms are permanently available through all time frames and dimensions. On a very practical level, ALL of the benefits from these amazing Gifts from On High are available to every single person no matter when he or she chooses to participate in them.

Regardless of how many times you participate in any of these activities of Light, your I AM Presence and the Company of Heaven will expand the benefits you receive one thousand fold. So pay attention to which activities of Light resonate most powerfully within you. Then ask your I AM Presence if it would enhance your Divine Plan for you to repeat that activity of Light or if your part in that particular activity is complete. Your I AM Presence will answer you through an intuitive inner knowing within the Divinity of your Heart Flame.

If you feel inspired to repeat a specific activity of Light, the Company of Heaven is encouraging you to do so. They said it will greatly benefit all of us to repeat any activity of Light we resonate with until we feel an inner sense of completion. Remember, our awakening is a unique and individual process. Sometimes we will be guided to repeat an activity one or two times before we feel a sense of completion. Other times we may be prompted to repeat an activity for a few weeks or months before it feels complete. It also happens that sometimes we feel complete with a particular activity of Light and then a few months or even years later we will be inspired to repeat it again. So listen to that intuitive inner guidance from your I AM Presence and you will know unerringly what is appropriate for you.

The myriad Gifts from our Father-Mother God and the Beings of Light in the Realms of Illumined Truth that are being revealed through our celestial sharings *will never become outdated or obsolete.* Even though the Company of Heaven may be referring to a specific time frame or date that has already past, that does not mean that you have missed the opportunity to benefit from the activity of Light they are talking about.

With every sharing we deliberately connect with the I AM Presence of every person on Earth and unite with the Love in their Heart Flame. We are able to do this because we are One and there is no separation. Consequently, every man, woman and child receives some benefit from the activities of Light being presented in our Weekly Vlogs, our Free Seminars, our Monthly Newsletters and our book The Bigger Picture. This is true whether or not the person is consciously aware of the blessings he or she is receiving from On High through their I AM Presence.

The Beings of Light want us to clearly understand, however, that when we participate on a conscious level in the activities of Light they are presenting to us, the benefits we are able to receive from our I AM Presence expand

exponentially. In order to receive that greatly intensified Gift of Heavenly Assistance, all we have to do is open
our heart and be willing to participate in the activities of
Light being given to us by our Father-Mother God and the
Company of Heaven.

With every celestial sharing you focus your attention
on your I AM Presence automatically aligns you within the
Eternal Moment of Now. This enables you to instantaneously
receive the maximum benefit from our Father-Mother God,
the Company of Heaven and the activity of Light you are
participating in.

1

THE FIRST STEP

When we see so many challenging things taking place around the world, it is obvious that this is a very confusing and sometimes frightening time. In many instances, it looks and feels like no matter how hard we try things seem to be getting worse. That is very disheartening and many people feel hopeless and helpless when confronted with all of the adversity occurring on this planet.

What we are learning, however, from the Beings of Light in the Realms of Illumined Truth, is that our interpretation of what we are witnessing in the outer world is inaccurate. Things are not getting worse. It is just that we have not been able to see the bigger picture of what is happening. We have been judging what is taking place in our lives and the world by outer appearances, but that is only a small fraction of what is actually occurring.

If we want to comprehend the bigger picture we must raise the focus of our attention above the chaos in our lives. Once we transcend the discordant frequencies of our human miscreations, we can clearly hear *"the still small voice"* pulsating within the Divinity of our heart. This is the voice of our God Self, that part of us that is known in the Realms of Truth as our I AM Presence. This is the part of us that is created in God's Image. It is the part of us that is One with the all-encompassing Presence of our Father-Mother God, the Cosmic I AM, All That Is.

When we listen to the inner guidance of our I AM Presence, we begin to *"see with new eyes and hear with new ears."* In the sacred knowledge revealed in this book, the Company of Heaven will help all of us learn how to do just that.

Even though the information being shared in this book may seem familiar to you, the Earth and ALL Life evolving upon her have passed through an unprecedented shift of energy, vibration and consciousness since the birth of the New Earth, which took place on December 21st and 22nd in 2012. That means that every person on this planet is now able to experience these Truths from a higher level of consciousness than ever before.

There will also be people for whom this information will seem brand new. Some of those people will be willing to accept this sacred knowledge as a possibility, but others may think it is too improbable to be true. If you are one of those people, the Beings of Light are lovingly encouraging you to be patient. This information is not new for you. It is just that you have forgotten. Know that your I AM Presence has magnetized this information into your sphere of awareness at this critical time to help you remember, so that you will be both able and willing to fulfill your Divine Plan.

The Company of Heaven is asking each and every one of us to open our heart and mind as we assimilate the information being shared in this book. As we reach, ever higher, into the Realms of Illumined Truth, we will easily remember who we are and why we are on Earth at this time. Then we will see the bigger picture of the Divine Plan that is unfolding on Earth day by day and finally everything will begin to make sense.

Once we fully comprehend the bigger picture, we will no longer feel helpless or hopeless. On the Contrary, we will be elated by the opportunity that is being presented to each of us that will allow us to participate in transmuting back into Light the painful things that are surfacing all over the planet. We will realize that *we* are instrumental in the process of cocreating the patterns of perfection for the New Earth tangibly in the lives of all Humanity. These are the exquisite patterns that reflect Divine Love, the Oneness of ALL Life, Eternal Peace and God's Infinite Abundance.

So let's begin. Why does it seem as though things are getting worse on this planet?

This phenomenon is happening because there is an unprecedented awakening taking place within the hearts and minds of Humanity. People everywhere are beginning to remember that they are here for a reason and that they have an important purpose for being on Earth at this time. Some of the people may not yet remember the specifics of this inner knowing on a conscious level, but that inner prompting is causing them to go within and to seek answers.

When a person focuses on the Divinity within their heart and asks for guidance and answers, this gives their I AM Presence permission to intervene in their life in powerful ways. When this happens, the person begins to intuitively know that by reaching out to God or a Higher Power, in whatever way resonates in their heart, they will receive the answers they are seeking.

We have all heard the statements from On High,

"Ask and you shall receive."
"Knock and the door will be opened."
*"Seek ye first the Kingdom of Heaven within
and all else will be revealed to you."*

These are not just lofty platitudes or religious rhetoric. They are profound Truths that apply to each and every one of us regardless of our beliefs.

Every single day, the awakening taking place at this time is inspiring literally billions of people to reach out to God or a Higher Power in one way or another. These heartfelt pleas ask for Divine assistance and as they are made the Light of God flows into the lives of billions of people on this planet. Humanity's pleas also invoke the Light of God into the painful situations and conditions manifesting everywhere on Earth. Our prayers and invocations are always heard and they are always answered whether we realize it or not.

As the Light of God flows into the person's life who is asking for assistance, their I AM Presence receives that Light and breathes it through the person's Heart Flame into the physical plane. The Light then flows into everything that conflicts with that Light and pushes it to the surface to be healed and transmuted back into its original perfection. Once that negativity is cleared, then the Light of God will fulfill the highest good of whatever the person is requesting.

The reason things seem to be getting worse is because the Light of God is exponentially increasing on this planet day by day, and it is pushing everything that conflicts with that Light to the surface. That is necessary so that awakening Humanity can heal and transmute our human miscreations, thus, clearing the way for the patterns of perfection that we are all destined to cocreate on the New Earth.

This is the time that was Biblically referred to as,

"The time of screaming and the gnashing of teeth."

That is because when we look at the outer world we can easily see the horrific negativity being pushed to the surface to be healed and transmuted back into Light. This makes it looks like things are getting worse, but what we cannot see is the incredible Light of God that is pushing those things to the surface.

The important thing for us to know is that this greatly intensified purging would not be occurring at this pace if it were going to cause more harm than good. This accelerated purging is happening because awakened Humanity is remembering that we are the ones who have either deliberately or inadvertently miscreated these painful things sometime during our Earthly sojourns. Consequently, we are the ones who are responsible for transmuting these gross mutations back into Light before we can cocreate the lives we have been longing for since our fall from Grace aeons ago.

We have agreed to experience the intensity of this purging process through our I AM Presence, because we know that the faster the negativity surfaces, the sooner we will be able to transmute it back into Light. Then the way will be cleared so that we can cocreate the patterns of perfection for the New Earth tangibly in our lives.

Dear One, to begin your healing process ask your I AM Presence to flood Love and Forgiveness into every single thing in your life that is causing pain or suffering of any kind. Then ask for that person, place, condition or thing to be held in the full embrace of our Father-Mother God's Infinite Perfection until it is healed and transmuted back into Light.

In the next chapter I will share with you information about a powerful Gift of Light from our Father-Mother God that is designed to help Humanity transmute the surfacing negativity at a greatly accelerated pace.

God Bless You, Dear One, I wish you Divine Love, Forgiveness and Enlightenment.

2

HOW TO TRANSMUTE
NEGATIVITY INTO LIGHT

By looking only at outer-world appearances, it is easy to come to the erroneous conclusion that things are getting worse on this planet. That is an illusion. In fact, nothing could be further from the Truth.

The reason it looks like things are getting worse is because we are not perceiving the bigger picture. In Truth, the reason the chaos in our lives seems to be increasing is because the Light of God is intensifying on Earth, and everything that conflicts with that Light is being pushed to the surface to be healed and transmuted back into its original perfection.

Everything manifesting in the physical plane of Earth that is causing pain or suffering of any kind is a *human miscreation*. There is not a single electron of precious life energy that is breathed forth from the heart of our Father-Mother God that is less than God's Infinite Perfection which means, literally, Heaven on Earth.

This includes Humanity's Life Force which is the unformed primal Light substance that flows into our body on electrical currents that pass through our chakra system and our acupuncture meridians. These electrical impulses activate our brain and beat our heart. We can see these electrical impulses flowing through the heart and brain monitors of people who are in the hospital.

When a person's Life Force is withdrawn from their body in the process we refer to as "*death*", these electrical impulses stop and the monitors go flat indicating that the person is no longer in that physical body. We cannot exist on Earth without the constant flow of our Life Force from our Father-Mother God.

When we receive our Life Force from God, it is always filled with Divine Light and it is pulsating with God's Infinite Perfection. Our Life Force enters our Crown Chakra at the top of our head and descends into the Divinity in our Heart Flame. There, our I AM Presence stamps this unformed primal Light substance with our own unique electronic Light pattern. The Life Force utilized by every Son and Daughter of God is stamped with his or her individual electronic Light pattern lifetime after lifetime.

No two people have the same Light pattern. This pattern is given to each of us at our inception when we are breathed forth from the Core of Creation by our God Parents. This is how the Universe knows what energy belongs to whom. The energy stamped with our unique electronic Light pattern flows out from us with every thought, feeling, word and action. Then it is magnetized back to the *identical* Light pattern which is pulsating within our Heart Flame. This is how the Law of the Circle is immaculately accomplished.

Once our I AM Presence has stamped the electronic Light substance of our Life Force with our individual pattern, then that Gift of Life is available for us to use in any way we choose. Through our freewill choices and our creative faculties of thought and feeling, every moment of every day, we are sending forth our Life Force qualified with whatever our frame of mind or emotional state happens to be at the time. We can use our Life Force any way we choose, but the important thing for us to remember is that *we are responsible for how we use our Gift of Life.*

If we have taken our precious Life Force and misqualified it into gross mutations resulting in pain and suffering for ourselves or any other part of Life, then that energy will return to us to be healed and transmuted back into its original perfection. If we fail to do that, the Universe will keep returning that negatively qualified energy to us lifetime after lifetime until we finally transmute it back into Light.

This is exactly what is happening in the unprecedented purging that Humanity is experiencing at this time. We have birthed the New Earth and the patterns of perfection associated with the New Earth are Divine Love, Oneness, Reverence for All Life, Eternal Peace and God's Infinite Abundance. In order for us to experience those wonderful things, we must first transmute back into Light our human miscreations and everything that conflicts with those patterns for the New Earth.

Everything that is being pushed to the surface at this time is the antithesis of the patterns for the New Earth. Everywhere we look we see evidence of our miscreations in the form poverty, disease, hate, war, greed, corruption, ignorance, the abuse of power and every other form of pain or suffering occurring on Earth. I know that the magnitude of those things seems overwhelming, but we have been given a powerful Gift from On High that will help us through this challenging time.

Our Father-Mother God have given us a powerful tool that will help us move through this purging process at warp speed. This tool will help us transmute literally lifetimes worth of negativity in what will be perceived as "*the twinkling of an eye*" compared to the aeons of time we have been buried in our painful miscreations.

This powerful tool is a Gift of Light that reflects the perfect balance of our Father God's Blue Flame of Divine Will, Power, Protection and Authority, and our Mother God's, the Holy Spirit's, Pink Flame of Transfiguring Divine Love, Oneness, Reverence for Life and Adoration. This Gift of Light is known throughout all Creation as "*The Violet Flame of God's Infinite Perfection.*"

This is the most powerful frequency of Light in all Creation for transmuting negativity back into Light. When the Violet Flame of God's Infinite Perfection is invoked through a person's I AM Presence, it will flow through their Heart Flame and enter the Core of Purity in every electron of the human miscreations the person is asking to be healed and transmuted back into Light. Amazingly, this Core of Purity still exists within the electrons of even Humanity's grossest mutations and miscreations.

Once the Violet Flame enters the Core of Purity it activates the original Divine Potential encoded within that precious electronic Light substance. As the atomic and sub-atomic particles and waves of Life existing in those painful mutations are accelerated into higher frequencies of Light, our human miscreations are cast into the Violet Flame and transmuted back into their original perfection.

Every time we invoke this powerful Violet Flame from our Father-Mother God, we transmute tons of our human miscreations. It is important for us to "*keep on keeping on*" every day until this purging process is complete and we are experiencing the heart-based patterns of the New Earth

The Violet Flame of God's Infinite Perfection is powerful beyond our knowing. Please join me now and together we will invoke this Sacred Fire to heal and transmute into Light the negativity being pushed to the surface in our lives and in the lives of all Humanity. And we begin.

Violet Flame Invocation

I AM my I AM Presence and I AM One with the I AM Presence of ALL Humanity. As one voice, one breath, one heartbeat, and one energy, vibration and consciousness of pure Divine Love we invoke the most intensified frequencies of the 5th-Dimensional Crystalline Solar Violet Flame of God's Infinite Perfection that Cosmic Law will allow.

We invoke the Company of Heaven and the Legions of 5th-Dimensional Violet Fire Archangels. Blessed Ones, we ask that you blaze, blaze, blaze the Violet Flame of God's Infinite Perfection with the power and might of a thousand Suns in, through and around every thought, feeling, word, action, memory and belief that Humanity has ever expressed in any time frame or dimension, both known and unknown, that is reflecting anything less than Heaven on Earth.

Transmute this energy cause, core, effect, record and memory back into its original perfection and seal it in an invincible forcefield of Divine Love, Eternal Peace and God's Infinite Abundance.

We accept that this activity of Light is being God Victoriously accomplished even as we call. We also accept and know that this powerful Violet Flame is increasing daily and hourly, moment by moment, with every breath we take until this sweet Earth and all her Life have Ascended into the 5th-Dimensional Realms of Light on the New Earth where Divine Love, Oneness, Reverence for All Life, Eternal Peace and God's Infinite Abundance are a tangible reality. And so it is.

3

HEALING OUR PAINFUL POLARIZATION

At this time, Humanity is experiencing painful polarization that needs to be healed. All we have to do is watch the news to see that people all over the world are as polarized as they have ever been. In fact, it seems like every day there is more hatred and fear being expressed through social media and a deeper level of incivility and disrespect for each other than we have known in the past. It is time for this self-destructive behavior to stop.

In the previous chapter we talked about the fact that people everywhere are awakening at an accelerated pace causing the Light of God to intensify on Earth. This Light is pushing everything that conflicts with the Light to the surface. This is why it appears as though Humanity's polarization is getting worse.

This influx of Divine Light is also increasing Humanity's vibrations. This is helping people to raise their heads above the negativity that is surfacing to be healed. Once we get our heads above the mud puddle of our human miscreations our I AM Presence is able to communicate with us much more easily.

The first thing our I AM Presence reveals to us when we begin to awaken is that we are *not* our fear-based human ego. Our ego is a fragmented part of our consciousness that is fighting tooth and nail just to survive in this chaotic world. We are a Beloved Son or Daughter of God and ALL that our Father-Mother God have is our Divine Birthright. I know that may sound too good to be true, but it is true. The only reason it is difficult for people to remember that Truth is because Humanity has been accepting for millennia the fallacy that separation and duality are real.

The belief that we are separate from each other has caused more problems than just about anything else. This erroneous belief gave our fear-based human ego the idea that whatever it needed to do to get what it wanted was okay. This self-centered consciousness is the basis of Humanity's "*dog-eat-dog*" and "*looking out for number one*" attitude.

As time progressed, we fell into the dense frequencies of our human miscreations and lost the awareness of our I AM Presence. Our ego started believing that our physical body is all that we are and that the physical plane is all that exists. When that happened, our fragmented ego started believing that its very purpose and reason for being was to gratify our physical senses. Our ego decided that even if it needed to lie, steal, cheat or kill to accomplish that self-obsessed goal of instant gratification that would be okay.

With that fateful decision, the horrific human miscreations of poverty, greed, corruption, violence, the abuse of power, oppression, hatred, selfishness, prejudice, pollution, disease, ignorance, and every other painful experience began manifesting on this planet.

Now, everything has changed. Humanity is awakening and our fallen human egos no longer have the ability to manipulate and control us the way they used to. We are beginning to hear the inner voice and to receive the Divine Guidance of our I AM Presence once again. From deep within the recesses of our heart, we are remembering profound Truths that will empower each of us to reverse the adverse affects of our human ego's distorted perception and painful miscreations.

The next vitally important thing our I AM Presence wants us to remember is that *we are One* and that there is no separation. This means quite literally that there is no such thing as *"us and them."* I know for many people that concept just boggles the mind. For others, the Oneness of Life seems like a sweet sentiment, but they do not comprehend the magnitude of what that profound Truth really means.

We are One means that every single atomic and subatomic particle and wave of Life throughout the whole of Creation is interrelated, interconnected and interdependent. Every miniscule expression of Life that has ever been breathed forth from the heart of our Father-Mother God lives, moves, breathes and has its Being in the all-encompassing Divine Matrix of our Father-Mother God's Body.

The astonishing thing that we have forgotten about the fact that we are One with all Life, is that every thought, feeling, word or action we express, day by day with every breath we take, affects every single facet of Life in our Father-Mother God's Divine Matrix. This means that depending on our frame of mind, daily and hourly, we are either adding to the Light of the world or we are adding to the pain and suffering. Just imagine.

When the masses of Humanity remember what *we are One* really means, they will understand that for a person to inflict harm on any person, place, condition or thing for their own personal gain, it is not only ludicrous, it is self destructive. With this awareness, no one will be willing to deliberately wreak the havoc in his or her own life that will result from such negative behavior.

When the reality that we are One resonates in every person's heart they will realize that every thought, feeling, word or action they express that is based in Divine Love, Oneness and Reverence for ALL Life will bless all Life and greatly enhance the Love and Harmony in their own life.

We are not the victims of circumstance. We are the cocreators of our lives. If we do not like the way things are going, by remembering that we are Beloved Sons and Daughters of God and that we are One with all Life, we can change our course of action. Then we will create a new life for ourselves based in Love, Oneness, Reverence for ALL Life and a heartfelt desire for the highest good for all concerned.

To begin this transformation within yourself make the heart commitment to focus on the Divinity within the Heart Flame of every person on Earth. Anything a person does that is not heart-based, simply ask their I AM Presence to take control of their thoughts, feelings, words and actions and guide them to their highest good. Then blaze the Violet Flame of God's Infinite Perfection in, through and around anything they may have done that conflicts with the Divinity pulsating in their heart.

God Bless You, Dear One, and may the Oneness of ALL Life be your true inner knowing.

4

How Did We Create Such a Patriarchal Society?

The Company of Heaven is revealing to us now just how we inadvertently created such a dysfunctional patriarchal society.

For millennia women have been relegated to the position of second class citizens. This is true in most religions and in secular societies around the world. This inequality affects women adversely in all walks of life including the work place, leadership roles and many times even in personal relationships.

In my quest for answers, whenever I asked knowledgeable people in the outer world why this was the case I often got the reflex response, "*It is because Eve ate that darned apple.*" Men have been blaming our Earthly woes on one woman's transgression for literally aeons of time. In many instances, men have felt obligated to suppress women and to keep us in our place ever since.

Now, with the guidance of the Company of Heaven we are learning and remembering what really caused this horrific imbalance between men and women.

In the Beginning

In the beginning, when we were first breathed forth from the Core of Creation, our Father-Mother God anchored the perfect balance of the masculine and feminine polarities of God within each of us. First our Father God anchored the masculine polarity within the left hemisphere of our brain. This polarity manifests as a *sapphire blue ray* of Light that pulsates with the masculine qualities of Divine Will, Power, Illumined Faith, Protection, and God's First Cause of Perfection. After our Father God's blue ray of Light activated our rational, logical left-brain hemisphere, it awakened the power center within our Throat Chakra. Then this Light was anchored in our heart as a powerful blue plume of Sacred Fire.

Next, our Mother God anchored the feminine polarity of God within the right hemisphere of our brain. This polarity manifests as a *crystalline pink ray* of Light that pulsates with the feminine qualities of Transfiguring Divine Love, Oneness, Reverence for Life, and the Sacred Fire Breath of the Holy Spirit. After our Mother God's pink ray of Light activated our creative, intuitive right-brain hemisphere, it awakened the Love center within our Heart Chakra. Then this ray of Light was anchored in our heart as a powerful pink plume of Sacred Fire.

Once the Blue Flame of our Father God's Power and the Pink Flame of our Mother God's Love were perfectly balanced in the right and left hemispheres of our brain and in our heart, the two Flames merged into a magnificent Violet Flame. This Violet Flame then blazed up from our heart into our physical brain structure activating our spiritual brain centers. These centers are associated with our pineal, pituitary, and hypothalamus glands, and the ganglionic center at the base of our brain.

Once the activation of our spiritual brain centers was complete, our Crown Chakra which is on the top of our head opened to full breadth. This allowed the enlightened consciousness of our I AM Presence which is known as Christ Consciousness to begin flowing through our pineal gland into our mental and emotional bodies. In the enlightened state of Christ Consciousness, we were fully aware of our Father-Mother God, the Company of Heaven, and our I AM Presence. In this natural state of awakened consciousness, we were able to easily communicate with the entire Company of Heaven through open heart and mind telepathic communication.

Christ Consciousness is our Divine Birthright as Sons and Daughters of God. It manifests as a *yellow-gold ray* of Light that pulsates with the Divine Qualities of Enlightenment, Wisdom and Illumination. Once our Crown Chakra was open to full breadth and we began to receive the flow of Christ Consciousness from our I AM Presence, that ray of Light was anchored in our heart as a powerful yellow-gold plume of Sacred Fire.

That event completed the physical manifestation of our Heart Flame which is known through all creation as the Immortal Victorious Threefold Flame. These three Flames—the Blue Flame of our Father God's Power, the Pink Flame of our Mother God's Love, and the Yellow-gold Flame of the Son and Daughter of God's Wisdom—represent the threefold activity of Life that is known as the Holy Trinity.

Christ Consciousness is the awakened state of awareness that our Father-Mother God invested us with in the beginning. The original Divine Plan was for the Sons and Daughters of God to remain in the elevated state of Christ Consciousness while receiving guidance from the Company of Heaven that would teach us how to become cocreators with our God Parents. The goal was for us to learn how to use our Life Force, our free will and our creative faculties of thought and feeling to cocreate new and previously unknown patterns of Divine Love, Peace, Abundance, Harmony, Balance, Happiness and Abounding Joy. The Divine Intent of this Earthly schoolroom was for the Sons and Daughters of God to learn how to expand the borders of the Kingdom of Heaven on Earth with every thought, feeling, word or action we expressed.

In order to insure the fulfillment of that facet of the Divine Plan and to keep their Sons and Daughters focused strictly on the Light, our Father-Mother God gave us one admonition,

"Do not partake of the Tree of Knowledge of good and evil."

Our God Parents knew that as long as their Sons and Daughters never used our free will or our creative faculties of thought and feeling to empower evil, *which is nothing more than thoughts and feelings that are not based in Love,* then we would not create the gross mutations of evil which manifest as poverty, disease, war, greed, crime, corruption, the abuse of power, inclement weather conditions and every other form of pain and suffering.

Tragically, there was a point in time when the Sons and Daughters of God made the free-will choice to experiment with our Life Force by empowering thoughts and feelings that were not based in Love or Reverence for Life. Once we made that horrific decision, we began to experience for the first time the painful effects of our actions. We became frightened and thought that maybe we could eliminate our suffering by closing our Heart Chakra and blocking our ability to feel pain.

Our Heart Chakra is the portal through which the Love of our Mother God enters the physical plane. Once we chose to close our Heart Chakra which blocked the flow of our Mother God's Love she was forced to withdraw. The Company of Heaven said, *"That fateful decision is the event that is overwhelmingly responsible for the imbalance between men and women that Humanity is experiencing to this very day."*

The infinitesimal amount of Divine Love our Mother God was able to project through our right-brain hemisphere after we closed our Heart Chakra was barely enough to sustain brain consciousness. This caused our right brain to become almost dormant and our spiritual brain centers to atrophy. When that happened, our Crown Chakra closed and we lost Christ Consciousness. This prevented us from communicating with our I AM Presence and the Company of Heaven.

Blocking the Divine Love of our Mother God and the Love Nature of the Divine Feminine within us is the event that caused what is known as Humanity's *"fall from Grace."* The *"fall"* was inadvertently created by the unintended consequences of Humanity's decision to close our Heart Chakra in an attempt to avoid the pain of our own miscreations. This was the result of a decision that was made by every man and woman evolving on Earth at the time. It was not because one woman named Eve ate an apple.

After the *"fall"*, without Christ Consciousness and the guidance of the Company of Heaven, we started to believe that the physical plane is our only reality and that all we are is our physical body. With that distorted perception, we developed a fragmented and fear-based lower human ego. Without the balance of our Mother God's Love, our ego began abusing our masculine power. When we were in male bodies our ego abused our power by being violent and aggressive. When we were in female bodies, our ego abused our power by suppressing it and allowing ourselves to be dominated and oppressed.

Our human ego developed the erroneous belief that its sole purpose was to gratify our physical senses, so it decided that whatever it needed to do to accomplish that goal would be just fine. This self-serving decision gave our ego permission to lie, cheat, steal and kill to get whatever it wanted.

For aeons of time, our fragmented and fear-based human ego has controlled and manipulated us by blocking the awareness of our Mother God. Our ego even convinced us that as Children of God we had a *single parent,* and that our only parent was our masculine Father God. Well, what child is ever born without a Father and a Mother? The Universal Law is,

"As Above, so below."

At long last, Humanity en masse is now beginning to remember the Love Nature of the Divine Feminine, our Mother God, who is the Holy Spirit. Women, men and children are opening their Heart Chakras once again. Even though we can see some powerful resistance surfacing in the outer world from Humanity's distorted patriarchal consciousness, remember,

"The Light of God is ALWAYS Victorious and WE are that Light."

Nothing is going to prevent the return of our Mother God. Take time each day to focus on the Divine Feminine and the Love of our Mother God which is now flowing through your awakening right-brain hemisphere and your Heart Flame.

5

THE RETURN OF THE
DIVINE FEMININE

The Company of Heaven is sharing this information with the Divine Intention of awakening within our Heart Flame the Truth about the return of our Mother God, who is the Holy Spirit.

Regardless of outer appearances, miraculous changes have taken place within every man, woman and child over the past several decades. These changes are reversing the negative effects of Humanity's descent into separation and duality, and they are occurring within every person whether he or she is consciously aware of it or not. Our I AM Presence has guided us through these changes in perfect alignment with our individual Divine Plan and our highest good.

One of the most important changes we have experienced so far is the return of our Mother God. This has occurred because Humanity is awakening at an unprecedented pace and millions of people are now opening their Heart Chakra to receive the influx of our Mother God's Love once again.

Our Mother God's Transfiguring Divine Love, which is now freely flowing through our right-brain hemisphere and our Heart Flame, is the foundation of all existing things and it is the purest essence from which all physical manifestations are brought into form. Our Mother God's Divine Love is embracing each of us, and we are being lifted up and freed from the illusions of our painful human miscreations.

Day by day, as we assimilate the Transfiguring Divine Love of our Mother God, we are becoming conscious, empowered and self-generating centers of Light. Our Mother God is now able to respond to Humanity's heartfelt pleas in new and profound ways. She is helping our I AM Presence to remove the shackles of limitation and the shadows of our miscreations that have blocked the Light and enshrouded us in darkness for aeons of time.

With the return of our Mother God, the Divine Masculine and the Divine Feminine are being balanced within every person's physical brain structure and Heart Flame. Now, in order to comprehend what an unfathomable blessing the return of our Mother God is for each and every one of us, we need to remember what our Mother God's Transfiguring Divine Love means in relation to our very existence. So, please center yourself and read these words within the Divinity of your Heart Flame.

So much has been written about Love that it has almost become a platitude, but the Transfiguring Divine Love of our Mother God is the mightiest force in the Universe. It is the vibration from which we were born out of the Heart of God and it is the vibration through which we must now evolve and Ascend back into the Heart of God. The Transfiguring Divine Love of our Mother God has no bonds, or barriers, or conditions. Within the infinite power of our Mother's Love there is no pain or sorrow, no lack or limitation. Her Love contains within its essence the full potential to rise above all human conditions, all self-inflicted suffering, and all manner of chaos, confusion, hopelessness and despair.

Our Mother God's Love heals the illusion of separation. It rejuvenates, revitalizes and makes whole all that
it embraces. It is the single greatest source of forgiveness,
and it reverberates with the full gathered momentum of
our eternal freedom in the Light. Our Mother's Love is the
foundation of all creation. It is the indivisible, unchanging
ecstasy that allows us to know Love in all things. When we
experience the Love of our Mother God, we understand
that we are all One. We *know* that every particle and wave
of Life is interconnected, interdependent and interrelated.
Whether we are a magnificent Sun, a person or a blade
of grass, we are united in the Body of our Father-Mother
God by the all encompassing cohesive power of our Mother
God's Transfiguring Divine Love.

As our Mother God reclaims this Earth and once again
anoints Humanity with her Infinite Love, we are beginning
to experience a deep Reverence for ALL Life. Our Mother's
Love is now pulsating within the core of our Beings, it is
not outside of us. We no longer need to seek the Divine
Feminine from afar. We need to merely accept that our
Mother God has returned, and that she is now abiding
within every person's Heart Flame. Her Love is pulsating
within the silent rhythm of every heartbeat, every breath.
It is the universal language now speaking to all Humanity
through our gift of Life. As we take the time to listen in the
silence of our Heart Flame, we hear the tones and whisperings of our Mother's Love inspired by the wonders of Nature
and the Music of the Spheres.

Our Mother God is now reestablishing her covenant of
Divine Love with the Children of Earth, which will enhance
our ability to once and for all accept the gift of Eternal Peace
and God's Infinite Abundance. Through this covenant, the
supply of all good things will forever and ever flood into the

hands and use of the Sons and Daughters of God. The glory of God's Eternal Peace and Infinite Abundance will be a manifest reality not only in this moment, but far beyond the Earth and time into Eternity.

The effulgence of our Heart Flame is creating an environment of Love and upliftment around each of us. When we turn our attention to the expression of our Father-Mother God within our Heart Flame, the illusion of separation is shattered. Our hearts are unified, and we once again experience the bliss of knowing that *we are One*, and that *Love is ALL there is.*

During this auspicious time, our Mother God is placing each of us within a mantle of her Divine Love, and our nervous systems are being recalibrated to withstand the highest possible frequencies of the Divine Feminine. Our Father-Mother God's Violet Flame in our heart is now penetrating into our atrophied spiritual brain centers. The Violet Flame is gradually reactivating our pineal, pituitary, and hypothalamus glands, and the ganglionic center at the base of our brain. This is allowing our I AM Presence to open our Crown Chakra in perfect alignment with our level of consciousness, and day by day Humanity is returning to Christ Consciousness.

At this time, our Mother God's radiant Transfiguring Divine Love is pouring through all of us without designating favor to a particular person, place, condition or thing. Her Love is giving a healing, impersonal benediction to every particle of Life. The magnetic Love of the Divine Feminine is blessing all Life with an equal opportunity to respond. Every person on Earth is being given both the blessing and the responsibility of becoming an Open Door for our Mother God's exquisite Love. Every Human Being now has the opportunity to become an instrument of God vested with the power to change the feeling worlds of all with whom we come in contact. This will be accomplished not through our human will, but through the power of the Flame of Divinity that is now pulsating in our heart. And so it is.

Precious Heart, please take this information from the Realms of Truth into your Heart Flame and ask your I AM Presence to help you assimilate the full magnitude of what the return of our Mother God means to you and to all Life evolving on this sweet Earth.

6

RECONNECTING WITH YOUR HIGHER SELF

One of the most important things that is happening at this time is that Humanity is in a position to reconnect with our Higher Self in ways that we have not experienced since our fall from Grace aeons ago. Our Higher Self is our I AM Presence which is the part of us that was created in God's Image.

Now that the masculine and feminine polarities of God are being balanced within the physical brain structure and Heart Flame of every person, our Crown Chakra is beginning to open and we are receiving more Light. This is permitting higher levels of consciousness to flow into our mental and emotional bodies which is raising our vibrations. This is allowing us to hear the *still small voice* of our I AM Presence once again.

This shift of consciousness is happening within every person at some level whether he or she is aware of it or not. Every person is now experiencing the gradual reopening of their Crown Chakra. This is initiating the return of Christ Consciousness within all of us which is a major factor in the unprecedented awakening that is taking place on Earth at this time. Now, the Company of Heaven is inviting us to deliberately accelerate this process by participating on a more conscious level in our awakening.

Over time, we have referred to our Higher Self by many different names, but now our Father-Mother God are encouraging us to intensify our connection directly with Them by referring to this aspect of our own Divinity as our I AM Presence. When we use the term I AM Presence, it serves as a code word that instantaneously connects us with our Father-Mother God, the Cosmic I AM, which is the Source of ALL that is.

Remember when Moses asked the burning bush *"Who are you?"*

The response was, *"I AM That I AM. I AM Alpha. I AM Omega. I AM the beginning and I AM the ending of all that is."*

"I" represents Alpha, the Masculine Aspect of our Father God. *"AM"* represents Omega, the Feminine Aspect of our Mother God. The words *"I AM"* are considered the Name of God. They mean, quite literally, that our Father-Mother God are the beginning and the ending of ALL that is.

Our I AM Presence has been patiently awaiting our remembrance of this Truth. This aspect of our own Divinity is elated that we are at long last becoming One with the part of our self that *knows* that we are One with our Father-Mother God. Of course, we have always been One with our Father-Mother God, and our I AM Presence has always been connected to us. We just lost awareness of that fact when we buried ourselves in our dense human miscreations and lost the ability to communicate with our I AM Presence and the Company of Heaven. Now that is over!

Everything has changed, and all that we have to do to start reconnecting with our I AM Presence on a consciousness level is to acknowledge that our I AM Presence exists and accept the fact that our I AM Presence is who we are as a Beloved Son or Daughter of God. This is not a complicated task. It simply involves a slight adjustment in our awareness. All we need to do is affirm that we are our I AM Presence and then ask our I AM Presence to guide us to that inner knowing. There is not another thing that is more worth our while than taking the time to remember and reconnect with our I AM Presence, which is our true God Self.

Reconnecting with our I AM Presence is not difficult. It is as easy as beginning every morning with this simple affirmation:

"I AM my I AM Presence and I AM One with my Father-Mother God."

Then we can go about our day knowing and living that Truth. With every situation we encounter and every person we interact with we will be aware that we are responding through the higher consciousness of our I AM Presence which is always striving toward the highest good of all concerned. Before acting, we simply need to pause and take a deep breath as we imagine how our I AM Presence would respond. It will help to remind our self that we *are* our I AM Presence which is One with our Father-Mother God. Then we will act out of that knowing in constructive and helpful ways.

When we affirm:

"I AM my I AM Presence and I AM One with my Father-Mother God."

we give our I AM Presence permission to intervene in our life and to take dominion of our thoughts, feelings, words and actions. Once we do this, we will find our self intuitively coming up with new and more positive ways of interacting with the people and situations in our life. Through our I AM Presence, we will think of new and very viable solutions to problems we may have been encountering over and over again for a very long time.

If we are patient and diligently take these simple steps every single day soon our realignment with our I AM Presence and our Father-Mother God will be automatic. Then we will prove to our self what an amazing difference it makes and how much our life improves when we lift above the chaos of our fragmented lower consciousness and give our I AM Presence permission to reclaim dominion of our thoughts, feelings, words and actions.

Precious Heart, if you would like more information about this process we are all going through on our journey back to Christ Consciousness, I have written a book and produced a set of two CDs titled *Return to Christ Consciousness*. These items include enlightening information that the Company of Heaven has given to Humanity to help us comprehend what we are all going through. These items also include very powerful invocations and meditations designed to help us return to Christ Consciousness much more quickly. The book and CDs are available on our website www.eraofpeace. org In addition to the physical book and CDs, these items are also available electronically as an E-book and MP3s.

God Bless you Dear One, have a glorious time reconnecting with your I AM Presence as you return to Christ Consciousness.

7

SHOULD I INVOKE THE
LIGHT ON BEHALF OF
MY LOVED ONES?

People often ask whether or not it is appropriate for us to help our loved ones through their challenges by praying for them and invoking the Light of God on their behalf. The Company of Heaven said if our prayers and invocations are done in the right way, they are the most powerful thing we can do to assist our loved ones during difficult times. When done correctly, our prayers and invocations can literally create miracles in another person's life.

There is a school of thought that believes if we invoke the Light on behalf of another person without them specifically asking for our help, we are interfering with the learning experiences they need to go through. Whether that is true or not depends on how our request for assistance is made.

It is true that everyone is going through the exact learning experiences they need and that *at some level of consciousness* they have agreed to go through. The only one who knows when the lesson is learned and when it is time for the experience to be over is the I AM Presence of the person involved.

Sometimes we observe a loved one's suffering and from a place of compassion, we decide it is time for the person to be healed. In an endeavor to help them, we begin invoking the Light and decreeing that they be healed immediately. When we try to force a healing without going through the person's I AM Presence, we can indeed interfere with their learning process. If we heal someone before they have completed the lesson associated with the particular challenge they are going through, their I AM Presence will have to recreate that experience all over again which can greatly delay the person's progress.

We are being taught by the Company of Heaven, however, that if we invoke our I AM Presence and the I AM Presence of the person involved before we invoke the Light of God on their behalf, that changes everything. When we take this important first step, it gives our I AM Presence and the I AM Presence of the person we want to help permission to receive the Light and to control how the Light is used.

Our I AM Presence works solely toward our highest good and the highest good of all concerned. It knows exactly what our unfolding Divine Plan is and it perpetually strives to help us expedite the fulfillment of that plan. Our I AM Presence knows why we are going through the particular challenge we are experiencing. It knows what we are going to learn by transmuting that experience back into Light and it knows how close we are to completing that process.

Our I AM Presence also knows precisely how to utilize the Light it is receiving for our highest good. That is true whether it is Light that we have invoked for our self or Light that has been invoked by another person on our behalf.

The process for ensuring that we always invoke the Light through our I AM Presence and the I AM Presence of the person or the people we want to help is very simple. All we need to do is state the following affirmation prior to our invocations, our prayers and our meditations:

"I AM my I AM Presence and I AM One with the I AM Presence of Name the person or persons."

Know that the Light of God is Infinite and there is no limit to the number of people for whom we can invoke the Light in a single invocation. Personally, before all of my prayers, invocations and meditations I affirm:

"I AM my I AM Presence and I AM One with the I AM Presence of ALL Humanity."

When that affirmation is stated, instantaneously, the I AM Presence of every man, women and child on Earth receives a signal from my I AM Presence and is alerted that I am invoking Light on their behalf. Every person's I AM Presence then stands in readiness to receive the Light I am invoking. The I AM Presence then assimilates the Light and uses it for the highest good, in perfect alignment with the person's Divine Plan. This happens every time no matter who is making the invocation.

This is what the Company of Heaven means when they tell us that we are powerful beyond our knowing. We literally have the ability to invoke the Light of God through the I AM Presence of every person on Earth simultaneously. Just contemplate what that really means for a moment. Instead of spending our time and energy invoking the Light for one person, with the same expenditure of time and energy we can invoke the Light on behalf of the over 7,000,000,000 people evolving on this planet.

It is time for us to develop the habit of setting aside some time every day to invoke the Light of God on behalf of our self, our loved ones and all of Humanity. Then we can easily take advantage of the fact that we truly are an Open Door through which the Light of God is flowing to transform Mother Earth and all her Life into the patterns of perfection for the New Earth.

8

INVOKING THE VIOLET FLAME

In the last sharing we learned how very powerful our invocations can be when they are done the right way. Now the Beings of Light are going to join us in an activity of Light that will demonstrate how our invocations can transmute into Light the tons of negativity that is being pushed to the surface all over the planet. As you participate in the following invocation, know that you are being joined by the Company of Heaven and Lightworkers around the world. Take a deep breath and center yourself now within the Divinity of your Heart Flame. Please focus on these words with the full power of your attention. And we begin.

Violet Flame

I AM my I AM Presence and I AM One with the I AM Presence of ALL Humanity. As One Voice, One Breath, One Heartbeat, and One Energy, Vibration, and Consciousness of Pure Divine Love we invoke the most intensified frequencies of the 5th-Dimensional Crystalline Solar Violet Flame of God's Infinite Perfection that Cosmic Law will allow.

We invoke the Legions of Light and the Violet Fire Archangels who are associated with this unfathomable frequency of the

Violet Flame. Beloved Ones come forth NOW! We ask that you blaze this Violet Flame with the power and might of a thousand Suns in, through and around all lower human consciousness and all of the human miscreations that are surfacing at this time. Transmute this negative energy cause, core, effect, record and memory back into its original perfection and seal it in an invincible forcefield of God's Transfiguring Divine Love.

a) *Blaze the Light of a thousand Suns through the thoughts, words, actions and feelings of every man, woman and child evolving on Earth until every person individually acknowledges and accepts the Divinity within ALL Life, and every expression made by Humanity is a healing benediction for every part of Life on this planet.*

b) *Blaze the Light of a thousand Suns through all incoming babies, the children, their parents and guardians until ALL of the youth are raised up in energy, vibration and consciousness to hear and carry out the directives of their I AM Presence.*

c) *Blaze the Light of a thousand Suns through all youth centers and activities, all schools, colleges and universities, all leaders, teachers, instructors and professors in every line of endeavor until the Flame of Wisdom, God Illumination and Enlightenment is manifest and eternally sustained within the heart and mind of every person.*

d) *Blaze the Light of a thousand Suns through all religions and all spiritual teachings until Divine Love, Truth, Tolerance, Respect, Oneness and Universal Sisterhood and Brotherhood are a manifest reality.*

e) *Blaze the Light of a thousand Suns through all doctors, nurses, healers, hospitals, insurance companies, pharmaceutical conglomerates and every institution associated with Healing of any kind until Divine Mercy, Compassion, Caring and Healing are tangible realities for every person.*

f) *Blaze the Light of a thousand Suns through all banking and financial institutions, all economic systems, all money and the people associated with monetary interactions of any kind until every person on Earth is openly demonstrating true integrity, honesty, generosity, fairness, abundance and the God Supply of all good things.*

g) *Blaze the Light of a thousand Suns through all places of incarceration and all employed there, through every correctional institution, and through every law enforcement officer, lawyer, judge, jury and court of law until Divine Justice is manifest and eternally sustained.*

h) *Blaze the Light of a thousand Suns through ALL of the governments of the world and through every person, place, condition and thing associated with the governments of the world at national, state and local levels. Intensify this Violet Flame until every government is focusing on Divine Love, Oneness, Reverence for ALL Life and the desire to cocreate the Highest Good for ALL concerned in every single instance.*

i) *Blaze the Light of a thousand Suns through all space activities throughout the world until every nation unites in cooperative service, so that God's Will may be manifest with our sisters and brothers throughout the Universe.*

j) *Blaze the Light of a thousand Suns through the physical, etheric, mental and emotional bodies of Humanity until all disease and human miscreation, its cause and core, is dissolved and transmuted into purity, vibrant health, eternal youth and physical perfection.*

k) *Blaze the Light of a thousand Suns through the food and water industries and through all of the food and water used for human consumption until every particle of food and every molecule of water is filled with Light. Empower this Elemental substance to raise the vibratory action of Humanity's physical, etheric, mental and emotional bodies until physical perfection becomes a sustained manifest reality for every Human Being.*

l) Now, blaze the Light of a thousand Suns in, through and around every remaining electron of precious Life energy until the Immaculate Concept of the New Earth is permanently manifest.

We accept that the activity of the Violet Flame of God's Infinite Perfection, which we have invoked this sacred and holy day, is being God Victoriously accomplished right here and right now, even as we Call.

We also accept and know that through every person's I AM Presence the Violet Flame of God's Infinite Perfection is increasing daily and hourly, moment by moment, with every breath we take which will continue until this sweet Earth and ALL her Life have completed our Ascension into the 5th-Dimensional Realms of Light on the New Earth.

And so it is! Beloved I AM, Beloved I AM, Beloved I AM.

Precious Heart, if you would like more assistance on how to use the Violet Flame and how it can help you transform your life, I have written a book and produced a set of two CDs titled THE VIOLET FLAME. They are available on our website www.eraofpeace.org. These items include important information and very powerful tools that have been given to Humanity by the Company of Heaven. In addition to the physical book and CDs, both items are available electronically as an E-book and MP3.

God Bless You. And I wish you a powerful time of clearing and transmuting the negativity that is surfacing in your own life and in the world as you invoke the Violet Flame.

9

DOWNLOADING THE PATTERNS OF PERFECTION FOR THE NEW EARTH

Several years ago the Company of Heaven asked awakening Lightworkers on Earth if we would be willing to begin the process of downloading the patterns of perfection for the New Earth from the Realms of Cause onto the newly formed fluid field of unmanifest Divine Potential in the mental and emotional strata of Earth. Everything begins in the Realms of Cause. In order for something from the Realms of Cause to then manifest in the physical world of form which is the world of effects, it must be drawn through the Divinity within the Heart Flame of the Sons and Daughters of God abiding in the physical plane.

The Beings of Light said that beginning the process of downloading the patterns of perfection for the New Earth was a necessary first step for eventually manifesting these patterns in the physical plane. Lightworkers accepted this mission and have been diligently downloading these patterns ever since. Now the Beings of Light have revealed that it is time for us to take the next step.

They said that the Violet Flame that Lightworkers around the world have been invoking on behalf of ourselves, Humanity and ALL Life on Earth has cleared enough of the surfacing negativity to allow a higher and more powerful frequency of the patterns of perfection for the New Earth to be downloaded onto the mental and emotional strata of Earth. Once again, the Beings of Light are asking for our assistance.

If you have the Heart Call to participate in this activity of Light, please join with me and Lightworkers all over the world who are empowering these patterns. Through our I AM Presences, we will offer the collective Cup of our unified Heart Flames as the Open Door through which these greatly enhanced patterns of perfection for the New Earth will be downloaded through the newly opened portal from the Realms of Cause onto the mental and emotional strata of Earth.

Take a deep breath, go within to the Divinity of your Heart Flame, and BE here now.

Downloading the Patterns of Perfection

I AM my I AM Presence and I AM One with my Father-Mother God, I AM One with the entire Company of Heaven and I AM One with the I AM Presence of every man, woman, and child on Earth.

As One Breath, One Heartbeat, One Voice and One Energy, Vibration and Consciousness of pure Divine Love we offer the Cup of our unified Heart Flames as the Open Door for this activity of Light which we are invoking on behalf of ourselves and every person on this planet.

Beloved Father-Mother God and the Legions of Light throughout Infinity download NOW from the Realms of Cause the highest and most exquisite frequencies of the patterns of perfection for the New Earth that Cosmic Law will allow.

As we invoke these patterns one by one, we ask that they be downloaded instantaneously onto the fluid field of unmanifest Divine Potential within the mental and emotional strata of Earth. We know and accept that this will occur through each person's I AM Presence in perfect alignment with their Divine Plan and the highest good for all concerned. And we begin.

1. *Beloved Ones download now the patterns of perfection from the Realms of Cause that are associated with the flow of Eternal Peace and God's Infinite Abundance, Opulence, Financial Freedom and the God-Supply of ALL good things.*

2. *Download now the patterns of perfection from the Realms of Cause that are associated with Eternal Youth, Vibrant Health, Radiant Beauty and Humanity's Flawless Form.*

3. *Download now the patterns of perfection from the Realms of Cause that are associated with perfect health habits including Eating and Drinking Habits, Exercise, Work, Relaxation and Recreation Habits, and Spiritual Devotion, Meditation and Contemplation Habits.*

4. *Download now the patterns of perfection from the Realms of Cause that are associated with Divine Family Life, Loving Relationships, Adoration, Divine Love, Divine Sexuality, True Understanding, Clear and Effective Communication, Open Heart Sharing, Oneness and the Unification of the Family of Humanity.*

5. *Beloved Ones download now the patterns of perfection from the Realms of Cause that are associated with Harmony, Balance, Oneness and Reverence for ALL Life.*

6. *Download now the patterns of perfection from the Realms of Cause that are associated with Empowerment, Success, Fulfillment, Divine Purpose, a Rewarding Career, Self*

Esteem, Spiritual Development, Enlightenment, Divine Consciousness and Divine Perception.

7. *Download now the patterns of perfection from the Realms of Cause that will initiate conscious open heart and mind telepathic communication through our I AM Presence with our Father-Mother God, the Company of Heaven, and the Angelic and Elemental Kingdoms.*

8. *Beloved Ones download now the patterns of perfection from the Realms of Cause that will inspire Creativity through Music, Singing, Sound, Toning, Dance, Movement, Art and Education.*

9. *Download now the patterns of perfection from the Realms of Cause that are associated with Laughter, Joy, Playfulness, Fun, Self-expression, Elation, Enthusiasm, Bliss, Ecstasy, Wonder and Awe.*

10. *And download now the patterns of perfection from the Realms of Cause that are associated with the tangible manifestation of Heaven on Earth and our NEW Planetary CAUSE of Divine Love.*

We now accept and know that these 5th-Dimensional patterns of perfection for the New Earth have been successfully downloaded through our Heart Flames and encoded on the fluid field of unmanifest Divine Potential in the mental and emotional strata of Earth. This activity of Light has been God Victoriously accomplished for the highest benefit of ALL Life evolving on this precious planet.

Now in deep Humility, Divine Love and Gratitude we decree,
It is done. And so it is.
Beloved I AM. Beloved I AM. Beloved I AM That I AM.

Thank you Precious Heart for your willingness to add to the Light of the world in this powerful way. God Bless You.

10

ARE YOU EMPOWERING YOUR PAIN AND SUFFERING?

In this sharing we are going to talk about whether or not you are inadvertently empowering and sustaining with your thoughts and feelings the very things that are causing you pain and suffering.

From the time I was a very small child I kept asking the question, *"Why is there so much pain and suffering in the world?"* Even from a child's perspective I knew that the negative things I was witnessing and experiencing were not the way things were supposed to be on Earth. When I was older, I studied the gamut of world religions and sought answers in the fields of science and psychology.

During my quest, I became aware that there is a unifying thread of Truth running through all of the various schools of thought. That Truth reveals that we are responsible for how we choose to use our Life Force and that we will experience the results of our actions. This means quite literally that the energy we expend in whatever we are thinking, feeling, saying or doing not only affects everybody and everything in our sphere of influence, it eventually returns to us through our everyday life experiences.

In the Realms of Illumined Truth this unifying thread of knowledge is known as the **Law of the Circle**. In Eastern philosophies this principle is referred to as karma or the Law of Cause and Effect. In Judeo-Christian teachings this Law is described by various phrases such as:

"We reap what we sow"
"When we cast our bread upon the water it returns to us"
"An eye for an eye and a tooth for a tooth."

Gandhi said if we follow that philosophy we will all end up blind and toothless. The statement should say,

"An eye for an eye, a tooth for a tooth, a hug for a hug and a kiss for a kiss" so we get the whole picture.

In science the Law of the Circle is demonstrated in statements such as

"Like attracts like"
"Radiation and magnetization"
"For every action there is an equal and opposite reaction."

In metaphysical terms the Law of the Circle is described as

"The outbreath and the inbreath of our Father-Mother God."

The Law of the Circle confirms that at any given moment our lives are reflecting back to us the sum total of our past experiences and whatever we are currently empowering with our thoughts, feelings, words and actions. This means that we are not just innocent victims of circumstance who, through no fault of our own, are being buffeted about by things that are beyond our control. On the contrary, we are cocreating our lives daily and hourly with every breath we take. If we do not like what is happening in our life by changing the way we are thinking, feeling and behaving we have the ability to create the life we want.

When I became aware of that Truth my overwhelming questions were, if every form of knowledge on Earth, both spiritual and academic, is revealing that both the good and the bad things taking place in our lives are the result of our own thoughts and feelings, then why hasn't Humanity taken the necessary steps to stop the pain and suffering? Why in the world are we in the mess we are in? Why do we dwell on our fears and negativity instead of focusing on the positive and wonderful things we want to create in our life?

After much contemplation, I knew that the answers to those questions were not outside of me, so I went within and asked my I AM Presence and my Father-Mother God to reveal the answers to me. After a time of patience and remaining in a state of listening Grace, the Truth that we ALL have pulsating within the Divinity of our Heart Flame began to surface into my conscious mind.

During the next few sharings, I am going to tell you what I learned. From my own experience and the responses of the thousands of people with whom I have shared this information, I know it is much more effective and life-transforming if we apply this sacred knowledge step-by-step as an experiential process.

So, the very first step is to begin taking control of your thoughts, feelings, words and actions. In order to do that, you have to be consciously aware of what you are thinking and feeling moment by moment throughout the day.

Unfortunately, the vast majority of people just go through the day without paying any attention to what they are allowing themselves to empower with their thoughts and feelings. Unless something is extremely wonderful or extremely painful, people just let their thoughts muddle through their mind and allow their feelings to whip around their emotions without any conscious direction at all. If something makes them happy, they just let it make them happy. If something upsets them, they just let it upset them. Consequently, every day the majority of people are on an up and down roller coaster mentally and emotionally.

This unconscious behavior is the main reason that we see so little progress when it comes to improving the quality of our lives. We take one step forward by deliberately thinking positive thoughts and working with the Light for a period of time. Then we go about our day and stop paying attention. Within a very short time, we are taking two steps backward with our oblivious thoughts and feelings. It is time for that counterproductive behavior to stop. We are awake now, and we can no longer use the excuse that we did not understand how important it is for us to pay attention to what we are empowering with our thoughts and feelings.

Now that we know that our Life Force is comprised of *intelligent* electronic Light substance which is our Gift of Life from our Father-Mother God, it is not only irresponsible for us to use our precious Life Force haphazardly, it is a sacrilege. The Company of Heaven and our I AM Presence are reminding us that our thoughts and feelings are creative and that whatever we are thinking and feeling we are empowering, sustaining and bringing into tangible form. Now that we are becoming consciously aware of that fact, we have an even greater level of accountability for how we use our Life Force.

Due to the shifts of energy, vibration and consciousness that have taken place within every person over the past few years, our I AM Presence now has the ability to intervene in our life in ways we have not experienced in the past. During this auspicious time, our I AM Presence is integrating into our mental and emotional bodies and will now be able to help us monitor our thoughts and feelings. All we have to do is ask for that intervention and affirm that Truth.

So start taking control of your thoughts and feelings by affirming every day:

"I AM my I AM Presence and I AM One with my Father-Mother God."

Then ask your I AM Presence to help you to be consciously aware of what you are thinking and feeling throughout the day. Ask yourself time and again,

"Is what I AM thinking and feeling this moment adding to the Light of my life or the shadows?"

If what you are focusing on is negative or not what you want to empower in your life ask yourself,

"What do I want to empower with my thoughts and feelings instead of what I AM thinking about now?"

Then focus on what you want to empower. It may be that you need to focus on the same thing, but that you just need to do so from a positive perspective instead of the negative perspective you are empowering at that moment.

Once you shift from the negative thought to the positive thought, ask your I AM Presence and our Father-Mother

God to blaze the Violet Flame of God's Infinite Perfection through the negative thoughtforms you were unintentionally empowering.

This is a very simple but necessary first step. Once you begin paying attention, you will realize how very often you allow yourself to slip into the habit of oblivious thoughts and feelings. In the beginning, you will need to repeat these simple steps many times every single day. However, with the help of your I AM Presence positive thinking will soon become automatic for you.

So remember, to begin, your moment to moment mantra is:

"Is what I AM thinking and feeling this moment adding to the Light of my life or the shadows?"

If what you are focusing on is negative or not what you want to empower in your life say to yourself,

"What do I want to empower with my thoughts and feelings instead of what I AM thinking about now?"

Then focus on what you want to empower and blaze the Violet Flame of God's Infinite Perfection through your negative thoughtforms and feelings.

God Bless You, Dear One. I wish you an enlightening time of empowering what you want to cocreate in your life.

11

THE POSITIVE EFFECTS OF THE
LAW OF THE CIRCLE

We have learned about the Law of the Circle and the fact that this Universal Law is instrumental in determining the various things that are taking place in our lives, both good and bad. Now the Beings of Light want to take this teaching to the next level. They are striving to inspire us to be more committed and more disciplined in the way we choose to use our precious Gift of Life and our creative faculties of thought and feeling.

For those of us abiding on Earth, the Law of the Circle is like the Law of Gravity. Even though we may not understand the Laws of Physics or comprehend just how gravity works, we are all subject to it just the same. It is immaterial whether or not we believe in gravity. If we jump off of a roof we are going to fall to the ground. It is just that simple.

The Law of the Circle is like gravity. It does not matter whether or not we believe that every single thought, feeling, word or action we express goes out into the world on an electromagnetic current of energy like a radio or television wave and then returns to us through our everyday life experiences. However, that is exactly what is happening scientifically to the letter with every breath we take.

Anything that is manifesting in our life at this time that is less than the wonders of Heaven on Earth is a human miscreation. These challenging and often painful things are being returned to us through the Law of the Circle so that we can experience the results of our actions and transmute back into Light the precious electronic Light substance that we misused at one time or another. The negative things that are occurring in our daily lives were either deliberately or inadvertently created during our Earthly sojourn when we made the free will choice to express our thoughts and feelings in ways that were not based in Love.

During this Cosmic Moment, you and I and the rest of Humanity are awakening. We are remembering who we are and why we volunteered to be on Earth to assist with the monumental event of Earth's Ascension process that we are now experiencing. Daily and hourly, the Light of God is increasing on this planet. Humanity is being raised up in energy, vibration and consciousness by our I AM Presence the maximum we can withstand in every 24-hour period. With this Divine Intervention, each and every one of us now has the ability to reverse the adverse effects of our fall from Grace. This means that at long last the Sons and Daughters of God are once again destined to cocreate Heaven on Earth. We just need to perceive the bigger picture of how we got into this mess in the first place.

The first thing we need to remember is how our Father-Mother God intended for the Law of the Circle to work while we are learning to become cocreators. At this point in our evolutionary process, we are so used to dealing with the pain and suffering in our individual and collective lives that it is difficult for us to fathom that there was ever a time when these horrific things didn't exist, but there was such a time prior to our fall from Grace.

In the beginning, the Law of the Circle was always a joyous experience and it functioned as God intended. Moment by moment, our I AM Presence gratefully received our Life Force from our Father-Mother God and breathed this intelligent Light substance through our Crown Chakra and into our Heart Flame. Once this intelligent Light entered the Divinity within our Immortal Victorious Threefold Flame, it was stamped with our individual electronic Light pattern. This electronic Light pattern is unique for every Son and Daughter of God and it is given to us at our inception by our God Parents. This unique pattern is how the Universe knows what energy belongs to whom and it is how the Law of the Circle is flawlessly accomplished for every single person.

Once our Life Force was imprinted with our individual pattern, the atomic and subatomic particles and waves of energy contained within this Gift of Life were available for us to use as we went about the business of our daily lives learning to become cocreators with our God Parents. We would observe the patterns of perfection in the Causal Body of God and then through our unique ways of thinking and feeling, we would use those patterns and our free will to cocreate new and previously unknown patterns of perfection. Since we had not created any painful human miscreations yet, we were able to focus our attention exclusively on expanding the boarders of Heaven on Earth as our Father-Mother God intended.

With every thought, feeling, word or action we expressed, our Life Force flowed forth from us on an electromagnetic current of energy very similar to the way radio and television waves pass through the atmosphere. Our current of energy reverberated with whatever frequency of vibration we charged it with depending on our frame of mind and the way we were feeling at the time.

As our current of energy traveled to its destination, it accumulated other energy along the way that was vibrating at the same frequency. Remember, like attracts like. For instance, if we were sending Love to someone our current of Love magnetized other currents of Love to itself as it traveled along the way. By the time our current of Love reached the person we were thinking of, it was vibrating at a much more powerful frequency of Love than we originally sent out. Our current of Love blessed the person in ways that were in alignment with his or her Divine Plan, and then this loving expression of our Life Force began its journey back to us and ultimately to our Father-Mother God, thus fulfilling the Law of the Circle.

The first phase of our Life Force's journey is called *involution*. The involution of our Life Force begins in the Heart of God, then passes through our Heart Flame and culminates when our Life Force reaches the furthest point of its destination once we send it into the physical world of form through our thoughts and feelings. After this intelligent electronic Light substance completes the path of *involution*, it must then return to our Father-Mother God, the Source of All That Is. The return phase of its journey is called *evolution*. *Involution* and *evolution* are the dual activities of Life that reflect the Law of the Circle, the outbreath and the inbreath of God.

On the return *evolutionary* path our current of Love is magnetized back to its identical electronic Light pattern which is pulsating within our Heart Flame. Once again, on the return journey our current of Love accumulates other frequencies of Love along the way. By the time our current of Love returns to us, it is greatly magnified over what we originally sent out. As a result of this amplification, it is possible that the positive energy magnetized to our original expression of Love gathered enough momentum on its return journey to manifest in our life as a healing, or a financial success, or a new friendship, or a success in our job, or myriad other *seemingly* unrelated things. This is the Divine Potential of all of the positive thoughts, feelings, words and actions we express every day.

After our positively qualified intelligent Life Force returns to our Heart Flame, and we tangibly experience whatever blessings were cocreated through our expression of Love, our I AM Presence is then responsible for returning that energy back to the Heart of our Father-Mother God. This process completes the Law of the Circle.

When our Life Force is qualified positively, this process works perfectly. If, however, we charge the intelligent electronic Light from our Life Force with negative thoughts, feelings, words and actions everything changes.

The important thing the Beings of Light want us to contemplate is the fact that when the intelligent electronic Light substance from our Gift of Life returns to us on its evolutionary path, it can *only* pass through our Heart Flame and return to our Father-Mother God if it is vibrating with the same or a higher frequency of Light than when we originally received it. Love, of course, fulfills that requirement, and so do many other positive things that we might empower with our thoughts, feelings, words and actions. But how many times every day are we obliviously using the precious Gift of our intelligent Life Force to empower things that are not based in Love or the pure and perfect frequencies of God's Light?

Pay attention and see if the things you are cocreating every moment with your thoughts and feelings are qualified with enough Love and Light to easily pass through your Heart Flame on their journey back to the Heart of God.

12

REVERSING THE NEGATIVE
EFFECTS OF THE LAW OF
THE CIRCLE

In the last sharing the Beings of Light reminded us of how our Father-Mother God intended for the Law of the Circle to work during our Earthly lives as we learned to become cocreators with our God Parents. Now we are going to learn how the Law of the Circle affected us in adverse ways once we made the fateful decision to experiment with our intelligent Life Force in ways that were not based in Love.

Prior to our tragic decision to misuse our Life Force, our Gift of Life flowed forth from our Heart Flame on electromagnetic currents of energy qualified with positive thoughts, feelings, words and actions. After completing its involutionary journey into the world of form, our Life Force began its evolutionary journey back to our Heart Flame bringing with it the wonderful experiences that were cocreated as the result of our positive behavior. After our Life Force returned to our Heart Flame, and we experienced the blessings and the positive results of our actions, our I AM Presence returned that positively qualified energy back to the Heart of our Father-Mother God. That event completed the Law of the Circle.

When we decided to experiment with our Gift of Life and began misqualifying the intelligent electronic Light substance from our Life Force with thoughts, feelings, words and actions that were not based in Love, everything changed. That is because our Life Force can *only* pass through our Heart Flame and return to our Father-Mother God if it is vibrating with the same or a higher frequency of Light than when we originally received it. What the Company of Heaven wants us to clearly understand at this time is what happens to the returning electronic Light from our Gift of Life once it is has been misqualified with negative thoughts and feelings. That sacred knowledge is a vitally important part of the bigger picture, and it explains why in the world we are in the mess we are in and why it seems as though terrible things are happening to good people.

Thoughts and feelings that are not based in Love include anything that does not reflect Love, Oneness and Reverence for ALL Life. Just for a moment, think about your own life and the things you are witnessing everyday in the world. How much of what you are perceiving is reflecting Love, Oneness and Reverence for ALL Life? If you are like most people probably not nearly enough.

Everything we see that is in any way associated with fear, anxiety, incivility, hatred, judgment, greed, corruption, violence, crime, poverty, abuse of power, war, disease, meanness, disrespect, ignorance, prejudice, religious fanaticism, terrorism or any other form of pain and suffering is a human miscreation that is not based in Love. The energy associated with these human miscreations cannot return to the Heart of our Father-Mother God once it returns to the Heart Flame of the person who sent it forth in the first place. So what happens to the grossly mutated electronic Light substance that our Father-Mother God originally gave to us as our precious Gift of Life?

Well, since that dense and grossly distorted intelligent electronic Light cannot return to the Heart of God in that form, it manifests in our everyday life experiences in painful ways that allow us to experience the results of our actions. The hope is that we will realize how self-destructive it is for us to misuse our Life Force, and that we will learn to not do that again. Once the lesson is learned, we have the ability to invoke the Violet Flame of God's Infinite Perfection and transmute that misqualified energy back into its original perfection. Then, that portion of our Life Force can return to the Heart of our Father-Mother God, thus completing its journey through the Law of the Circle.

The problem is that when this heavy, discordant energy returns to us it is greatly amplified over what we originally sent out. Like our positive thoughts and feelings, our negative thoughts and feelings also accumulate energy along the way that is vibrating at the same frequency, like attracts like. On the involutionary journey our misqualified current of energy enters the space of the person, place, condition or thing we were thinking of when we sent it forth and creates whatever learning experience is appropriate in that moment. Then on the evolutionary journey back to our Heart Flame our current of misqualified energy accumulates more discordant energy along the way. When we observe the horrific things that are happening in the world at this time, it is easy to see why things seem to be so out of proportion. Just look at the tons of negative and fear-based energy that is being expressed by the masses of Humanity every single day. All of that energy is reverberating through the atmosphere and it is being drawn to our own electromagnetic currents of negative thoughts, feelings, words and actions.

With so much pain and suffering in the world, it is truly amazing that we can even get out of bed in the morning with all of the negative energy that is returning to us. This energy is returning to us from not only this lifetime, but from the hundreds of previous lifetimes we have experienced since our fall from Grace. By the time this greatly amplified energy returns to us, it often manifests as all kinds of unrecognizable things. It could manifest as a car accident, a financial challenge, a dysfunctional relationship, a health problem, a family problem or myriad other things that do not seem like they could possibly be our own miscreations.

To complicate the problem even further, for aeons of time our fragmented human ego has manipulated us into believing that we are victims and that both the good and the bad things that are happening in our lives are just a coincidence and don't have anything to do with our behavior. This fragmented and fear-based level of our fallen consciousness knew that if we awakened and gave the power it usurped from us back to our I AM Presence, it would no longer be able to manipulate us through fear and anxiety. Well guess what? That is exactly what has happened over the past several years.

We are awakening and our I AM Presence is once again taking full dominion of our life. Our human ego is no longer in charge. That is what has brought us to this unprecedented moment in time during which we are experiencing the most intensified purging process that Humanity has ever been able to withstand. Our I AM Presence is pushing hundreds of lifetimes worth of our returning misqualified energy to the surface to be transmuted back into Light.

That is enabling this precious electronic Light substance to return to the Heart of our Father-Mother God, so that it can complete the Law of the Circle.

We are not being punished for our past transgressions, and this cleansing process would not be occurring at this pace if it was going to cause more harm than good. This unique purging process is being allowed by our Father-Mother God because millions of people are now awake and they remember who they are and why they are here. They know what their responsibility is for what is happening on Earth at this time and they remember that they volunteered to transmute lifetimes worth of misqualified energy back into Light in what the Company of Heaven has referred to as, *"The twinkling of an eye."*

Contemplate the challenging things that are returning to you through your daily experiences in order to be healed and transmuted back into Light. Ask your I AM Presence to help you learn the lessons involved in that returning energy. Then invoke the Violet Flame of God's Infinite Perfection to help you quickly transmute the negative energy from your past that is causing those challenging experiences. You have been training for lifetimes so that you will be able to do this, and you have everything you need within you to be God Victorious. Trust yourself and know that your I AM Presence is in charge.

Next the Company of Heaven will help you perceive the progress you are making even though that progress may not be obvious to you at this moment.

13

WHEN WILL WE SEE PROGRESS?

Now we are going to explore the progress we are making in improving the quality of our individual and collective lives. There are very dedicated people who have been invoking the Light of God for decades and yet outer world appearances often do not reflect their heartfelt efforts. In fact, in many instances things seem to be getting even worse, which I know is incredibly disheartening. As a word of encouragement, I want you to know that the Beings of Light assure us that things are not getting worse. On the contrary, they say that we are succeeding beyond the greatest expectations of Heaven. The reason things seem to not be progressing is because of our limited perception and the fact that we are not seeing the bigger picture. This sharing will help to solve that problem.

One of the most important things for us to remember is that we are multidimensional Beings functioning in several Realms of Consciousness simultaneously. Our invocations and our prayers and meditations are first formed in the Realms of Cause where everything begins. Then they are magnetized through various dimensions of consciousness into the physical plane of Earth which is known as the world of effects. Even though we think of the physical plane as being very real, it is actually the *least real* of all of the Realms of Consciousness we abide in, and it is the *very last* dimension to reflect the changes we are invoking.

When we invoke the Light of God without seeing the results in the outer world that we would like to see, it gives us the impression that our invocations and meditations are not working and that our prayers are not being answered, but that is never the case. The Light of God responds to our invocations and meditations each and every time we participate in these activities, and our prayers are always heard and they are always answered. If before we begin our invocations, meditations and prayers we affirm,

"I AM my I AM Presence and I AM One with the I AM Presence of ALL Humanity,"

our efforts will expand exponentially and we will invoke the Light of God into the lives of the more than seven billion people evolving on this planet.

The moment we invoke the Light of God, in any way, a matrix for the thoughtform we want to cocreate begins forming in the Realms of Cause. Each time we repeat our invocations or our prayers and meditations our matrix grows and becomes more powerful. Once something is formed in the Realms of Cause, *nothing* can prevent it from eventually manifesting in the world of effects, which is the physical plane of Earth. The only variable is how long that will take and that is up to you and me and the rest of awakening Humanity.

The Earth is subject to the Laws of Physics. There is a factor that we learn about in Quantum Mechanics that determines when the changes we are invoking and praying for will manifest in the physical world of form. That factor is called the *critical mass*. Everything is comprised of atomic and subatomic particles and waves of intelligent energy that are vibrating at various frequencies. The negative things manifesting in our lives are the result of heavy and discordant energy that we misqualified in the past through thoughts, feelings, words and actions that were not based in Love. The positive things manifesting in our lives are the result of positive and harmonious thoughts, feelings, words and actions we expressed in the past that were based in Love.

In order to change the negative things that are happening in our lives into positive things, we need to raise the vibration of the energy that is manifesting in negative ways and transmute it back into frequencies of Light. This unstoppable shift occurs when the negative energy reaches a *critical mass* of the higher frequency of Light. The fastest and most powerful frequency of Light available for transmuting negativity back into Light is the Violet Flame of God's Infinite Perfection. This particular Gift from our Father-Mother God is designed to help each of us reach a critical mass of positive energy faster than any other frequency of Light. So why are we not seeing more tangible results in the physical plane? It is because we often give up before we invoke enough Light to reach the critical mass of whatever it is we are striving to cocreate.

A very common scenario is that when we awaken and become aware of how powerful our creative faculties of thought and feeling are our I AM Presence inspires us to change our behavior. We are prompted to control our thoughts and feeling, and we are motivated to invoke the Violet Flame so we can transmute the negative things manifesting in our life. We decide to think positively and to control our emotions, and we focus our attention on what we want to manifest in our life. Sometimes, after what seems like a valiant effort we continue to experience some of the same old problems. That is when we often become discouraged and lose trust in our ability to change our life.

When this happens, we usually give up and stop trying to improve our situation. We no longer invoke the Violet Flame, and we stop doing our affirmations. This causes us to regress back into our old, negative behavior patterns. We start dwelling on our fears, problems and challenges instead using our thoughts and feelings to empower our goals, our hopes and our dreams. As a result of that relapse, things in our life get worse, and our situation appears to be even more hopeless. This phenomenon occurs because we stopped invoking the Light before we reached a critical mass of whatever it is that we were trying to cocreate. So what do we have to do to reach the unstoppable shift of critical mass? We have to *"keep on keeping on"* even when it seems as though we are not making progress, because that is never the case.

There are many variables that determine when something reaches critical mass, but to make things easy the Beings of Light said for us to think of critical mass as being 51% of the energy, vibration and consciousness of whatever it is that we want to cocreate. When an electron is increasing in vibration and 51% of its vibration reaches the higher frequency, an unstoppable shift occurs and the remaining 49% of the electron is instantly absorbed into the new vibration and the entire electron ascends into the higher frequency.

So for example, if we are striving to cocreate prosperity, 51% of our energy, vibration and consciousness from all time frames and dimensions, both known and unknown, must be vibrating with a frequency of prosperity consciousness instead of poverty consciousness. When we reach that critical mass of 51% prosperity consciousness, an unstoppable shift occurs and nothing can prevent prosperity from manifesting in our life. This is true for every single thing we are striving to cocreate in our life. If something that we have been working toward has not manifested in our life yet, it just means that we have not reached critical mass and we must "*keep on keeping on*" with our efforts. If we don't, what we are trying to cocreate will never manifest.

I know it is very daunting when we realize that we have to reach a critical mass of our energy from all timeframes and dimensions, both known and unknown, but miracles have taken place over the past several years and reaching a critical mass for our positive goals is far easier than it has ever been before. For one thing, our manipulative human ego is no longer able to block our efforts, and our I AM Presence is once again taking command of our life. Another critical factor is that the Light of God is exponentially expanding on Earth every single day. Light is infinitely more powerful than the fragmented and distorted patterns of our human miscreations. The Beings of Light have revealed that one person invoking the Light through their I AM Presence and the I AM Presence of ALL Humanity can transmute centuries worth of misqualified energy in a very short period of time.

In addition to those miracles, because of the need of the hour our Father-Mother God have granted the Company of Heaven a sacred Cosmic Dispensation that allows the Legions of Light to amplify our efforts every single time we add to the Light of the world. We are being told from On High that this is a Gift of Divine Grace unprecedented in any system of worlds.

Even though it is impossible for us to know when we will reach that magical moment of critical mass, it could be with the very next breath we take. So the Company of Heaven is encouraging us to invoke the Light of God with the enthusiasm that our goals could be reached with the very next breath, but with the heart commitment that, in the Eternal Moment of Now, we are going to *keep on keeping on* no matter how long it takes.

Precious Heart, *keep on keeping on* in whatever you are striving to accomplish know full well that *The Light of God is ALWAYS Victorious and YOU are that Light.*

14

TRANSCENDING YOUR
HUMAN EGO

In this sharing we are going to learn about transcending our bad habits and our negative behavior patterns. These are behaviors that we were coerced into by our manipulative human egos. In many instances, these negative habits are still affecting us adversely even though our egos are no longer in charge.

The Company of Heaven has revealed how we inadvertently created our fragmented and fear-based human ego. This aspect of our fallen consciousness has been a key factor in the painful situations we have been inflicting on ourselves for lifetimes. If you have not read the sharing in Chapter 4 please do so. That information will give you a foundation for the sacred knowledge the Beings of Light want you to comprehend at this time.

In 2010, after decades of work and innumerable activities of Light that were victoriously accomplished through the unified efforts of embodied Lightworkers and the Company of Heaven, a critical mass was reached on Earth that changed the lives of Humanity forever. That event involved Humanity, en masse, reaching a frequency of vibration which caused an unstoppable shift. That shift enabled every person's I AM Presence to burst the paralyzing grip our human ego has had on our Earthly Bodies.

For millennia our human ego has held us in bondage and fought tooth and nail to convince us that our physical body is who we are, and that the physical plane of Earth is all that exists. Our ego was terrified that if we remembered that we are multidimensional Sons and Daughters of God, we would reclaim our Divine Birthright and give dominion of our life back to our I AM Presence. Our ego was afraid that if that happened it would die and cease to exist.

That is not an unfounded fear. Our ego developed that concern because for centuries well meaning religious teachers have inaccurately taught us that Humanity is innately evil and that we are worthless sinners and worms in the dust. Unfortunately, we believed them and we accepted the erroneous idea that the only way we could free ourselves from the evil aspect of our ego was to destroy it.

Even now, there are schools of thought that are teaching that in order to become a spiritual Being one must suppress the ego through *"the mortification of the flesh."* To try and accomplish that impossible feat, Initiates have taken vows of celibacy and vows of poverty. They have even participated in self-flagellation and extreme fasting to try and eliminate the ego and separate themselves from that fallen consciousness. To the Initiate's dismay, those futile battles actually empowered the ego and caused it to hold on tighter and to fight even harder to maintain its control.

All efforts to suppress or eliminate our ego are futile, because we are One with ALL Life and there is no separation. Our ego is part of us and we cannot move forward in the Light without transforming, and Loving free, that fragmented and fear-based aspect of our own consciousness.

In 2010, awakening Humanity reached a critical mass of that profound knowing. Collectively, with the assistance of every person's I AM Presence and the entire Company of Heaven, we invoked a frequency of Light from the Heart of our Father-Mother God that raised the vibration of our Earthly Bodies beyond the grasp of our human ego. With this powerful influx of Light, the manipulative hold our human ego had on our physical, etheric, mental and emotional bodies was burst asunder. Once Humanity en masse was freed from the paralyzing grip of our human ego, our I AM Presence invoked Archangel Michael and his Legions of Power and Protection to encapsulate our ego in an invincible Forcefield of Light that is known as *"Archangel Michael's Ring Pass Not of God's First Cause of Perfection."* This is a Circle of White Lightning that prevents anything that is not of the Light from passing in or out of the circle. Only the Light of God can pass through this Forcefield of Light.

Once our ego was secured in this Circle of Light, our I AM Presence Inbreathed this aspect of our fallen consciousness into its Heart Flame. This is where our ego will remain until it voluntarily surrenders into the Light. With every breath, our I AM Presence is flooding our ego with our Father-Mother God's Transfiguring Divine Love. Even though in many instances our ego was breathed into the Heart Flame of our I AM Presence kicking and screaming, slowly but surely the Divine Love that our ego is being bathed in daily and hourly is softening its resistance. In the not too distant future, our ego will be permanently transformed and Loved free.

So of course the question is, if we were each freed from the manipulative control of our human ego in 2010 why are so many of us still acting out of those negative habits and obsolete behavior patterns? Well, that is the very thing that the Beings of Light in the Realms of Illumined Truth want us to understand at this critical juncture in our Ascension process.

Our Etheric Body is known as *"the seat of all memory."* Everything we have experienced through all of our Earthly sojourns is recorded in our Etheric Body. That means that the memories of our human ego's devious schemes, deceptions and self-obsessed behavior patterns are recorded in this vehicle. Since we are all creatures of habit, if we do not deliberately stay focused on our I AM Presence, it is very easy for us to just have reflex responses to our life situations that imitate our ego's past behavior. We respond in those obsolete but familiar ways because of our etheric memories and the simple fact that we are acting out in the same old way because it is the way we are used to doing things. In other words, it is just a habit and not because our human ego is able to manipulate us into behaving that way anymore.

Our human ego is no longer in control of our life. Now, the Beings of Light want us to understand that even though that is the case, it is our responsibility to stop acting out of old counterproductive habits. We have the absolute ability to correct this situation, but in order to do so we need to discipline ourselves. It is very important for us to stay focused on our I AM Presence and for us to be consciously present throughout the day.

This may sound difficult, but it is easily accomplished by remembering that you *are* your I AM Presence. By affirming that Truth and taking a moment to feel aligned with your I AM Presence before you respond to any situation in your life, you will begin to clearly hear the *"still small voice"* of your I AM Presence's inner guidance and experience your intuitive inner knowing in ways you were not able to when your human ego was in control.

This is incredibly liberating. Your I AM Presence has wonderful innovative ideas and viable solutions for all of the challenges in your life. The guidance from your I AM Presence is very practical and will always enhance your life and the lives of others. In my experience, it is impossible for a person to keep resisting this kind of positive and effective inner guidance. Consequently, even the most resistant person will sooner or later transcend the old habits of their human ego and begin joyfully responding to the inner directives of their I AM Presence. So to begin this process, before you respond the way you normally do to any situation in your life, align with your I AM Presence by affirming;

I AM my I AM Presence and I AM One with My Father-Mother God."

Then ask yourself;

From this level of Divine Consciousness, how will I respond to this situation?
How will I add to the Light of the world through my thoughts, words, feelings, actions, beliefs, and attitudes in this instance?

Then take a moment and listen to your heart. When you feel a sense of inner peace, respond to what you feel your I AM Presence is intuitively guiding you to do. If you have any doubts, there is an easy test to be sure you are responding to the guidance of your I AM Presence and not merely acting out of old habits from your ego. Ask yourself these three questions:

Is my response free from fear?
Am I handling this situation in the most Loving way?

Does my response reflect the highest good for all concerned?

If your answer is "no" to any of those questions, the guidance is not coming from your I AM Presence. You are responding from your Etheric Records and the residual habits of your ego. Instead of continuing with your old habits, center yourself and ask your I AM Presence for guidance again. Do this as many times as you need to until you are able to answer "yes" to all of those questions.

Practice being in the moment. Stay aligned with your I AM Presence and pay attention to how you are responding to everything in your life.

15

WHAT IS YOUR PURPOSE ON EARTH?

Your I AM Presence has magnetized this book into your sphere of awareness because of who you are and why you are on Earth during this auspicious time. This information which is being shared with you from the Company of Heaven is something you are very aware of on a higher level of consciousness, but that you may not have been able to remember in this dense physical plane. The Divine Intent is to remind you of what you have forgotten, because the time for you to fulfill your purpose and reason for being on Earth is now. Please open your heart and mind and let these words resonate within the Flame of Illumined Truth in your Heart Flame. Your I AM Presence will lift the veil and confirm this for you as an inner knowing.

Because of the unprecedented events being cocreated on Earth at this time through the unified efforts of awakening Humanity and the Company of Heaven, we are being told from On High that the greatest privilege and honor for any Son or Daughter of God is physical embodiment on Planet Earth during this Cosmic Moment. The Beings of Light want all of us to remember this Truth, because they are very aware of how difficult the challenges are that Humanity is facing on a daily basis.

We all knew it was going to be like this when we volunteered to embody on Earth during this unparalleled time. We agreed to come in spite of how daunting it might be because we knew we had all of the skill, knowledge, strength, courage and willingness necessary to succeed in this monumental mission. As a word of encouragement, we are being reminded that for every person who was granted permission to embody on Earth at this time, there were thousands more who were turned away. That is not because we are better or more enlightened than anyone else. It is because our Father-Mother God and the Company of Heaven felt that because of our past life experiences we had a better chance than our sisters and brothers of awakening and staying focused on the Light in the face of the adversity we were destined to encounter.

From the time Humanity made the fateful decision to experiment with our Life Force in ways that were not based in Love the Earth and all her Life were catapulted into the abyss of separation and duality. When that occurred our Father-Mother God set a plan into motion with the Divine Intent of reversing our fall from Grace. Of course, we are responsible for our human miscreations so the only way this plan could be fulfilled is if the Sons and Daughters of God made the freewill choice to reverse the adverse effects of the fall. In order to do that, we had to open our hearts and reclaim the path of Divine Love that our Father-Mother God originally intended for us to experience in this Earthly schoolroom.

Lifetime after lifetime, when we were between embodiments, our I AM Presence and the Company of Heaven evaluated our progress and our karmic liabilities. Together we came up with a plan that we thought would be most effective in moving us forward in the Light during our next embodiment. Part of that plan was always to help us learn our lessons and clear up as many of our past mistakes as possible. In order to accomplish that, we volunteered to be born into some very challenging situations. Once we began to experience the dense physical plane of Earth, without any conscious knowledge of why we had volunteered to experience such difficult situations, we were often overwhelmed which made things even worse. That gave our manipulative human ego the upper hand. That meant that many times by the end of that lifetime we ended up with even more karmic liabilities than we had when we started.

Fortunately, our I AM Presence never gives up. Ever so slowly, through many lifetimes of trial and error, we made incremental progress in our attempt to move forward in the Light. There were often lifetimes where we spent the majority of our life *"weeping and wailing through our valley of tears,"* but nothing is ever lost. Every difficult experience we endured actually strengthened our resolve and prepared us to stand our ground in the face of adversity. That difficult training prepared us for the mission we have volunteered to accomplish during this lifetime. That mission includes holding the sacred space for Humanity's and Earth's Ascension by staying focused on the Light no matter how horrific outer world events seem to be.

When we observe what is taking place in the outer world it is obvious that something big, but very confusing, is happening. There are two statements in the Bible that describe what we are experiencing.

"This is the time of screaming and the gnashing of teeth," and *"All that is hidden must now be revealed."*

The reason this is referred to as *"The time of screaming and the gnashing of teeth,"* is because when we look at the outer world we can easily see the horrific negativity being pushed to the surface to be healed and transmuted back into Light, which makes it look like things are getting worse. However, what we cannot see as easily is the incredible Light of God that is pushing those things to the surface.

The other statement, *"All that is hidden must now be revealed,"* is also the result of God's Light pushing everything to the surface. That statement involves not only pushing to the surface the greed, corruption and abuse of power that has been manipulating Humanity at a clandestine level since our fall from Grace, it also involves revealing the profound Truth of who we are as Sons and Daughters of God. This influx of God's Light is helping our I AM Presence push to the surface of our finite mind the memory of why we are on Earth during this particular time. It is also revealing what we have volunteered to do to assist this planet and ALL her Life to Ascend up the Spiral of Evolution into the 5th-Dimensional frequencies of the New Earth. Earth's Ascension will victoriously fulfill the next phase of our evolutionary journey back to the Heart of our Father-Mother God.

Your I AM Presence wants you to know that you have been preparing for lifetimes for this moment on Planet Earth. In spite of how overwhelmed, or how hopeless, or how inadequate or powerless you may feel, that is an illusion. Those thoughts and fear-based emotions are just residual memories from your human ego that are recorded in your Etheric Body. You are powerful beyond your knowing, and your I AM Presence is standing in readiness, awaiting the opportunity to reveal to you your facet of this unprecedented Divine Plan.

Your I AM Presence is the *only* one who can accurately reveal to you what your purpose is and what you have volunteered to accomplish in this lifetime. So center yourself every day, and ask your I AM Presence to guide you unerringly to fulfill your highest Divine Potential with every thought, feeling, word and action you express. Then, pay attention.

Nothing in your life is happening by accident. Every single thing that enters your sphere of awareness is part of your Divine Plan. Be consciously aware that every moment, of every day, with every breath you take, you are being given the opportunity to fulfill your PURPOSE and REASON for BEING on Earth by adding to the Light of the world. Your I AM Presence knows exactly how to do this, so be open and receptive to that intuitive inner guidance moment to moment.

16

WHY IS THIS SUCH A CRITICAL TIME ON EARTH?

In this sharing the Beings of Light are going to remind you of why this is such a critical time on Earth. You already know this or you would not have been allowed to embody at this time. If you have forgotten these Truths, this information will make it much easier for you to lift your head above the chaos so you can stay focused on the Light as you move through these wondrous but often challenging times.

The Earth and all Life evolving upon her are in the midst of a Cosmic event known as the "*Shift of the Ages.*" This event is a natural step in our evolutionary process back to the Heart of our Father-Mother God. The Shift of the Ages affects every particle and wave of Life throughout the whole of Creation and it occurs only once in several million years.

The Shift of the Ages involves a very rare alignment during which celestial and galactic cycles within cycles within cycles throughout the whole of Creation dovetail into one synchronized pulsation with the Heartbeat of our Father-Mother God. During that awesome moment, our God Parents inbreathe every particle and wave of Life within the all encompassing Divine Matrix of their Body up the Spiral of Evolution into the next wave of our evolutionary process. This is the Ascension that awakening Humanity is becoming aware of on a conscious level.

This event has been alluded to in the ancient scriptures of various world religions. In the Bible it is referred to as the Rapture and described as a mystical event during which the Righteous will be raised up into the air. The Raptured souls will experience a New Heaven and a New Earth, and the old Earth will pass away. These prophecies of old predicted that when the time comes, only a few people will be in position to make this shift. Some foretold that only 144,000 people would be pure enough to make this shift. Others said it would be only 10 percent of the people on the planet who would make it through the Shift of the Ages, and that the rest of Humanity would be left behind with the old Earth. Others have taught that only those who belong to a particular religion will be Righteous enough to make it through this Ascension process.

It is true that there was a time in the very recent past when millions of people had the potential of being left behind during the Shift of the Ages, but that is no longer the case. Now the Beings of Light want you to know that miracles have been cocreated through the unified efforts of Heaven and Earth over the past several decades. Your I AM Presence was an intricate part of that victorious facet of the Divine Plan. That is true even if you were not aware of it on a conscious level.

Several of the Divinely Inspired prophecies indicated that the reason so many people would be left behind is because of the dense and discordant frequencies of vibration Humanity fell to after our fateful decision to use our Gift of Life in ways that were not based in Love. Due to our painfully slow progress in reversing the adverse effects of that decision, there was a great possibility that many of us would not be able to raise our vibrations and reclaim the path of Divine Love in time to make it through the Shift of the Ages. The concern was that millions would be left behind, not because God was punishing us, but because our vibrations were so dense that we would not be able to withstand the 5th-Dimensional frequencies of Crystalline Solar Light associated with the New Earth. The Beings of Light warned that if Humanity tried to Ascend into the 5th-Dimensional frequencies of Light on the New Earth from the depth of vibration we had fallen to, it would be like trying to move through a lightning bolt and we would be vaporized.

Many people have accepted these prophecies literally and they are anxiously wringing their hands and waiting for catastrophic events to occur so they can be Raptured. Some fanatical religions are trying to expedite the Rapture by instigating events that would trigger a global world war. They realize this is the time for this long awaited Ascension process and they believe that Armageddon is a precursor to the Rapture. Both of those interpretations are inaccurate.

The Company of Heaven assure us that the only time prophecies are Divinely Inspired that foretell a potentially negative outcome as this one does, is if the Sons and Daughters of God abiding on Earth have the ability to do something to avert the negative outcome. Prophecies of this nature are revealed to demonstrate to Humanity what will occur if we continue on the path we are on. These prophecies are specifically designed to motivate us to change course so that we will avert the potential negative outcome being revealed. In this case, that would be potentially millions of people being left behind during the Shift of the Ages.

The Beings of Light said a fulfilled negative prophecy is a *failed prophecy*. If in fact the negative outcome revealed in the prophecy does occur, it means that Humanity did not rise to the occasion and improve our behavior patterns effectively enough to accomplish the change that was intended by the Divinely Inspired prophesy.

To the exquisite joy, wonder and awe of the Heavenly Realms, this prophecy did not fail. Awakening Humanity succeeded beyond the greatest expectations of everyone involved. Not only did millions of people not get left behind during the Shift of the Ages, every single recalcitrant person on Earth made the conscious choice through his or her I AM Presence to do whatever is necessary to heal and transmute their human miscreations so they can complete their Ascension process and move forward into the Light.

The Cosmic Moment of the Shift of the Ages was God Victoriously accomplished through ALL Creation during the Solstice on December 21st and 22nd in 2012. In the Eternal Moment of Now, as the Earth aligned with the Galactic Core of the Milky Way, our Father-Mother God instantaneously inbreathed every particle and wave of Life within the Body of God up the Spiral of Evolution into the next octave of their evolutionary process. During that unprecedented moment in the evolution of this planet, the New Earth was birthed in the Realms of Cause in all of her resplendent glory.

According to the Company of Heaven, this was the most difficult thing the Sons and Daughters of God have ever been called to do. This was a unique experiment that had never been attempted in any system of worlds. Never in the history of time has a planet that has fallen to the depth of pain and suffering the Earth is experiencing been given the opportunity to move through two dimensional shifts is such a short period of time. We moved from the 3rd-Dimension through the 4th-Dimension and into the initial impulse of the frequencies of the 5th-Dimensional New Earth in a matter of a few short decades. This is what was meant when the prophecies said Earth's transformation will take place in what will be perceived as *"the twinkling of an eye."* But this is just the beginning of the mission you and I and the rest of awakening Humanity have volunteered to accomplish on behalf of Mother Earth and all Life evolving upon her.

We have victoriously birthed the New Earth and every person evolving on this planet made it through the Shift of the Ages. This was an act of Divine Grace by our Father-Mother God that is truly beyond the comprehension of our finite minds. This merciful Gift of Divine Grace was given to the recalcitrant Sons and Daughters of God because every one of them, through their I AM Presence, made the heart commitment to do whatever is necessary to complete their lessons and transmute their human miscreations back into Light.

When every single person has completed this unparalleled Ascension process, and the New Earth in all of her exquisite beauty has reclaimed her rightful place in our Solar System, we will have cocreated a new octave of Godhood for the Sons and Daughters of God throughout all Creation. From this time on, the Children of God will be able to learn about the perils and the agony of separation and duality from the records of our life experiences without ever having to go through the pain and suffering we inadvertently miscreated through our lack of awareness.

Everything we have ever endured from our tragic self-inflicted fall from Grace is now recorded in the Halls of Knowledge in the Realms of Illumined Truth. The Sons and Daughters of God throughout Infinity will now be able to learn about these painful miscreations by studying about them. This means they will never have to physically experience the horrific challenges we have endured. The Beings of Light want us to know that because of that Truth, the Universe is rejoicing and the Gratitude flowing forth from the Heavenly Realms is unwavering.

17

A CONTINGENCY PLAN
FOR EARTH

During the past century, our sisters and brothers in the awakening Family of Humanity have been holding the sacred space for our awakening. These dedicated Lightworkers have been invoking our I AM Presence and weaving the Light from all of our Earthly experiences into every activity of Light that our Father-Mother God and the Company of Heaven have inspired the Sons and Daughters of God on Earth to participate in. Through this unified effort, miracles have taken place that moved this sweet Earth forward in the Light in ways that transcended the greatest expectations of everyone involved.

The Beings of Light are going to share some information about those miracles with you. The Divine Intent of this sharing is to help you clearly see that in spite of outer appearances amazing things are happening on this planet. This Earth and ALL Life evolving upon her are in the process of Ascending into the full embrace of the New Earth. The reason it is important for you to understand what is happening is because it is time for you to participate in this holy endeavor on a conscious level. This knowledge will enhance the efforts of your I AM Presence which will accelerate the tangible manifestation of the patterns of perfection for the New Earth in your life and in the lives of all Humanity.

In the previous sharing, we learned that what is occurring on Earth at this time is a unique experiment that has never been attempted in any system of worlds. When we succeed in completing this experiment, we will have cocreated a new octave of Godhood that will benefit all of the Sons and Daughters of God from this moment forth. For this reason, the Earth is receiving more assistance from the Company of Heaven and the Sons and Daughters of God throughout Infinity, than has ever been allowed by Cosmic Law. The entire Universe is focused on this one tiny planet. The Beings of Light from every Ascended Realm and Galaxy are holding the sacred space for Earth's and Humanity's ultimate Ascension in the Light.

Even with this unprecedented level of assistance, it was clear by the end of the 1800's that without super-human Divine Intervention the masses of Humanity were not going to awaken soon enough to change our course from the path of separation and duality to the path of Divine Love in time to make it through the Shift of the Ages. With that realization our Father-Mother God issued a Cosmic Edict that initiated a contingency plan with the Divine Intent of accelerating Humanity's awakening.

Knowing the urgency of the hour, our Father-Mother God sent forth a Clarion Call asking highly evolved Beings from the Ascended Realms of Light if they would be willing to embody on Earth to assist Humanity in transmuting our human miscreations and reclaiming our path of Divine Love. The goal was for these Beings to help the masses of Humanity who were still asleep to raise their heads above the mud puddle of their miscreations effectively enough to once again hear the still small voice and the inner guidance of their I AM Presence.

The Beings of Light said that never before had so many Sons and Daughters of God volunteered to assist their sisters and brothers under such difficult circumstances. In order to withstand the discordant frequencies of Humanity's miscreations, these Beings had to lower their vibrations to a frequency they had never experienced. They were also compelled to enter the Earth with the Band of Forgetfulness just like the rest of Humanity. That meant that they would not initially remember who they are or why they had volunteered to be born on Earth. Since these Beings would not be encumbered by the karmic liabilities the Children of Earth were enduring, the hope was that they would be able to awaken quickly and remember their selfless missions in time to help Humanity through the Shift of the Ages.

Our Sisters and Brothers throughout the Cosmos agreed to make this sacrifice because they were shown what would be accomplished on behalf of the Sons and Daughters of God throughout all Creation once Earth's Ascension was complete and this unprecedented experiment was victoriously accomplished. Out of the billions of highly evolved Beings who volunteered to embody on Earth, several hundred million were chosen for this vitally important facet of our Father-Mother God's new contingency plan.

Once the decision was made the floodgates of Heaven opened and these Beings began to embody on Earth through the natural process of birth. During the past 100 years, hundreds of millions of these powerful Beings have embodied in every corner of the world. Many of these selfless Sons and Daughters of God embodied into areas of the planet that are reflecting the most horrific frequencies of

Humanity's miscreations. These are areas where people's fragmented and fear-based egos have been inflicting atrocities on other human beings for millennia.

The highly evolved Beings made the sacrifice of being born into these painful situations on Earth because they believed that they would be able to transcend the pain more easily than the Children of Earth who had been beaten into the depths of despair and hopelessness by their ego's destructive behavior and their gross miscreations.

In addition to the Beings who volunteered to embody into the densest frequencies of Humanity's pain and suffering, there were Beings who chose to embody in areas that would allow them to speed up Humanity's technological advancement. When these Beings awakened, they lifted up in consciousness and tapped into the patterns of perfection in the Causal Body of God. Their goal was to improve the conditions of the world through advanced technology.

The discoveries and inventions these Beings have revealed to the world over the past 100 years accelerated our technology in ways that cannot be logically explained through Humanity's typical evolutionary process. During the latter part of the 1800s, we had barely discovered the telephone, the combustion engine and electricity. The quantum leaps we have made in technology since that time far transcend any previously known rate of development.

Unfortunately, some of the technology has been hijacked by Humanity's wayward human egos. It has been corrupted and used for destructive purposes that have caused a great deal of harm. Misguided people have created things like nuclear weapons and designer diseases. Some industries have abused technology in ways that have caused the catastrophic pollution of the Earth. These gross abuses of power have resulted in levels of greed and corruption that boggle the mind. They have also created obscene imbalances in the distribution of wealth and a level of poverty that is beyond the comprehension of anyone who has a compassionate Heart.

Now, the egos of even the most recalcitrant and asleep people are no longer in control and are in the process of being Loved free. This means that the Divine Intent of our Father-Mother God's contingency plan is now in full swing and the Earth and all her Life are moving forward in the Light at warp speed.

It is quite possible that you may be one of the advanced Beings who have come to assist the Earth and all her Life into the 5th-Dimensional New Earth. Only your I AM Presence can reveal that to you, and that will only happen if that knowledge will somehow help you to fulfill your Divine Mission in this moment.

It is actually immaterial whether we are one of the highly evolved Beings from the Realms of Light who have come to help the Children of Earth, or if we are one of the original Children of Earth. We are all One, and no person's part of this Divine Plan is more important than another person's part of the plan. We are all Sons and Daughters of God with exactly the same Divine Potential, and we are here to help our sisters and brothers in the Family of Humanity to return to the path of Oneness and Divine Love. It is through our collective and unified efforts that we will succeed.

The Company of Heaven wants us to know about this contingency plan on a conscious level, so that we will realize the incredible assistance we are receiving from On High. They want to encourage us and to motivate us to stay focused on the Light in spite of any adversity surfacing in our life or in the outer world.

Next the Beings of Light will share some of the amazing and life-transforming events that have taken place during the past 30 years. These were vitally important facets of Earth's Ascension process that you participated in through your I AM Presence whether you were consciously aware of it or not.

18

SOME CLARITY ABOUT
THIS TIME AND THE TERM
"NEW AGE"

The Company of Heaven is aware that this information may seem new to you and may be a little technical. However, they affirm that knowing this Truth on a conscious level will greatly enhance the ability of your I AM Presence to reveal to you the extensive experiences you have been through in preparation for this Cosmic Moment in your evolutionary process.

In the last sharing we learned about the Cosmic Dispensation from our Father-Mother God that allowed hundreds of millions of our Sisters and Brothers from the Higher Realms of Illumined Truth to embody on Earth during the latter part the 1800s and the beginning of the 1900s. That was the first phase of the Divine Plan involving the urgent push to awaken Humanity in time for the Shift of the Ages.

The second phase of the Divine Plan involved a Dispensation from our Father-Mother God that gave the Company of Heaven permission to come through the dense veil of Humanity's miscreations in the psychic astral plane in order to meet us halfway. This Divine Intervention made it much easier for awakening Humanity to reach up in consciousness and once again connect with the Beings of Light in the Realms of Illumined Truth through our I AM Presence.

As the Enlightened Beings who were embodied on Earth began to awaken and reach up in consciousness, several Mystery Schools began forming on Earth. Each school was under the tutelage of the Company of Heaven and revealed one of the various paths that would assist Humanity to awaken and return to Christ Consciousness. As the sacred knowledge for the various Mystery Schools began flowing into the mental and emotional strata of Earth, people around the world began awakening in massive numbers. This caused the Light of God to expand exponentially through every person's Heart Flame. People began remembering who they are and why they are on Earth during this auspicious time.

This awakening terrified our human egos because they knew that if we regained Christ Consciousness and our I AM Presence reclaimed dominion of our physical, etheric, mental and emotional bodies, they would lose the ability to manipulate and control us. This fear caused an all out rebellion in the most asleep and recalcitrant people on Earth. In order to try and stop Humanity's awakening these people, through the fallen consciousness of their human egos, proceeded to wreak havoc wherever they could. World War I, World War II, the creation of the atom bomb, the Korean War and the other wars that took place during the last century including the Vietnam War were all instigated through the fear-based consciousness of Humanity's fragmented egos.

In addition to the catastrophic wars some people's egos tried to block Humanity's awakening through greed, corruption and the abuse of power. That interference caused the stock market crash in the 1920s and 1930s, and the obscene imbalance in the distribution of wealth that we are experiencing to this very day. In spite of the ego's horrific attempt to block Humanity's awakening, its malevolent efforts failed and the Divine Plan continued to unfold step by step.

The Light of God is infinitely more powerful than the fragmented and fear-based thoughtforms and behavior patterns of our fallen human egos. The Enlightened Beings embodied on Earth continued to awaken, and the influx of Light and the sacred knowledge they invoked into the hearts and minds of the masses of Humanity through each person's I AM Presence began raising the energy, vibration and consciousness of each person above the chaos and confusion manifesting in their life.

In the 1950s and the 1960s, the Oneness of ALL Life began to be resurrected within the hearts of awakening Humanity. In the United States of America the Civil Rights movement became a powerful force for good. Once again our fear-based egos tried to block this compassionate and vitally important movement toward equality and Oneness, but in most instances their attempts failed.

During the 1960s and 1970s, the youth around the world began rejecting the consciousness of war and greed. Young people in the USA and around the world began Peace movements and expressed en masse the concept of "*making Love not war.*" These awakening young people professed the need to reconnect with nature and to honor Mother Earth as the living, breathing organism she is. They rejected the ego's quest for the almighty dollar and its wayward desire to accumulate wealth and personal gain regardless of the negative effects that obsession for money may have on Humanity or the Earth.

During those decades, young people *"tuned in and dropped out"* and connected with a new level of spirituality that inspired them to remember their own Divinity as Sons and Daughters of God. This awareness set them on a quest for answers that catapulted the Earth and all her Life into the full embrace of the Dawning New Age of Enlightenment.

When our egos realized that sacred knowledge was flowing into Humanity's hearts and minds on the waves of consciousness associated with the Dawning New Age of Enlightenment, they knew they had to do something or our I AM Presence would be able to once and for all reclaim the power our ego had usurped from us aeons ago. The only thing our egos knew to do was to discredit the profound Truth flowing from the Heart and Mind of God into the mental and emotional strata of Earth during the Dawning New Age.

Our egos created fear-based misinformation and disinformation about the term "New Age." They knew that whenever there is new information coming to the forefront that challenges our present belief systems, our first response is to become suspicious and afraid. Once we let go of our fear and open our hearts and minds, however, our I AM Presence is able to help us perceive things in a higher Light with greater clarity.

In case you are confused about what the term *"New Age"* really means, let me briefly share with you what a New Age is. First of all a New Age is not a new religion, or a movement, or a new philosophy, or the work of the devil as some are professing. The Dawn of a New Age is nothing more than a span of time. It involves the natural astronomical cycle known as the Precession of the Equinoxes, which the Earth has been going through since her inception.

As our Earth revolves on her axis every 24 hours, we experience a new day. As she orbits in a clockwise movement around the Sun every 365 and ¼ days, we experience a new year. On the orbit around the Sun, the Earth passes through the force fields of the 12 natural constellations that form our zodiac. During this annual orbit, the Earth and all Life evolving upon her are held in the Light and influence of these constellations for 28 to 31 days depending on the month. These are the Sun cycles that we are all familiar with: Capricorn, Aquarius, Pisces, et cetera. Each of these constellations pulsates with one of the Twelve Solar Aspects of Deity, which the Company of Heaven will discuss in detail in another chapter. During the time we are held in the forcefield of each Sun cycle, the Earth is bathed with the Light and Divine Qualities of that particular Solar Aspect of Deity. All Life on Earth receives the blessings from this Light regardless of whether or not we are aware of it or are in anyway associated with astrology.

In addition to the very obvious time frames of a new day and a new year, the Earth is part of a much larger celestial cycle that is called the Precession of the Equinoxes. This precession is created by the wobble the Earth makes due to the tilted position of her axis. This is a counterclockwise rotation that once again moves the Earth very slowly through the forcefields of the 12 constellations. The Earth's movement in this precession is measured at the point where the Sun passes the equator during the March Equinox each year. This point moves about 50.2 seconds per year, so it takes about 70 years for the Earth to move one degree, or about 26,000 years to move through the forcefields of all 12 constellations. Earth is held in the Light of the Solar Aspect of Deity associated with each constellation for approximately 30 degrees or a little over 2,000 years. These 2,000-year cycles are called Ages.

The Dawn of a New Age is the period of time during which the energies from the Age we are leaving begin to recede and the energies from the Solar Aspect of Deity of the constellation we are moving into have not fully embraced the Earth. It is during this ebb of energy that our Father-Mother God and the Company of Heaven evaluate the progress Humanity made during the Age that is ending and determine what information will enhance our spiritual growth in the Dawning New Age. Once the decision is made, that sacred knowledge is projected into the mental and emotional strata of Earth so that awakening Humanity will have easy access to it.

In the latter part of the 1800s we began leaving the Age of Pisces and we had not begun to receive the full influx of Light from the Dawning Age of Aquarius. This opened the door for the influx of information our Father-Mother God and the Company of Heaven felt would be most beneficial in helping Humanity through the Shift of the Ages and Earth's Ascension into the 5th-Dimensional frequencies of the New Earth.

Contemplate this information and ask your I AM Presence to reveal to you how your awakening process has been affected by this Dawning New Age.

19

How Did We Create Such Divisive World Religions?

So much of the chaos that is surfacing around the world at this time is based in Humanity's fallen ego's manipulation and misinterpretation of the sacred knowledge that was revealed to Humanity by our Father-Mother God and the Company of Heaven during the Dawning New Ages of the past. In many instances that knowledge, which was designed to assist ALL of Humanity to move forward in the Light, was hijacked by our egos and crystallized into the divisive world religions that are doing battle with each other today.

Our fear-based egos are no longer in control, but in order to stop the masses of Humanity from continuing to act out of the destructive habits of separation and duality, we need to perceive the bigger picture. How did our egos come up with the distorted beliefs that are causing so much pain and suffering at this time? Once we understand that, our I AM Presence will be able to assist us more effectively in transmuting back into Light the intelligent atomic and subatomic energy associated with those gross mutations. So let this information resonate within the Divinity of your Heart Flame and your I AM Presence will assist you to comprehend this Truth in perfect alignment with your Divine Plan and your highest good.

Prior to the fall, when the Dawn of each New Age arrived it was easy for our God Parents and the Company of Heaven to determine the next level of sacred knowledge that would assist us the most in learning how to become cocreators with our Father-Mother God. This new information was projected into the mental and emotional strata of Earth and was then assimilated by our I AM Presence and reflected into our conscious mind. Since we were aware that we are Sons and Daughters of God and understood our purpose and reason for being embodied on Earth, we accepted this new information with enthusiasm and gratitude.

After the fall, this process changed dramatically. Once we began misqualifying our Life Force, we no longer came to Earth with the sole purpose of learning the joy-filled lessons of becoming cocreators. After the fall we came to Earth not only to learn our lessons of cocreation, but also to transmute the distorted patterns we had created through the misuse of our thoughts and feelings in our previous lives.

Without the balance of our Mother God's Love and the inadvertent creation of our fragmented and fear-based human ego, our perception was totally distorted. We forgot about the Oneness of all Life, so we just allowed our fallen ego to keep abusing our Masculine Power. During this time, the windows of opportunity provided by the Dawning New Ages had very little influence in changing our direction. We were so buried in the oppressive energy of our human miscreations that we were not able to perceive the guidance from On High that our I AM Presence was trying to filter into our conscious mind. It seemed as though we were never going to be able to stop our downward spiral, but our Father-Mother God would not give up on us.

Several Ages ago our God Parents made the decision to allow an advanced Cosmic Being to embody on Earth during the Dawn of each New Age. These Enlightened Beings were Avatars who were not associated in any way with Earth's fall from Grace. The Divine Intent of this dispensation was for the Avatar of each New Age to reveal and physically demonstrate to Humanity the lessons our Father-Mother God wanted us to learn during the next 2000-year cycle. Because of the patriarchal consciousness of Humanity's human egos at the time, our God Parents initially chose masculine Avatars for this Divine Mission. There were several Avatars over the Ages, but the ones we are most familiar with prior to the Piscean Age are Krishna, Buddha and Moses.

The lessons the Avatar brought to Earth from our Father-Mother God were always designed to help Humanity awaken, so that we would reconnect with our I AM Presence and reverse the adverse effects of our fall from Grace. This meant initiating the return of our Mother God by opening our Heart Chakra and placing our feet on the path of Divine Love. It also meant reclaiming our Divine Birthright as Sons and Daughters of God by returning to Christ Consciousness.

Unfortunately, we were so beaten down by the victim consciousness of our egos that we misunderstood the lessons the Avatars were trying to teach us. We assumed these Beings had come to save us and we began separating ourselves from them and worshiping them. We Deified them and expected for them to do for us the very things they were trying to teach us that we must learn to do for ourselves.

Humanity formed cult like attachments to these Enlightened Beings and began organizing other people who would accept their particular interpretation of what the Avatars were demonstrating through their teachings.

Since it was the person's fragmented human ego that was interpreting the lesson the Avatar was teaching, much of the information was grossly distorted and infused with a patriarchal and victim consciousness. This limited perception omitted the Divine Love Nature of our Mother God and the reality that Christ Consciousness is the Divine Birthright of every Son and Daughter of God. These groups became the foundations for the crystallized and often divisive "religions" that have formed over the Ages.

When it was time for the Dawn of the Piscean Age our Father-Mother God and the Company of Heaven knew that the Earth was swiftly moving toward the momentous event known as the Shift of the Ages. They were profoundly aware that the masses of Humanity were still buried in the painful effluvia of our miscreations. They knew that the embodiment of the Avatars during the previous New Ages had helped to a degree, but not nearly enough to raise the energy, vibration and consciousness of Humanity high enough to make it through the Shift of the Ages.

All of the Legions of Light in the Realms of Illumined Truth knew that if the Earth and ALL Life evolving upon her were going to make it through the Shift of the Ages, we were going to need superhuman Divine Intervention. With that knowing, a Divine Plan was set into motion that changed the course of history for this sweet Earth and all Life evolving upon her.

In the next sharing the Company of Heaven will reveal the Truth about the life-transforming events that occurred during the Piscean Age through the unified efforts of Heaven and Earth. Those events changed the course of history and paved the way for an unprecedented influx of Light that catapulted the Earth and all her Life into the Dawning New Age of Aquarius.

20

THE AVATARS OF THE PISCEAN AGE JESUS AND MARY MAGDALENE

The Beings of Light want to share with you some important information with the Divine Intent of bringing a
new level of clarity to the events that occurred during the
Dawning New Age of Pisces. Those events were a critical factor in assisting Humanity to reverse the adverse effects of
our fall from Grace. The success of that facet of the Divine
Plan paved the way for the missions you and I and the rest of
awakening Humanity have volunteered to accomplish during this unprecedented moment on Earth.

Please ask your I AM Presence and our Father-Mother
God to take full dominion of this moment, so that you can
set aside any preconceived ideas that would prevent you
from *"seeing with new eyes and hearing with new ears"* as this
information is revealed to you. This is sacred knowledge
that you know through the higher consciousness of your
I AM Presence, but that the Company of Heaven said will
greatly accelerate your comprehension about what is occurring on Earth at this time if you know it on a conscious level.

When our Father-Mother God and the Company of Heaven evaluated Humanity's progress during the Dawn of the New Age of Pisces, it was clear that the growth we had attained during the Age of Aries was almost nonexistent. Our egos were still misleading us by perpetuating the myth that our physical body is all that we are and that the physical plane is all that exists. Those who were beginning to remember God accepted our ego's distorted perception that even though we are Children of God, we only have one parent and that parent is our Father God. We were oblivious to the fact that we also have a Mother God.

It was clear to the Beings of Light evaluating Humanity's progress that even though the masculine Avatars of the past Ages had indeed demonstrated to Humanity the path of Divine Love, the fact that they were all male perpetuated the belief that God is masculine. The Beings of Light knew that if Humanity was going to make it through the Shift of the Ages, which was looming in the not too distant future, we had to remember that we have a Father and a Mother God.

Only then would we know to open our Heart Chakra to full breadth and invoke the return of our Mother God. Only then would our Mother God's Divine Love be available to reawaken the dormant hemisphere of our right brain. Only then would our I AM Presence be able to reactivate our atrophied spiritual brain centers, so that we could once again open our Crown Chakra and reclaim our Divine Birthright as Sons and Daughters of God by returning to Christ Consciousness.

Christ Consciousness is the state of Enlightenment that our Father-Mother God invested each of us with at our inception when we were first breathed forth from the Core of Creation. It is this elevated state of consciousness which we must all return to in order to complete the Ascension process we are now experiencing.

Knowing the urgent need of the hour, our Father-Mother God and the Company of Heaven devised a plan in cooperation with the I AM Presence of every man, woman and child on Earth. That plan set into motion events they hoped would open the door for the return of our Mother God and initiate Humanity's return to Christ Consciousness.

A Beloved Son and Daughter of God who had been preparing for this possible service to Humanity for aeons of time were summoned from the Great Silence by our Father-Mother God. This time there would not be one masculine Avatar but rather a male and a female Avatar who would model to Humanity the perfect balance of the Masculine and the Feminine Aspects of our Father-Mother God, which originally pulsated within the Divinity of every person's Heart Flame.

These precious Beings are Twin Flames who selflessly volunteered to embody on Earth through the natural process of birth in order to anchor the Divine Matrix and the archetypes for the return of our Mother God and the path of Divine Love that would enable Humanity to return to Christ Consciousness. The Avatars of the Piscean Age are the Ones we have known as Jesus the Christ and Mary Magdalene.

Jesus and Mary Magdalene knew that because of Humanity's ingrained belief in the patriarchal authority of a single Father God, Mary's role would initially be as a silent partner. Her part of the Divine Plan was cloaked in secrecy to prevent the plan from being blocked through the abuse of power being wielded by Humanity's patriarchal human egos at the time. Jesus and Mary Magdalene were husband and wife. They served as equal partners in this facet of the Divine Plan. Through their unified efforts they God Victoriously accomplished the Immaculate Concept of their Divine Mission.

During what is referred to as *"the lost 18 years,"* Jesus and Mary Magdalene studied in the Mystery Schools of India, Tibet, and Egypt. When it was time to begin their mission of anchoring the Divine Matrix and the archetypes for the return of our Mother God and Humanity's return to Christ Consciousness, Jesus and Mary Magdalene demonstrated the imperative first step for all the world to see.

At the age of 30, after completing their lessons in the Mystery Schools, Jesus and Mary Magdalene traveled to the banks of the Jordan River where they consecrated their Life Force to serve as surrogates on behalf of ALL Humanity. Water represents the emotional strata of the Earth as well as Humanity's heart centered Emotional Bodies. Jesus immersed himself in the sacred waters of the Jordan River and participated in a Divine Ceremony conducted by John the Baptist. During that ceremony, Jesus opened his Heart Chakra to full breadth and invoked through his Heart Flame the return of our Mother God on behalf of every man, woman and child on Earth.

When John the Baptist Baptized Jesus with the sacred Water Element, our Mother God projected her Love through Jesus' right-brain hemisphere. The Dove of the Holy Spirit entered Jesus' Crown Chakra and activated his spiritual brain centers to their full Divine Potential. This permanently anchored into the physical plane of Earth the Divine Matrix and the archetypes for the return of our Mother God and Humanity's return to Christ Consciousness.

I imagine we have all seen pictures of Jesus standing in the Jordan River with the Dove of the Holy Spirit descending into his Crown Chakra after he was Baptized by John the Baptist. When Jesus' Baptism was complete, Mary Magdalene experienced the same anointing through a Baptism of the Holy Spirit. At that moment they both became the Christ grown to full stature, and their mission of modeling Humanity's Divine Potential as Beloved Sons and Daughters of God began in earnest. They were now officially the Avatars of the Piscean Age.

For the next three years, Jesus and Mary Magdalene modeled to the world the path of Oneness and Divine Love that each of us must follow in order to return to Christ Consciousness. They were very aware of how Humanity's egos had distorted the message of the Avatars in past Ages and they worked continuously to prevent that from happening this time.

They affirmed through their teachings that the path of Divine Love is a path we must all follow in order to return to Christ Consciousness and that no one can do this for us. In spite of all of the miracles Jesus demonstrated as "*the Christ*" he reiterated over and over,

> "*These things I do you shall do and even greater things than these shall you do.*"

Jesus taught that "*the Christ*" within him is the same as "*the Christ*" within each of us, and that "*the Christ*" within each of us is the only begotten Son or Daughter of God. Jesus also said,

> "*Is it not written in your Law, I said, 'YE ARE GODS'? YE ARE GODS, and all of you are Children of the Most High.*"

For three years Jesus and Mary Magdalene demonstrated what being "*the Christ*" and Christ Consciousness truly are by modeling the path of Divine Love through their dedication to each other and their Reverence for ALL Life. When Jesus' part of the mission was complete he volunteered to go through one final demonstration with the Divine Intent of proving to Humanity once and for all that not even he can save us. Only by following the path of Divine Love and Returning to Christ Consciousness can we reverse the adverse effects of our fall from Grace.

Dear One, in the next sharing the Company of Heaven will reveal information regarding that profound Truth and clarify the final message that Jesus left for Humanity through his crucifixion and his Resurrection.

21

THE TRUE PURPOSE OF JESUS' CRUCIFIXION AND RESURRECTION

The Company of Heaven will continue bringing us greater clarity about the Divine Mission Jesus and Mary Magdalene fulfilled as Avatars during the Piscean Age. This is important for us to understand because it is a critical part of what we must each do now to fulfill our own Divine Missions. So please, center yourself within the Divinity of your Heart Flame and as you read these words ask your I AM Presence to help you *"see with new eyes and hear with new ears."*

From the time aeons ago when we inadvertently created our fragmented and fear-based human ego, that aspect of our fallen consciousness has been fighting tooth and nail to convince us that we are worthless sinners and worms in the dust. The intent of that blatant lie was to prevent us from remembering that, in Truth, we are Beloved Sons and Daughters of God and that ALL our Father-Mother God have is ours.

Unfortunately, for millennia our egos were very success-ful. That is why when the Avatars came during the Dawn of each New Age we did not accept that they were here to demonstrate to us what we must learn to do for ourselves in order to reverse the adverse effects of our fall from Grace. Instead our ego convinced us that the Avatars had come to save us because we were too evil and worthless to be able to save ourselves. Of course, nothing could be further from the Truth. In fact, no one can save us and that lie is exactly what prevented us from grasping the true message of the Avatars.

Jesus and Mary Magdalene were very aware of our ego's deception and they were determined not to let Humanity's egos interfere with their message. At the age of 33, Jesus and Mary had completed the mission of anchoring the Divine Matrix and archetypes for the return of our Mother God and Humanity's return to Christ Consciousness. Thirty-three is the master number that reflects "*The Christ made manifest.*" There is a lot of discussion at this time as to whether Jesus was actually crucified and whether or not he Resurrected his body. Jesus and the Company of Heaven have confirmed that both of those events did occur and were vitally important to the fulfillment of Jesus and Mary Magdalene's Divine Plan.

Contrary to the guilt-inducing things we are often told, the reason Jesus was crucified was not to save us because we are so evil we cannot do it for ourselves. Our Father-Mother God gave each of us the gift of free will and no one is allowed to do this for us. We are each responsible for how we have used our gift of Life.

We lost the awareness of our own Divinity through our free will choices and the misuse of our creative faculties of thought and feeling. Consequently, the only way we will return to Christ Consciousness is through our own endeavors. We must open our hearts and invoke the return of our

Mother God, and we must follow the path of Oneness and Divine Love that Jesus and Mary Magdalene modeled for us.

Jesus agreed to be crucified in order to prove to the world that we are not just our physical body, and that there is *nothing* the fallen human ego can do to our body that will destroy the Divinity within us. His crucifixion and Resurrection proved that even if one's physical body is abused, tortured, and crucified, *"the Christ"* within each of us is eternal and lives on in our Light Body.

After Jesus' crucifixion and his Resurrection into his Light Body, he had one more very important Truth to reveal to Humanity. It was obvious that the Children of God had been beaten down into a consciousness of unworthiness. Jesus realized that because of this low opinion of ourselves, the chances were great that we would misunderstand his mission as we had the previous Avatars.

Jesus and Mary Magdalene came to anchor the archetypes for the return of our Mother God, and to demonstrate for us the path of Oneness and Divine Love that each of us must follow if we are to return to Christ Consciousness. Jesus knew that our lack of trust in ourselves was overwhelming and that the potential was great that we would misconstrue his mission. He was very aware that our egos would try to convince us that Jesus was Divine in ways that we as Sons and Daughters of God are not, and that therefore we do not have to do anything because Jesus saved us by his physical presence alone.

To try and avert that misconception, Jesus' final demonstration was designed to clearly reveal to Humanity that he cannot save us and that no one is saved simply because he was here. Jesus' final demonstration left an example to prove that no matter how much we Love him or how dedicated we are to him and his teachings, we are each responsible for our return to Christ Consciousness. In order to accomplish this facet of the Divine Plan, Jesus invoked the assistance of his Beloved Disciples who are also referred to as the Apostles.

After Jesus' resurrection, he remained on Earth for 40 days. During that time, he demonstrated to the Disciples what it was like to experience Christ Consciousness. Jesus expanded his Light Body to envelop the Disciples and lifted them into the enlightened state of Christ Consciousness. Within that radiant Light, the Disciples were able to experience what it was like to reconnect with their I AM Presence and the Realms of Illumined Truth.

In that elevated state, the Disciples remembered their Divine Heritage as Beloved Children of God. Once they were reconnected with their I AM Presence, the Disciples were able to perform all of the miracles Jesus performed. They quickly learned the lessons that would enable them to continue the mission that had been started by their beloved brother, Jesus. They prepared to spread the Truth about our Mother God and Humanity's Divinity to the world. They also learned how to teach the path of Oneness and Divine Love that would lead to Christ Consciousness for every person on Earth.

At the end of the 40 days, it was time for Jesus to Ascend into the next phase of his mission. When the Heavens opened and Jesus Ascended into the Realms of Illumined Truth, it was no longer possible for him to sustain the Disciples in the elevated frequency of Christ Consciousness by enveloping them in his Light Body. Since the Disciples had not attained Christ Consciousness through their own endeavors, once Jesus withdrew his Light Body they began to falter and became afraid.

The Disciples realized that in spite of their great Love for Jesus and their dedication to him and his teachings, he could not save them or sustain them in Christ Consciousness. They clearly understood that it was not enough for them to Love him, or for them to say that they accepted him as their personal savior.

Jesus' demonstration revealed to the Disciples and the world that reaching Christ Consciousness was something each of us would have to accomplish on our own. The most Jesus and Mary Magdalene could do was anchor the Divine Matrix and the archetypes for the return of our Mother God and model the path of Oneness and Divine Love that we must each follow in order to return to Christ Consciousness. However, that in no way minimized what their Mission accomplished. Their selfless service to the Light on behalf of Humanity catapulted each of us forward in the Light in ways the Company of Heaven said are beyond our comprehension at this time.

For ten days following Jesus' Ascension into the Realms of Illumined Truth the Disciples struggled with their predicament. On the 50th day after Jesus' Resurrection, the day we now call Pentecost, the Disciples realized what they must do in order to attain and sustain Christ Consciousness. On that day, the Disciples entered what was called the *Upper Room*. This was a higher state of consciousness that they each attained by Consecrating their lives to the Path of Oneness and Divine Love. In that elevated state of consciousness, each of the Disciples opened his Heart Chakra to full breadth and from the depths of his Being invoked the return of our Mother God through a Baptism of the Holy Spirit. This time, the Baptism was by Sacred Fire instead of water.

In that instant, the Disciples' right-brain hemispheres were brought into perfect balance with their left-brain hemispheres. Their spiritual brain centers were activated, and their Crown Chakras were opened to full breadth. This allowed the Disciples to reconnect with their I AM Presence. I am sure many of you have seen paintings that depict the Disciples after their Baptism by the Holy Spirit on Pentecost. They are all shown with a Flame pulsating from their Crown Chakra indicating that they had regained Christ Consciousness, and that their mission of spreading Jesus' teachings to the world was at hand.

On that holy day of Pentecost, the Disciples were also given what has been called *the gift of tongues*. The *gift of tongues* enabled the Disciples to travel the face of the Earth and to teach the Truth about our Mother God, Humanity's Divinity and the Path of Oneness and Divine Love in the language of the people with whom they were speaking. This eliminated the language barriers and ensured the clarity of Jesus' and Mary Magdalene's message.

So with the success of Jesus' and Mary Magdalene's mission, why did we not comprehend their message during the Piscean Age? Well, that is the question the Company of Heaven will answer next. Precious Heart, contemplate what has been shared with you and in the next sharing the Company of Heaven will reveal how Humanity's egos suppressed this sacred knowledge.

22

How Did Jesus' and Mary Magdalene's Message Become so Misconstrued?

The Beings of Light want to share with us how Jesus' and Mary Magdalene's message got so misconstrued. It is difficult when we try to reconcile the information being given to Humanity by the Beings of Light in the Realms of Illumined Truth with what we are being taught by the various world religions. That is because the new information from the Realms of Truth that is flooding into the mental and emotional strata of Earth during the Dawning New Age of Aquarius is often diametrically opposed to what we have been taught.

We have been told by many of the various world religions that the Bible is Divinely Inspired and that every word should be taken as literal Truth. That is not what the Beings of Light have revealed or what has been confirmed through historical documentation.

When Jesus and Mary Magdalene were fulfilling their Divine Mission as Avatars of the Piscean Age, those who followed their teachings were well aware of their relationship and the message they were bringing about our Mother God and the Path of Divine Love each of us must follow in order to return to Christ Consciousness. After they left the physical plane, Humanity's egos once again did everything they could to confuse the issue and to block the Truth of Jesus' and Mary's message.

Even with all of the groundwork that was carefully laid out during the Piscean Age, Jesus and Mary Magdalene knew that it would be millennia before Humanity would really understand their message and awaken effectively enough to reclaim our Divine Birthright as Christ Conscious Sons and Daughters of God. It was obvious that our human egos were not going to relinquish their patriarchal control easily. The resistance would be great, and every possible effort would be made to suppress the role of Mary Magdalene and the Truth of our Mother God. Jesus confirmed this knowing in Revelations when he stated to John the Beloved,

"In the Day of the Seventh Angel, when he begins to sound, the mystery of God will be fulfilled and time will be no more."

Jesus said that would occur during the Second Coming of the Christ.

The predominant Light of God that bathes the Earth during the Age of Pisces, as well as the annual Sun Cycle of Pisces, is the Sixth Solar Aspect of Deity. This Aspect of our Father-Mother God is known as the Sixth Angel and it pulsates with an exquisite Ruby-Gold Radiance that reflects the Divine Qualities of Peace, Healing, Devotional Worship, Ministering Grace, and frequencies of *"the Christ"* made Manifest. These Divine Qualities were the perfect support that Jesus and Mary Magdalene needed in order to accomplish their Missions.

The Piscean Age was the Day of the Sixth Angel and Jesus is known as the Prince of Peace because of the influences of the Sixth Solar Aspect of Deity. Jesus' symbol is the fish because he and Mary Magdalene were the Avatars of the Piscean Age, which is represented by the symbol of the fish.

The Day of the Seventh Angel is the Age of Aquarius which we have now entered. This is the time Jesus was referring to when he said *"In the Day of the Seventh Angel, when he begins to sound, the mystery of God will be fulfilled."* Access to the Realms of Truth will indeed fulfill the mystery of God. This will happen when each of us returns to Christ Consciousness which is what Jesus meant when he talked about *"the 2nd Coming of the Christ."*

When we return to Christ Consciousness, we will once again be able to communicate with our I AM Presence and the Company of Heaven through the natural process of open heart and mind telepathic communication. Jesus also said, *"Time will be no more."* This is true because we are Ascending into the full embrace of the New Earth which exists in the timeless, spaceless Realms of Light in the 5th Dimension. The constraints of a time and space continuum only exist in the 3rd and 4th Dimensions.

The Aspect of Deity that bathes the Earth during the Age of Aquarius, and the annual Sun Cycle of Aquarius, is the Seventh Solar Aspect of Deity. This is *"The Seventh Angel."* This Aspect of our Father-Mother God pulsates with the Violet Flame of God's Infinite Perfection which is the perfect balance of our Father God's Blue Flame of Divine Will and Power and our Mother God's Pink Flame of Divine Love and Reverence for ALL Life. This Sacred Fire is the perfect support Humanity needs in order for us to return to Christ Consciousness.

After Jesus' crucifixion, Resurrection and Ascension, plans were set into motion to protect Mary Magdalene from the interference of Humanity's patriarchal human egos who were intent on blocking the awareness of our Mother God and the fact that Mary Magdalene was Jesus' wife. The Essene Brotherhood and Sisterhood, along with Mother Mary, Joseph of Arimathea, John the Beloved, and some of the other Disciples, guarded Mary Magdalene. She was safely guided to various locations on the planet where she was able to anchor the Divine Matrix and the archetypes for the return of our Mother God. Her protectors were well aware of her mission, and after her Ascension, they steadfastly held the Immaculate Concept for the return of our Mother God on behalf of ALL Humanity. These selfless exponents of God's Will formed Mystery Schools and passed the information on in veiled and mysterious symbols that could not be deciphered by the common man or woman.

The patriarchal leaders of the newly formed Christian churches had difficulty blocking the ground swell of information that kept surfacing in mysterious ways about Mary Magdalene and her relationship with Jesus. Various gospels were being circulated which gave conflicting accounts of what really occurred during the pageantry of Jesus and the founding of what was being considered the Christian Dispensation. Each gospel was an account of the experiences and the beliefs of the person who wrote it. These interpretations were made through each person's consciousness which was usually controlled by their flawed human ego.

In 325 AD the Roman Emperor Constantine decided that the confusion in the Christian doctrine needed to be stopped and that the various factions needed to be unified into one belief system. He called a meeting of over 300 bishops and organized what has been noted as the first

Ecumenical Council. This gathering was the Council of Nicaea.

During that meeting, Constantine denounced Arianism which was founded by the theologian Arius. These teachings taught that Jesus was a Son of God, and that all of the Children of Earth are Sons and Daughters of God. He reiterated that God is within every person, and that people do not need to depend on Human Beings outside of themselves in order to communicate with God or to receive God's Forgiveness.

This belief system interfered greatly with the power and control of the patriarchal priesthood and the Church, so Constantine ordered Arius to cease and desist in teaching such heresy. At the end of the gathering, Constantine ordered a vote, and all but three bishops signed the Nicaean Creed forbidding Arianism. Constantine felt this vote of support gave him the right to proceed with his mission. He gathered the 48 gospels that were being circulated amongst the various factions of the Church. He went through all of them carefully and selected just the gospels that indicated that Jesus was Divine in ways the rest of Humanity was not and that Jesus alone was—the *only* begotten Son of God. In all of the 48 gospels, there were only four that indicated that Jesus alone was the Son of God, and that every other Child of God is less than Jesus in God's eyes. These four gospels were unnamed, as were many of the 48 gospels. Constantine is the one who made the decision to name the gospels that he specifically chose to be included in the Bible. He named them Matthew, Mark, Luke and John.

Constantine then proceeded to go through the rest of the teachings to decide what he wanted to include in the Bible. In order to maintain the supreme power of the Church and the patriarchal priesthood, he removed any reference to our Mother God or the Divine Feminine. He also removed any reference to the relationship between Mary Magdalene and Jesus and any teachings he could identify regarding reincarnation. Constantine's actions redefined the status of Christianity, and formed the basis for the Bible used today throughout the Christian world.

Even with this obvious betrayal of the Truth, the mission of Jesus and Mary Magdalene could not be suppressed. To the total consternation of the Church, the reality of their spiritual and intimate relationship kept surfacing. One by one the seekers of Truth were guided to the Mystery Schools and secret societies. Little by little they learned about the sacred mission of Jesus and Mary Magdalene.

In 590 AD Pope Gregory decided that enough was enough. He was determined to once and for all put an end to this threat to the patriarchal supremacy of the Church. With the stroke of his pen, Pope Gregory declared that Mary Magdalene was a prostitute and asserted that she was seething with seven evil spirits. This was the very first time that Mary Magdalene was said to be a prostitute. That unconscionable lie was written nearly 600 years after her embodiment. As far as the Church was concerned, this concocted story squelched the rumors about Jesus and Mary Magdalene's marriage.

In order to maintain a semblance of damage control, the Church leaders tried to transfer the attention from Mary Magdalene to another Mary, Jesus' Mother. This was a futile effort in their attempt to block the awareness of our Mother God because Mother Mary was also holding the sacred space for the return of the Divine Feminine. Mother Mary protected the Truth about Mary Magdalene while she held the outer world's attention on her own mission of being the Divine Mother of Jesus.

For centuries, the Immaculate Concept of Mary Magdalene's Divine Mission with Jesus was guarded from the outer world by her valiant protectors. With unfailing tenacity these selfless souls prepared for the Day of the Seventh Angel when the return of our Mother God would be brought to fruition.

Throughout history there are bits and pieces of information regarding the souls who were fulfilling the service of protecting the mission of Mary Magdalene and Jesus, but most of them are terribly distorted and contaminated with misinformation from the fallen egos of those associated with the patriarchal Church. The groups most noteworthy of protecting the information regarding the return of our Mother God are the Essenes, the Cathars and the Knights Templar. Within the historic documentations of England, Spain, France, Malta and other places throughout the Mediterranean, the mystical stories of the protectors of the sacred knowledge about Mary Magdalene and the return of our Mother God can still be found.

The most blatant proof of the ego's attempt to block this information is reflected in accounts of the Church's horrific persecution and the brutal demise of these dedicated protectors during the Crusades and the Inquisition. For the past several decades, Lightworkers have been making pilgrimages to the areas where these atrocities took place. The intent of these pilgrimages is to transmute the etheric records of the pain and suffering involved in protecting the Truth about the return of our Mother God.

Precious Heart, we have moved into the full embrace of the Aquarian Age and the mystery of God is being revealed. Now it is time for you and me and the rest of awakening Humanity to fulfill the next phase of this unprecedented Divine Plan.

23

THE NEXT PHASE OF THE DIVINE PLAN

The Earth recently completed her transition through the window of opportunity that occurs during the Dawn of the New Age. We have now moved into the full embrace of the Age of Aquarius. The Seventh Angel is beginning to sound and the mystery of God is being revealed. The I AM Presence of every person on Earth is integrating into his or her physical, etheric, mental and emotional bodies the maximum that Cosmic Law will allow every 24 hours. This is gradually raising each person up in consciousness. Now we are ready for the next phase of the Divine Plan.

In August 2017, Earth and ALL her Life were held in the forcefield of one of the most life-transforming Eclipse Series Humanity has ever experienced. This Eclipse Series began with a powerful Full Moon Lunar Eclipse on August 7, 2017, and ended with an unprecedented New Moon Solar Eclipse on August 21, 2017. The Company of Heaven encoded that activity of Light in the Eternal Moment of Now, so know that no matter when you are reading these words your I AM Presence is weaving your Light into the full Divine Momentum of this facet of the Divine Plan.

This Eclipse Series is being heralded as unprecedented by the Company of Heaven for two reasons. The first is that due to the monumental shifts of energy, vibration and consciousness the Earth and all her Life have experienced over the past few years, Humanity is now able to receive and assimilate higher frequencies of Light than we have ever been able to withstand at a cellular level. This means that the Divine Light bathing the Earth during this Celestial alignment moved every person further up the Spiral of Evolution into higher 5th-Dimensional frequencies of the New Earth.

The second reason this Eclipse Series was such a monumental benefit to ALL Life on this planet is that there are now millions of people who are awakening and remembering that they have embodied on Earth at this time to be Instruments of God and to serve as the Open Door through which the Light of God and the patterns of perfection for the New Earth will be anchored in the physical plane. These precious Ones are holding the sacred space and serving as surrogates on behalf of unawakened Humanity during this Cosmic Moment.

The most critical time of any New Age is at its inception. It is during this time that the sacred knowledge from the Realms of Illumined Truth, and the Divine Plan revealing the greatest need of the hour for Humanity's evolutionary progress, are encoded into the mental and emotional strata of Earth. For the past several Ages there have been Avatars who were chosen by our Father-Mother God to embody on Earth during the inception of the Age in order to serve as the Open Door for the Light of God on behalf of Humanity. This was necessary because the vast majority of people on Earth were very asleep. They were buried in the effluvia of their miscreations and were trapped in that lower state of consciousness by their fear-based human egos. But now, during the inception of this Aquarian Age, everything has changed.

During the inception of this Age, there will not be one or two Avatars who will embody on Earth to serve as the Open Door for the Light of God on behalf of Humanity. This time there is going to be an all-encompassing *Group Avatar*. The Group Avatar will be comprised of every awakened man, woman and child on Earth who has returned to the enlightened state of Christ Consciousness. This is the consciousness of our I AM Presence and it is the Divine Birthright of every Son and Daughter of God. It is the Enlightened Consciousness our Father-Mother God invested each and every one of us with when we were first breathed forth from the Core of Creation. Eventually, this Group Avatar will involve every single person evolving on Earth.

The return to Christ Consciousness will be an individual process for every person. However, the Beings of Light in the Realms of Illumined Truth want you to know that your I AM Presence magnetized this information into your sphere of awareness because the process of your return to Christ Consciousness has begun and your Light is needed NOW!

During this Eclipse Series the first patterns of perfection for the Aquarian Age and the New Earth are being encoded into the mental and emotional strata of Earth. Our Father-Mother God have determined that these particular patterns are the greatest need of the hour for awakening Humanity, and they will be the greatest help in awakening the Sons and Daughters of God who are still asleep and continue to act out of the obsolete habits and behavior patterns of their fallen human egos.

You and I and the rest of awakening Humanity are being asked to be the Open Door through which the archetypes and the Divine Matrix for the new 5th-Dimensional patterns of *Eternal Peace and God's Infinite Abundance* will be encoded into the mental and emotional strata of Earth. Once these patterns are anchored they will be tangibly available for every person who is willing to reach up in consciousness and magnetize them through their Heart Flame into their own life and the lives of ALL Humanity.

The Company of Heaven has provided us with an activity of Light that will help each of us to be the Open Door for these exquisite patterns of Eternal Peace and God's Infinite Abundance on behalf of every man, woman and child on Earth. If you have the Heart Call to participate in this Gift from On High, please join with me now and be the Open Door for the Light of God that you have been preparing to be for literally Lifetimes.

This activity of Light is stated in the first person so we will each experience it on a personal level. Please breathe in deeply and go within to the Divinity of your Heart Flame. Ask your I AM Presence to take full dominion of your Earthly Bodies and follow me through this visualization with the full power of your attention. And we begin.

Invocation for Eternal Peace and God's Infinite Abundance

I AM my I AM Presence and I AM One with the I AM Presence of ALL Humanity. What I invoke for myself this sacred and holy day I invoke on behalf of every man, woman and child on Earth in perfect alignment with each person's Divine Plan and the highest good for all concerned. This is possible because WE ARE ONE and there is no separation.

As One Energy, Vibration and Consciousness of Pure Divine Love, we invoke our Father-Mother God and the entire Company of Heaven to assist the I AM Presence of every person on Earth to God Victoriously accomplish this facet of the Divine Plan.

Beloved Legions of Light throughout Infinity, I ask that you gather up every electron of precious Life energy being expended by Humanity in any way during this sacred time. Purify this energy with the power and might of a thousand Suns using the New Solar Frequencies of the 5th-Dimensional Violet Flame of God's Infinite Perfection.

Weave this purified energy into the collective Cup of Humanity's Consciousness, so that every single electron of precious Life energy being released by the Sons and Daughters of God on Earth at this time will be used to cocreate and tangibly manifest Eternal Peace and God's Infinite Abundance for every person belonging to or serving the Earth at this time.

The Golden Rays of Eternal Peace and God's Infinite Abundance from the Causal Body of our Father-Mother God are now flowing through the Cup of my consciousness into the Heart Flame of every person on Earth. This Golden Light is pulsating with frequencies of Eternal Peace and God's Infinite Abundance beyond anything Humanity has ever experienced. Contained within the essence of this Flame of Eternal Peace is God's Infinite Abundance, and contained within the essence of God's Infinite Abundance is the Flame of Eternal Peace.

I breathe in deeply, and I become One with this Golden Light as I enter the secret place of the Most High Living God within my Heart Flame. As I enter this sacred space on the Holy Breath, I AM open and receptive to the impulses pouring forth from the Heart and Mind of God. The hour has at last arrived, and the Divine Fiat has been issued by my Father-Mother God for the Divinity pulsating within my Heart Flame to be given full liberty and freedom of expression. My I AM Presence rejoices in this Divine Edict and will now give me every possible assistance in manifesting Eternal Peace and God's Infinite Abundance in my Life.

Now, in accordance with my Divine Destiny, I AM becoming a Keeper of the Golden Flame of Eternal Peace and Abundance. Through my I AM Presence my Earthly Bodies are being brought into perfect alignment. The latent powers encoded within my Heart Flame are being released. The abilities I developed over aeons of time that will assist me in cocreating Eternal Peace and God's Infinite Abundance on Earth are now surfacing and being brought into a balanced state of true mastery within me.

I AM now reaching into a new octave of my Godhood, and my Father-Mother God are able to easily move through me. My eyes become blazing rays of Light through which the Light of God blesses all Life. My hands become mighty conductors of God's Healing Power. My lips become the instruments through which God's words are formed and directed into the physical plane of Earth. My feet walk the Path of Light. And my Life Force becomes the vehicle through which God enters the world to Love and serve all Life.

Now… In the name of the Infinite Presence of God, I AM, I affirm:

Beloved I AM Presence enfold me now in God's Eternal Peace and Infinite Abundance as I become an Eternal Golden Sun of this Divine Light.

I AM an Eternal Golden Sun of God's Peace and Abundance now made manifest and permanently sustained by Divine Grace.

I AM an Eternal Golden Sun of God's Peace and Abundance now made manifest and permanently sustained by Divine Grace.

I AM an Eternal Golden Sun of God's Peace and Abundance now made manifest and permanently sustained by Divine Grace.

And so it is.

24

ABUNDANCE AND ETERNAL PEACE ARE PART OF OUR COVENANT WITH GOD

Through the unified efforts of Heaven and Earth the first patterns of perfection associated with the 5th-Dimensional Crystalline New Earth have been God Victoriously encoded within the mental and emotional strata in the body of Mother Earth. These are the patterns within the Causal Body of God that pulsate with the tangible manifestation of *Eternal Peace and God's Infinite Abundance.*

Now that these patterns are readily available to each and every one of us, it is our responsibility to lift up in consciousness and magnetize them into our everyday life experiences through our thoughts, feelings, words and actions. In order to inspire us to do this, the Company of Heaven wants to share with us the bigger picture of how we lost our Divine Birthright of Eternal Peace and God's Infinite Abundance in the first place.

In the beginning, when it was time for the Sons and Daughters of God to master the skill of becoming cocreators with our God Parents, a plan was set into motion to help us learn this process quickly and effectively. Our Father-Mother God decided that if their Children learned to use our free will and our creative faculties of thought and feeling within the constraints of a time and space continuum, we would experience the results of what we were creating much faster. This would enable us to develop our cocreative skills at an accelerated pace. Since time and space only exist in the 3rd and 4th Dimensions, the Sons and Daughters of God volunteered to descend into the stepped down frequencies in the 3rd-Dimensional schoolroom of Earth.

To ensure our success during our Earthly sojourn our Father-Mother God formed a Covenant with us. This Covenant was designed to provide us with a continual flow of the patterns of perfection within the Causal Body of God that pulsate with *Eternal Peace and God's Infinite Abundance.* Our Father-Mother God asked the Mighty Elohim, who are the Builders of Form, and the Directors of the Elemental Kingdom to provide us with everything we would need to sustain our physical, etheric, mental and emotional bodies while we were learning our lessons of cocreation in the 3rd Dimension. The Divine Intent of this Heavenly Gift was to prevent us from being distracted from our lessons by having to work to sustain our Earthly Bodies while we were abiding in the physical plane.

The Elohim and the Directors of the Elements responded by cocreating the Earthly Paradise we've known as the Garden of Eden. This resplendent expression of nature provided all of the sunlight, air, water, food and material for clothing and shelter we needed in order to sustain our bodies. In addition to these gifts, our Father-Mother God agreed to provide us with the perpetual flow of our Life Force, so that we would always have whatever we needed to cocreate the new patterns we were learning to manifest from the Causal Body of God.

In harmony with the Universal Laws that govern all Creation, there must always be a balance between the outbreath and the inbreath of God. The outbreath of God is the Life Force we receive as our Gift of Life from our Father-Mother God, and the inbreath of God is the Life Force that the Sons and Daughters of God qualify with Love and send back to our God Parents in appreciation for our Gift of Life. In the original Covenant, our Father-Mother God's outbreath ensured that their Sons and Daughters abiding on Earth would receive the infinite abundance of our Life Force and everything we would need to sustain our Earthly Bodies. In return, our Covenant with God promised that we would fulfill our responsibility of balancing the inbreath of God by using our Life Force in Loving ways that would add to the Light of the world and reflect our appreciation for our Gift of Life.

In order to accomplish this we made the heart commitment to respect our Earthly Bodies which the Elemental Kingdom had provided for us, and we agreed to honor and revere the myriad gifts Mother Earth and the Elemental Kingdom were providing to sustain our bodies in the physical plane. We also promised that we would use our Life Force, our free will and our creative faculties of thought and feeling to cocreate new patterns of perfection that would enhance the manifestation of Heaven on Earth.

Prior to our fall from Grace we fulfilled our part of this Covenant perfectly. Through our I AM Presence we observed the patterns of perfection in the Causal Body of God and then we used our free will and our unique ways of thinking and feeling to combined these patterns in previously unknown ways. Every day we used our Life Force through our thoughts, feelings, words and action to cocreate new expressions of Divinity, thus fulfilling our purpose and reason for Being by adding to the Light of the world. We continually acknowledged the blessings we were receiving on a daily basis with reverence, gratitude and abounding Love.

After we fell from Grace into the abyss of separation and duality everything changed. We became so buried in the negativity of our human miscreations that we lost Christ Consciousness and the ability to communicate with our I AM Presence and the Company of Heaven. We forgot that we are multifaceted and multidimensional Sons and Daughters of God abiding on Earth to learn how to become cocreators with our Father-Mother God. We also forgot about our Covenant with God which guaranteed that we would experience Eternal Peace and God's Infinite Abundance if we would just fulfill our part of the Covenant by using our Life Force in Loving ways that added to the Light of the world, and by honoring Mother Earth and our Earthly Bodies.

Once we lost the awareness of our own Divinity and forgot about our Covenant with God we inadvertently created our fear-based ego. This distorted aspect of our fallen consciousness manipulated us into believing that there was not enough of whatever we needed to survive. We developed poverty consciousness, and our ego began creating gross thoughtforms of lack and limitation. When our ego projected negative thoughts and feelings onto the Elemental substance in the Garden of Eden the Elemental Kingdom was forced to outpicture the distorted patterns of decay, aging and inclement weather conditions. These gross mutations manifested as famines, droughts, floods, plagues, pestilence and other painful miscreations that intensified our ego's fear-based consciousness of scarcity and lack.

As time passed, we created a monetary system to help us acquire the things we thought we needed to survive. We started working from morning to night to earn money to pay for food, clothing, shelter and whatever else we needed to sustain our Earthly Bodies. These were the very things our Covenant with God promised the Elemental Kingdom would provide for us during our Earthly sojourn. All we had to do in order to be blessed with this infinite flow of God's Abundance and Eternal Peace was to fulfill our part of the Covenant, but tragically we no longer remembered what that was.

The more our ego entrapped us in the consciousness of poverty the less money we had for anything other than supplying the needs of our physical bodies. We were spending all of our time and energy working to make money to pay for the very things our Father-Mother God had originally provided to us for free. Our ego's fear-based struggle for survival manipulated us into believing that there was not time for us to do anything else. As a result, we were not fulfilling our part of the Covenant. We were no longer using our Life Force to cocreate patterns of perfection that added to the Light of the world, and we had totally forgotten our agreement to honor and revere our Earthly Bodies and Mother Earth. This devastating state of affairs blocked our Divine Birthright which was the natural flow of Eternal Peace and God's Infinite Abundance that our Father-Mother God gave to us in the beginning.

To this very day the masses of Humanity are being adversely affected by this extreme imbalance between the outbreath and the inbreath of God. Our ego's destructive behavior has created a void that has kept us trapped in poverty consciousness for aeons of time.

Now, Humanity is awakening and we are in the process of reversing the adverse effects of our fall from Grace. New

5th-Dimensional patterns of perfection from the Causal Body of God, which pulsate with the tangible manifestation of *Eternal Peace and God's Infinite Abundance,* have now been encoded within the mental and emotional strata of Earth. At long last, Humanity has the ability to transmute our ego's poverty-based consciousness back into Light, so that we can reclaim our Divine Birthright and once again experience Abundance, Eternal Peace and the Gifts of our Covenant with our Father-Mother God.

In the next chapter the Company of Heaven will guide us through a process that will help us to transmute the residue of our ego's poverty consciousness, and then we can reclaim our Divine Birthright.

25

TRANSMUTING POVERTY
CONSCIOUSNESS

We have been given an activity of Light by the Company of Heaven that will help us to transmute poverty consciousness. This is the residue of our fear-based ego's belief in lack and limitation which has led to not only the dire poverty that is plaguing the masses of Humanity, but also the obscene levels of greed and corruption we are witnessing around the world.

Transmuting poverty consciousness is a critical step in paving the way so the new patterns of Eternal Peace and God's Infinite Abundance can be magnetized through our Heart Flames into our everyday life experiences. In addition to transmuting our own poverty consciousness, you and I and the rest of awakening Humanity have the ability to serve as surrogates on behalf of the masses of Humanity who are unaware of this monumental opportunity. If you have the Heart Call to do so, please join with me now and together we will greatly accelerate the process of manifesting God's Infinite Abundance and Eternal Peace on Earth.

A Clarion Call from our Father-Mother God is now ringing through the Cosmos. In response, the I AM Presence of every person on Earth and the entire Company of Heaven are standing in readiness to assist in this Holy Endeavor. And we begin.

Decree for Transmuting Poverty Consciousness

I AM my I AM Presence and I AM One with the I AM Presence of every man, woman and child belonging to or serving the Earth at this time. What I invoke for myself this sacred and holy day I invoke for every person on Earth in perfect alignment with his or her Divine Plan and the highest good for all concerned.

My I AM Presence now takes full dominion of my physical, etheric, mental and emotional bodies. As this occurs, my I AM Presence recalibrates and brings into balance the right and left hemispheres of my brain. This allows the fragmented pathways in my brain which have prevented me from communicating with the multidimensional aspects of my own Divinity and the Company of Heaven to be reconnected.

This Healing process activates my spiritual brain centers and restores them to their full Divine Potential. As these centers within my brain are reactivated, the Light flowing through them from the Heart and Mind of my Father-Mother God awakens the dormant DNA structures within my body. This allows my DNA to receive higher frequencies of Divine Light than I have ever experienced.

My DNA is a shimmering, waveform configuration that is now being modified by the Golden Light, solar radiation, magnetic fields, sonic impulses, thoughtforms and emotions associated with the newly encoded archetypes and the Divine Matrix of Eternal Peace and God's Infinite Abundance. These patterns are now pulsating within the mental and emotional strata of Mother Earth awaiting the opportunity to tangibly manifest in the lives of awakening Humanity.

During this Cosmic Moment, my I AM Presence and the Company of Heaven are imprinting the genetic codes for Eternal Peace and God's Infinite Abundance within my DNA. These patterns are igniting every cell in my body and lifting me into alignment with the 5th-Dimensional frequencies of the New Earth. The 5th-Dimensional Crystalline patterns of Eternal Peace and God's Abundance are flowing through my Heart Flame and being secured within the nucleus of every atomic and subatomic particle and wave of my Earthly Bodies.

A reactivation and initiation into multifaceted awareness is occurring within me. I step through the doorway into multidimensional reality and I AM empowered with even more rarified frequencies of my own Divinity. In this realm I recognize, and I AM willing to release and let go of, attachments and behavior patterns that are based in poverty consciousness. These are the obsolete beliefs of my fallen human ego that have trapped me in the painful illusions of lack and limitation for lifetimes.

Through the multifaceted and multidimensional aspects of my Divinity I now release all patterns I have ever empowered in any time frame or dimension, both known and unknown, that reflect a consciousness less than God's Infinite Abundance and Eternal Peace. The obsolete beliefs of my fallen human ego are cast into the most intensified frequencies of the Violet Flame of God's Infinite Perfection that Cosmic Law will allow. Instantaneously, the patterns of poverty consciousness are transmuted cause, core, effect, record and memory back into their original perfection.

I now ACCEPT and KNOW that my I AM Presence and the Company of Heaven will intensify this activity of Light daily and hourly, moment by moment, with every breath I take until Eternal Peace and God's Infinite Abundance are a manifest reality in the lives and experiences of every person on Earth.

This is the time of my new beginning. From this moment forth, I will empower my Divine Potential as a Beloved Son or Daughter of God with every thought, feeling, word and action I express.

I AM Divine Integrity.
I AM Illumined Truth.
I AM Trustworthy and Honest.
I AM Divine Love, I AM Oneness, I AM Reverence for ALL Life.
I AM Worthy and Deserving of God's Infinite Abundance and Eternal Peace.

I now Consecrate my Life Force to be the Open Door through which the newly encoded patterns of Eternal Peace and God's Infinite Abundance will perpetually flow to bless all Life on Earth.

And so it is. Beloved I AM, Beloved I AM, Beloved I AM That I AM.

26

RECLAIMING OUR COVENANT WITH GOD

The Company of Heaven has revealed to us how we inadvertently blocked our Divine Birthright which promised we would receive a constant flow of God's Abundance while we were learning to become cocreators with our Father-Mother God in this schoolroom of Earth. This tragedy occurred when we fell from Grace and forgot that we had made a Covenant with our God Parents.

The Beings of Light have taught us that the Universal Laws that govern all Creation require that there be a balance between the outbreath and the inbreath of God. The outbreath of God is the Life Force we receive as our Gift of Life from our Father-Mother God, and the inbreath of God is the Life Force that the Sons and Daughters of God qualify with Love and send back to our God Parents in appreciation for our Gift of Life.

In the original Covenant our Father-Mother God's outbreath ensured that their Sons and Daughters abiding on Earth would receive an infinite Abundance of our Life Force and everything we would need to sustain our Earthly Bodies. In return, our part of the Covenant with God promised that we would fulfill our responsibility of balancing the inbreath of God by using our Life Force in Loving ways that would add to the Light of the world and reflect our appreciation for our Gift of Life.

After we fell into the abyss of separation and duality, we totally forgot about our part of the Covenant. Since that fateful time aeons ago, we have been struggling from morning to night to acquire what we need in order for our physical bodies to survive on Earth. For the masses of Humanity this struggle has been all-consuming. The concept of using our Life Force to balance the inbreath of God by adding to the Light of the world has been virtually forgotten. In most instances, even awakening Humanity spends a relatively small portion of our time and Life Force adding to the Light of the world through our meditations, prayers, decrees, invocations and activities of Light. The rest of the time we are focused on working like everybody else to make money to pay for the things we need in order to survive.

In my experience, most people are so overwhelmed and exhausted with trying to survive that they cannot fathom having even 30 minutes a day to add to the Light of the world. What the Company of Heaven wants us to realize is that this erroneous belief is precisely what is keeping us trapped in poverty, lack and limitation.

The fact is, we have received and utilized the outbreath of our Father-Mother God's Life Force since we began our Earthly sojourn myriad lifetimes ago. Now, in order to reclaim our Divine Birthright and the Infinite Abundance and Eternal Peace promised in our Covenant with God, we have no other option than to fulfill our part of the Covenant. Remember, Universal Law requires that the Sons and Daughters of God balance God's outbreath with God's inbreath. The only way we fulfill that responsibility is by using our Life Force in Loving ways that add to the Light of the world and reflect our appreciation for our Gift of Life.

What the precious Beings of Light in the Realms of Illumined Truth want us to know is that this is not a time consuming or difficult task. Adding to the Light of the world and reflecting back to God our appreciation for our Gift of Life is easily accomplished with a slight adjustment in our awareness. We actually have the ability to do this every single day with every breath we take.

No matter where we are or what we are doing, all we have to do is align our heart and mind with our I AM Presence in Loving Gratitude for our Gift of Life. Then, we can ask our I AM Presence to Consecrate every thought, word, feeling and action we express throughout the day with Divine Love and Infinite Gratitude for the opportunity to add to the Light of the world. This is just a mind set and a heart commitment that does not take a single minute out of our day. It is as easily available to us as breathing and can be sustained with every beat of our heart through our Divine Intentions. This knowing will enable each of us to add to the Light of the world every minute of every day.

Know that when you develop this new perspective you will effortlessly add your Light and Love to every single thing you are thinking, feeling, saying and doing. This means that every moment of every day you will be adding to the Light of the world. This is how you will reclaim your Covenant with our Father-Mother God.

It is important for you to Trust your ability to be a force of Light even in the moments when you feel you are doing what might seem like a mundane task. When you have the consciousness that you are adding to the Light of the world no matter where you are or what you are doing, there is no such thing as a mundane task.

As you align more and more with the profound Truth that you have the ability to add to the Light of the world just by shifting your perception, you will become aware of the fact that with the intervention of your I AM Presence you have all of the time you need to accomplish whatever you have the Heart Call to do. When this happens you will find that you are motivated to participate in various activities of Light that your I AM Presence magnetizes into your sphere of awareness, then the Light you are adding to the world will exponentially expand.

The Company of Heaven assures us that if we begin every morning with the following simple affirmation and reaffirm it throughout the day, in *"the twinkling of an eye"* our I AM Presence will shift our awareness and empower us to be the Light Bearers we are destined to be.

So before you get out of bed every morning simply affirm from the deepest recesses of your Heart:

"I AM my I AM Presence and I AM One with my Father-Mother God. In Loving Gratitude, I accept my Gift of Life. I ask my I AM Presence to Consecrate every thought, word, feeling and action I express throughout this day with Divine Love and Infinite Gratitude for the opportunity to add to the Light of the world. And so it is."

Dear One, I AM so very grateful for your willingness to become the powerful force of Light you have been preparing for lifetimes to be during this Cosmic Moment on Earth.

27

THE KEY TO FINANCIAL FREEDOM

The Company of Heaven shared with us how very easy it is for us to reclaim the Covenant we made with our Father-Mother God prior to our embodiment on Earth. This Covenant was intended to assure that the Sons and Daughters of God would have a constant flow of God's Abundance and Eternal Peace throughout our Earthly sojourn. After we created a monetary system, however, our methods of receiving Abundance became very distorted and we lost our way.

Since we did not function from a monetary system in the beginning money was not a factor in whether or not we had Abundance. However, once we fell into the distorted illusion of separation and duality, we developed the oppressive mind set of poverty, lack and limitation. This caused us to come to the conclusion that we needed something we could use as barter for the things we needed in order to sustain our physical bodies and survive on Earth. Hence, we made the choice to create a monetary system. Now, having money seems to be the only determining factor in whether or not we are financially free. No matter how much Abundance we have in other areas of our life, if we do not have money we are not financially free.

When we complete our Ascension into the 5th-Dimensional frequencies of the New Earth we will not need money to survive. In the meantime, we need money. The Company of Heaven wants to remind us of the KEY to our Financial Freedom.

We have probably all heard about this essential KEY to our Financial Freedom, but we have often rejected it because of the manipulative way in which it is usually presented. Before I was shown the bigger picture and decided to set aside my preconceived skepticism and take the chance of experimenting with this information being given to Humanity from On High, I too rejected the concept of this information. I AM delighted to say that I proved the Truth of this process to myself beyond a shadow of a doubt.

For this reason, I ask you to please set aside any preconceived notions you may have about this subject and just read this information with an open heart and mind. Pay attention to how these words resonate in the Divinity of your Heart Flame. It will be well worth your time and effort. This information changed my life by increasing my flow of money.

First let's briefly talk about the Universal Law that determines the ebb and flow of our money. Money is just energy and every particle and wave of energy in the physical plane is subject to the Laws of Physics, which are reflected in what is known as the Universal Law of the Circle. The Law of the Circle is another way of describing the outbreath and the inbreath of our Father-Mother God.

The Law of the Circle is demonstrated in the activities we refer to as cause and effect, radiation and magnetization, reaping what we sow, action and reaction and giving and receiving. There must always be a balance between these two activities. For every cause there is an effect, and for every action there is an equal and opposite reaction. If these two activities are not balanced, a block is created that limits the flow in either the outbreath which is the energy we are sending out, or the inbreath which is the energy flowing back into our life.

What is causing such a financial crisis at the present time is that people are often in the position of having to spend all of the energy they receive in the form of money on the basics that they need to just sustain their physical bodies. These are the very things that our original Covenant with God provided to all of us in the beginning. When we spend all of our money on things that our Father-Mother God have already provided to us for free, it means we are not giving any energy back to God, in the form of money, in Loving appreciation for our Gift of Life.

Remember, like attracts like. If we want to increase the flow of money into our life, we need to add to the Light of the world with our money. It is just that simple. When we are only spending our money on our bodily needs, such as food, clothing, shelter, utilities, transportation, doctors, medical and health needs, and on and on, a void is created that causes stagnation which blocks our flow of money. This is what has been trapping us in the difficult position of barely receiving enough money to pay for our bodily needs no matter how hard we are working.

In order to remove the block, so that we can receive an abundant flow of money into our life, we need to use a portion of our money in ways that add to the Light of the world. This means not just paying for the things our Father-Mother God gave to us for free in their Covenant, but by donating an additional portion of our money to persons, places, conditions and things that are enhancing Life on this planet and literally adding to the Light of the world. This is the *KEY* to our Financial Freedom.

I know that on a logical level this may not seem realistic. After all, how could spending more money increase our Financial Freedom? But that is exactly how the Law of the Circle works, like attracts like. Whatever we are sending out through our thoughts, words, actions and feelings goes out and returns to us greatly expanded. This is true whether we are sending out Love, Joy and Happiness or anger, frustration and hatred. It is also true if we are sending out *money*.

Our problem is that we have been sending out just enough money to cover the cost of our bodily needs, which our Father-Mother God already gave to us for free. This is like not giving anything back at all as far as our Life Force goes. Consequently, no matter how hard we work it seems as though we receive back just enough money to cover our bodily needs. If we want to attain Financial Freedom, we need to send an *additional portion* of our money out, over and above what we spend for our bodily needs that will add to the Light of the world.

I know that when we are financially strapped the thought of having to spend more money in other ways can feel overwhelming. However, if we truly believed and accepted that by doing this we would increase the flow of money back into our life, we would not hesitate to do it. I realize that leap of faith is sometimes difficult, but take some time and contemplate this Truth. Let your I AM Presence awaken this inner knowing in the Divinity of your Heart Flame. Your I AM Presence wants you to be Financially Free and will help you grasp the magnitude of what this essential KEY will really mean as far as creating your Financial Freedom.

If you happen to feel motivated to experiment with this vital KEY to your Financial Freedom, this is the best way to begin the process.

First of all, decide in what way you would like to use a portion of your money to add to the Light of the world. Imagine that you are wealthy and that you have all of the money you need to survive and much, much more. What would you like to financially support that you feel would benefit Humanity and the Earth the most? There are literally thousands of people, places and organizations that would fulfill this requirement. Which of these options are you drawn to the most? Which ones just make your heart sing? That is where you need to start donating your money. When your money is supporting something that makes your heart sing, it is much easier for you to Trust the process and to release your donation without fear.

Next, your attitude and the consciousness with which you donate your money that is going to add to the Light of the world are very important. Before you give your money to whomever or wherever you have chosen to give it, consciously affirm to yourself:

"This money is a Gift of Love that I AM giving back to my Father-Mother God in appreciation for my Gift of Life. It is adding to the Light of the world and blessing everyone and everything in its path.

"In fulfillment of the Law of the Circle, I accept and know that this money is returning to me greatly expanded over what I AM sending out. This is occurring with the highest good of all concerned. And so it is."

Maintain that attitude and consciousness with every single donation you make.

Dear One, the newly anchored patterns of perfection for the New Earth that are associated with God's Infinite Abundance and Eternal Peace have been permanently encoded into the mental and emotional strata of this planet. The Beings of Light in the Realms of Illumined Truth assure us that the influx of these new patterns will greatly accelerate our flow of money when we utilize this KEY to our Financial Freedom and use a portion of our money to add to the Light of the world.

God Bless You, and I wish you God's Infinite Abundance here and now.

28

COCREATING ABUNDANCE

In the last sharing we learned from the Company of Heaven that the KEY to our Financial Freedom involves giving a portion of our money back to God in ways that add to the Light of the world and reflect our Love and appreciation for our Gift of Life. This always brings up the question of just how much money do we need to donate in order to reclaim our Divine Birthright and receive the flow of God's Abundance. The Beings of Light said that if we will donate as little as *10 percent* of our income to add to the Light of the world, we will receive such a flow of abundance back into our life that we will not be able to handle it all.

If you are struggling financially I know that 10 percent of your income sounds monumental, but let me share my personal experience with you. Please know that I do not ever teach something that I have not proven to myself to be true beyond a shadow of a doubt. That is the case even if the information is coming from the Company of Heaven. If I cannot prove what I am learning, I do not teach it. That does not mean that the information being given to Humanity from On High is not true. It just means that I will not teach something that I have not been able to prove to myself.

The concept of 10 percent of our income being the *critical mass* necessary for us to reclaim the Infinite flow of God's Abundance is something I have proven to myself beyond a shadow of a doubt, and witnessed with many people over the years.

Decades ago, when I was shown the bigger picture by the Company of Heaven and decided to set aside my preconceived skepticism about what is commonly called tithing, I did what people usually do. When I received my paycheck I paid all of my bills and then with the money that was left over I decided how I was going to use a portion of that money to add to the Light of the world. With every donation I affirmed:

> *"This money is a Gift of Love that I AM giving back to my Father-Mother God in appreciation for my Gift of Life. It is adding to the Light of the world and blessing everyone and everything in its path.*
>
> *"In fulfillment of the Law of the Circle, I accept and know that this money is returning to me greatly expanded over what I AM sending out. This is occurring with the highest good of all concerned. And so it is."*

I then paid attention to the money that was flowing back to me through various means. My flow of abundance did increase to a small degree even though the amount I was donating never was as much as 10 percent of my income.

Then one day during my meditation the Beings of Light asked me,

> *"How much do you tip a server who brings you a meal in a restaurant?"*

I said without hesitation that I always tip 20 percent of whatever the bill is. They responded,

"Isn't it amazing that you don't think twice about tipping 20 percent to someone who serves you a meal, but you do not think you can afford to give 10 percent back to God in appreciation for your Gift of Life?"

I had never thought of it that way. I was shocked when I realized how true their words were. So I decided to change the way I was making my donations. Instead of paying all of my bills first and donating my Gift of Love to God from whatever I had left over, I started donating 10 percent of my income before I paid my bills.

I will admit to you that initially there was a period of adjustment, but that did not last too long. After several months, I was in the flow. Since that time decades ago I have never been unable to pay my bills or to give my monetary Gift of Love to God in appreciation for my Gift of Life.

So let me share some words of encouragement with you. Again, I will say that if you truly believed that when you give a portion of your money in ways that will add to the Light of the world it will greatly expand and return to you, you would not hesitate to donate your money even if you thought you could not afford it. If you are hesitant to do this it simply means that you do not know if this is true or not, and you are afraid to take the risk which is perfectly normal.

The only way you will prove to yourself whether or not this Universal Law is true is by taking the chance of experimenting with it. If you have a lot of fear about giving 10 percent of your income in appreciation for your Gift of Life then do not begin with that much money. Instead chose the amount of money that feels safe to you and donate it somewhere that makes you heart sing and adds to the Light of the world. Before you donate your money state the affirmation:

> *"This money is a Gift of Love that I AM giving back to my Father-Mother God in appreciation for my Gift of Life. It is adding to the Light of the world and blessing everyone and everything in its path.*
>
> *"In fulfillment of the Law of the Circle, I accept and know that this money is returning to me greatly expanded over what I AM sending out. This is occurring with the highest good of all concerned. And so it is."*

After you donate your money, pay attention to every penny that flows back into your life. People with a fixed income usually feel that this process will not work for them because they do not have another avenue through which to receive more money, but that is not true. God is infinitely creative and very practical, so do not limit God's ability to increase the flow of money back into your life with your doubts and fears.

Be open and receptive to everything that increases your money.

If you go out with a friend for lunch and you thought you were going to pay for the lunch but your friend pays for it instead, accept that as your money flowing back to you.

If you need to buy something and it happens to be on sale, accept that is also your money flowing back to you.

If someone gives you something you want or need and now you do not have to spend money buying it for yourself that too is your money flowing back to you.

If your utility bills or your grocery bills or the gas for your car are less than normal accept that as your flow of money returning to you.

If you receive a larger tax return than you thought you were going to receive or if anything else in your life saves you money and gives you more cash in your pocket accept that as your Gift of Love flowing back into your life.

Know that this is an ongoing process. Don't donate money and then wait for money bags to appear at your doorstep before you give your next donation. *Keep on keeping on,* and as you create the habit of giving and receiving you will become more and more confident about this process. Before long you will prove to yourself that using your money to add to the Light of the world is truly the Key to your Financial Freedom, and the way you will reclaim your Divine Birthright by cocreating God's Infinite Abundance and Eternal Peace tangibly in your life.

Precious Heart, have fun with this. Develop an attitude of joyous expectation and remember... The Light of God is ALWAYS Victorious and YOU are that Light.

29

LOVING ALL LIFE FREE

As higher and higher frequencies of the 5th-Dimensional Crystalline Solar Light associated with the New Earth flow in, through and around every particle and wave of Life on Earth, the events taking place in the outer world are becoming more and more chaotic. There are many challenging things happening around the world and people everywhere are responding in a multitude of ways.

Awakening Humanity realizes that this purging process is a necessary part of Earth's Ascension, and millions of people are invoking the Light in powerful ways that will help us to move through this part of the Divine Plan more quickly. On the other hand, our sisters and brothers in the Family of Humanity who are still asleep, and those who are deliberately resisting moving forward in the Light, are responding from their basest fears and lashing out at anything and everything that is different from them.

This consciousness is exacerbating the *"us and them"* belief systems and the illusions of duality and separation that are perpetuating the vast majority of pain and suffering people are experiencing at this time. This destructive and polarized thinking is also creating the greatest stumbling blocks as Earth moves forward in the Light.

The reality is "*We are One*" and there is no such thing as "*us and them.*" Every single person on this planet is interrelated, interconnected and interdependent. It is impossible to harm any other person without our behavior reflecting back and harming us. Awakening Humanity is very aware of this Truth. For this reason, if we have the Heart Call to do so, the Company of Heaven is invoking our assistance. They are asking if we are willing to be our recalcitrant brothers and sisters keepers during this critical Cosmic Moment.

The people who are acting out in the most deplorable ways are acting out of fear. They are terrified and feel that what is happening on Earth will not only eliminate their ability to manipulate and control the masses, but that it will ultimately result in their demise. They are so buried in their own painful miscreations that they cannot comprehend that the Earth and all her Life are Ascending into the New Earth's 5th-Dimensional frequencies of Divine Love, Oneness and Reverence for ALL Life.

The Company of Heaven said the only way our recalcitrant sisters and brothers will be able to perceive that Truth is for awakening Humanity to flood them with so much Love that their I AM Presence will be able to lift their heads above the mud puddle of their human miscreations. When this happens, our sisters and brothers will be able to transcend their fear and at long last perceive the Light of their own Divinity.

The Company of Heaven is imploring every awakened Son and Daughter of God to respond to their Heart Call, and if this vitally important facet of the Divine Plan resonates with you, please participate in this activity of Light which is specifically intended to Love our sisters and brothers free.

And we begin.

Activity of Light for Loving ALL Life Free

I AM my I AM Presence and I AM One with the I AM Presence of every person on Earth. As One Unified Heart, we invoke our Father-Mother God and the entire Company of Heaven to help us raise every person on Earth from a consciousness of separation and duality into a consciousness of Oneness and Reverence for ALL Life. This is being accomplished by every person's I AM Presence in perfect alignment with his or her Divine Plan and the highest good for all concerned.

Beloved Father-Mother God, we ask that you expand your Flame of Transfiguring Divine Love which is pulsating within the Divinity of every person's Heart Flame. Allow a Heart of this Divine Love to expand and expand through each person's 5th-Dimensional Heart Chakra until it envelops the entire Planet Earth. As this unfathomable influx of Divine Love bathes the Earth, every facet of Life on this planet is being lifted into a Higher Order of Being.

Each person's I AM Presence now creates a sacred space that allows that person to open their 5th-Dimensional Crown Chakra of Enlightenment to full breadth. This allows each person to Ascend ever higher into the awakened state of Christ Consciousness.

As this occurs, multidimensional and multifaceted 5th-Dimensional Crystalline Solar Light expands from the Heart of our Father-Mother God into every cell of Humanity's Earthly Bodies allowing the I AM Presence of every person to take full dominion of their physical, etheric, mental and emotional bodies.

Now, all is in readiness. Through their I AM Presence, every person on Earth is participating at both inner and outer levels in this activity of Light, which is raising the consciousness of the masses of Humanity and assisting every recalcitrant soul to shift from the illusion of separation and duality into the Reality of Oneness and Reverence for ALL Life.

I now reach up into the Infinity of my own Divine Consciousness. As I AM lifted up, all of Humanity is lifted up with me. In this frequency of Divine Consciousness, I see that Humanity's free will is becoming One with God's Will. And the I AM Presence of each person affirms,

"I AM ready to Love ALL Life FREE!"

Instantaneously, I see the Truth of every person on Earth. I see all of my sisters and brothers in the Family of Humanity, even the most recalcitrant souls, as precious Sons and Daughters of God no matter how far their behavior patterns or their life experiences may be from reflecting that Truth. I perceive all of the painful human miscreations associated with my sisters and brothers as innocent primordial energy entering my awareness now to be transmuted back into Light and Loved free.

I happily greet all of these Children of God and all of their misqualified energy the same way my Father-Mother God would greet them. I greet them with Love from within the embrace of Eternal Peace, Detachment, God Confidence and Supreme Authority.

Within an Invincible Forcefield of God's Infinite Love I take my sisters and brothers into the Divinity of my Heart Flame, and I hold them in my arms of Light as I would an injured child. They cannot overwhelm me or control me in any way, nor do I need to fear them or shun them. I simply hold them and Love them until they surrender to the Love of God, desiring on their own to rejoin the Kingdom of

Heaven which is pulsating within the Divinity of their own Heart Flames.

Now rather than feeling rejected and thus perpetuating their negative behavior patterns, my sisters and brothers feel accepted and Loved as the innate Sons and Daughters of God they are. They voluntarily release themselves into the Light, and they begin to remember who they are.

I rejoice that recalcitrant souls and their unascended energies are at long last finding their way Home through me and I release myself into the Peace of knowing:

"My I AM Presence is handling ALL imperfection perfectly."

As these precious souls surrender to the Light, they realize that they are Beloved Sons and Daughters of God. With this sacred knowledge, they once again find their proper place in the Family of Humanity. In perfect Divine Order, they are set free to live and cocreate the patterns of Love, Oneness, and Reverence for ALL Life on the New Earth.

And so it is.

Dear One, the Beings of Light have confirmed that the more we hold this vision for our sisters and brothers in the Family of Humanity the sooner they will awaken and reclaim their Divine Birthright as Beloved Sons and Daughters of God.

The Company of Heaven is embracing you in their Eternal Gratitude for your willingness to be such a powerful force of Light on this sweet Earth.

30

YOU ARE POWERFUL BEYOND YOUR KNOWING

One of the concerns expressed to me most often is by people who are beginning to remember who they are and why they are here. As they awaken, they start to remember that there is a reason why they volunteered to come to Earth during this auspicious time. They realize that they have a purpose and that they volunteered to accomplish an important facet of the Divine Plan. Initially, these awakening souls feel very motivated to fulfill their Divine Mission and they are determined to accomplish whatever it is that they have come to Earth to do.

Every day they pray and meditate and do whatever they can to add to the Light of the world. As time passes, however, they start to feel as though their humble efforts cannot possibly make much of a difference with the enormous challenges taking place on the planet. Whenever they question their ability to really make a difference or initiate change, their I AM Presence encourages them to empower their efforts by joining together with other people. The problem is, they don't know of any like-minded groups in their area and they feel very alone and isolated. This is frustrating and very discouraging which often causes them to give up and stop trying.

This is a unique moment on Planet Earth. All of us have spent Lifetimes preparing to be in the physical plane during this tumultuous, but wondrous, time. The Earth and all her Life are Ascending into the 5th-Dimensional frequencies of the New Earth, and you and I and the rest of awakening Humanity are here so that we can invoke the Light of God to help awaken our sisters and brothers who are still asleep and unable to do it for themselves just yet. There is no way that our I AM Presence is going to let us just give up on this vitally important part of the Divine Plan. Consequently, if we try to stop doing our Lightwork we feel miserable and unfulfilled which causes us to think of ourselves as failures. This happens no matter how successful we may be in other areas of our life. So giving up is not an option, at least not an option that we can endure happily.

The Company of Heaven wants to remind all of us that we are never alone and that regardless of how isolated we feel or how limited our perception might be, the Truth is, we are multidimensional Beings and we are powerful beyond our knowing. It is true that it greatly empowers our Lightwork when we are able to gather together physically with other people for our invocations, meditations, prayers and activities of Light and we should do that whenever we can. However, there are also powerful ways we can join together in consciousness when we are not able to be together physically.

Remember, we are One with every other person on Earth and there is no separation. We often hear or say those words, but the Beings of Light want us to grasp the magnitude of what those words really mean. Quite literally, the statement "*We are One*" means that every person on Earth is interrelated, interconnected and interdependent with every other person on Earth. That is true whether we are aware of it or not on a conscious level.

What the Beings of Light want us to know is that even if this Truth is difficult for us to comprehend with our finite mind, our I AM Presence is absolutely aware of this fact. Our I AM Presence knows that in order for us to invoke the Light of God on behalf of every other person on Earth during our invocations, meditations, prayers and activities of Light, all we have to do is align with our I AM Presence and affirm that we are One with the I AM Presence of every other person. This is accomplished by simply saying:

I AM my I AM Presence and I AM One with the I AM Presence of every man, woman and child on Earth.

Once we make that statement, instantaneously, our I AM Presence sends a signal to the I AM Presence of each of the more than seven billion Sons and Daughters of God evolving on Earth. Our I AM Presence alerts each person's I AM Presence that a sister or brother is invoking the Light of God on their behalf and directs them to stand in readiness to receive that Blessing from On High.

In that instant, we shift from being the microcosm of one person's I AM Presence receiving the Light of God on Earth, to being the macrocosm of over seven billion people's I AM Presences receiving the Light of God on Planet Earth.

I will share with you that in my personal endeavors, experiencing this profound Truth was one of the most shocking and amazing experiences I have ever had. Beloved Archangel Michael is the Being of Light who demonstrated this to me.

One day many years ago, I was invoking my I AM Presence as I always did before beginning my meditation. In my mind's eye I saw my luminous I AM Presence expand through my Heart Flame and take full dominion of my physical, etheric, mental and emotional bodies. My I AM Presence became a brilliant Sun and enveloped everything in my sphere of influence, including my family, my home, my city and the surrounding area.

As I said my invocations and prayers, the Light of God flowed through my Heart Flame and expanded out to the periphery of the Sun being formed by my I AM Presence. Wave after wave of Light filled the Sun and blazed in, through and around every person, place, condition and thing within the Sun. When my I AM Presence determined that the activity of Light was complete, the Light I had invoked on behalf of my family and friends was secured in their Heart Flame by their I AM Presence.

When I thought my meditation was over, Archangel Michael appeared within the spectrum of my Inner Vision. He said that if I was willing, he would teach me how to exponentially expand my Lightwork to include every person on Earth. There are not words to express the Love and Gratitude I felt for this opportunity and I Gratefully accepted his offer.

Archangel Michael asked me to repeat the invocation I made to my I AM Presence before the invocations and prayers I had just completed, so I affirmed, "*I AM my I AM Presence.*" When I said those words once again, in my mind's eye I saw my I AM Presence expand through my Heart Flame and my Earthly Bodies and become a brilliant Sun that enveloped everything in my sphere of influence.

Archangel Michael said, "*Now affirm,*

I AM my I AM Presence and I AM One with the I AM Presence of every man, woman and child on Earth."

When I repeated those words, instantaneously the Sun of my I AM Presence exploded into a tremendous Starburst of Light that enveloped the entire Planet Earth. A Ray of Light from this exquisite Starburst of Light entered the Heart Flame of every person on Earth and signaled each person's I AM Presence to stand in readiness to receive the Light being invoked on their behalf.

Archangel Michael then asked me to repeat the invocations and prayers I had just completed. As I repeated the words the Light of God not only blazed through the Sun that was formed by my I AM Presence, but also through the Suns being formed by the I AM Presences of every person on Earth. I do not have words that can adequately describe the monumental expansion of Light I witnessed that day, but I understand now, beyond a shadow of a doubt, what the Beings of Light mean when they say that we are powerful beyond our knowing.

When we affirm that we are One with the I AM Presence of another person and invoke the Light of God on their behalf, the person's I AM Presence knows exactly how to use that Light in perfect alignment with the person's Divine Plan and their highest good. We do not need to figure out just what their Divine Plan is or worry that we may be interfering with their Divine Plan by trying to force our Will on them.

Simply by affirming that we are One with the person's I AM Presence and invoking the Light on their behalf, we give the person's I AM Presence permission to go into action and to utilize the Light we are invoking in ways that are in perfect alignment with their highest good and their Divine Plan.

Precious Heart, knowing this Truth will inspire you to *"keep on keeping on"*, and it will prevent you from erroneously thinking that if you are by yourself you are not making much of a difference. On the contrary, once you accept how powerful you are it will be impossible for you to feel like your efforts are in vain.

31

You Are Here to
Make a Difference

This is a New Day on Planet Earth, and Humanity is in the midst of the most intensified purging and the greatest shift of energy, vibration and consciousness we have ever experienced. The Company of Heaven has been granted permission by our Father-Mother God to come through the veil to meet us halfway. Sacred Knowledge from the Realms of Illumined Truth is flowing at an accelerated pace into the mental and emotional strata of Earth.

This information is filtering into the awakening consciousness of people everywhere and enlightenment is being received in new and profound ways. People are beginning to *"see with new eyes and hear with new ears."* At long last, Humanity is realizing the awesome power we have within us to transform this planet and all her Life into the infinite perfection of the New Earth which is her Divine Destiny. This is truly an auspicious moment and an unparalleled opportunity for all of us.

After decades of dedicated service to the Light by embodied Lightworkers and the entire Company of Heaven, our unified efforts have resulted in reaching a critical mass that has allowed the first 5th-Dimensional archetypes for the New Earth to be anchored into the mental and emotional strata of this planet. These archetypes contain the Divine Matrix for *God's Infinite Abundance and Eternal Peace*. These are inseparable aspects of our Father-Mother God's Divine Qualities. Infinite Abundance cannot be sustained without Eternal Peace, and Eternal Peace cannot be sustained without God's Infinite Abundance.

Now, through the unified Heart Calls and the invocations of embodied Lightworkers around the world these archetypes will be drawn into our Heart Flames and projected into the physical plane of Earth, so that every man, woman and child will eventually experience God's Abundance and Eternal Peace tangibly in their lives.

The successful anchoring of the very first 5th-Dimensional archetypes for the New Earth has paved the way for Lightworkers to anchor the remaining 5th-Dimensional patterns of perfection for the New Earth into the mental and emotional strata of this planet. Once this occurs, those exquisite patterns will also be readily available for every awakened person to draw into their Heart Flame and project into the physical plane of Earth for the benefit of all Humanity.

These patterns pulsate with the Immaculate Concept of the New Earth in all of her resplendent glory and perfection. They transcend every frequency of vibration that is less than the Oneness and the Divine Love, Harmony, Balance and Reverence for Life of our Father-Mother God.

This is the moment we have all been working toward for aeons of time. Every single one of us has all of the skill, wisdom, knowledge, strength and courage we need to succeed God Victoriously in this mission. All we have to do is remember the awesome ability we have to make a difference through the incredible power of our spoken words and our invocations, prayers and decrees.

The I AM Presence of every person abiding on Earth and the entire Company of Heaven are standing in readiness, awaiting the opportunity to assist us in this holy endeavor. However, not even our I AM Presence or the Company of Heaven can intervene to help us without us asking them to do so. No one is allowed to interfere with our free will.

That is why the Avatars of the Ages have continually reiterated,

"Ask and you shall receive"
"Knock and the door will be open".

The Beings of Light have told us there is a Universal Law that declares,

"The call for assistance must come from the Realm where the assistance is needed!"

This means quite literally that those of us abiding on Earth must invoke the Light of God and ask for the assistance we desire from our I AM Presence and the Company of Heaven in order for these Divine Beings to have permission to intervene in our lives and to respond to our Heart's Call.

At this time, we are being called to a higher octave of service. Our Father-Mother God are asking us to remember who we are and why we are on Earth during this unprecedented Ascension process that we are all experiencing. We are Beloved Sons and Daughters of God which means that ALL our Father-Mother God have is ours.

You and I and the rest of awakening Humanity have been given permission to be on Earth during this critical time, because we have been preparing for Lifetimes to be a force of Light in the face of all adversity. We are here because we willingly volunteered to be the Open Door for the Light of God on Earth. We volunteered to hold the sacred space for our sister's and brother's awakening. We volunteered to be God in Action in the physical plane during Humanity's Ascension process into the 5th-Dimensional frequencies of the New Earth.

Dear One, your I AM Presence and the Company of Heaven are standing in readiness awaiting your invitation to assist you in remembering who you are and what you have volunteered to do to assist this sweet Earth and ALL her Life up the Spiral of Evolution into the frequencies of the New Earth.

Take some time to quiet yourself and ask your I AM Presence and the Company of Heaven to awaken within your Heart Flame and your conscious mind the knowing that you have an important reason for being on Earth, and that the time for you to begin fulfilling that Divine Purpose is NOW!

32

THE POWER OF THE
SPOKEN WORD

This is a vitally important time on Earth and the Company
of Heaven is reminding us of ways that we can enhance
our effectiveness as Lightworkers. One of the most powerful
ways we can enhance our Lightwork is through the spoken
word. We can easily accomplish this through our invocations, prayers and decrees. Remember...

> "In the beginning was the Word, and the Word was with
> God, and the Word was God."

Within each spoken word is the Holy Breath, the Creative
Power of our Father-Mother God, which molds unformed
primal Light substance into form. Each thoughtform and
physical manifestation we create corresponds to the vibration of the words being spoken.

After Humanity's fall from Grace aeons ago, we inadvertently charged and surcharged our gift of speech and
our spoken words with vibrations of imperfection and dis-
cord. Unfortunately, to this very day in many instances we

are still misusing our gift of speech in this way. Every one of our distorted thoughtforms and the manifestations created by negative speech continue to pulsate in the atmosphere of Earth until they are transmuted back into harmony and balance.

With sacred knowledge from the Realms of Illumined Truth now flowing into the hearts and minds of awakening Humanity as never before, we are becoming acutely aware of the urgency of the hour. It is now clear how vitally important it is for every awakening man, woman and child to take an active role in transmuting back into Light Humanity's human miscreations from both the past and the present. This may seem like a difficult task but actually it is not.

Negative speech creates negative thoughtforms and negative manifestations. Positive speech creates positive thoughtforms and positive manifestations. The Beings of Light have revealed that when we use our Holy Breath to speak words that are invoking the Light, the power of our words is increased exponentially.

When we invoke the Light through spoken invocations, prayers and decrees our words are infinitely more powerful than the words used to express negativity and darkness. When we invoke the Light through the power of our spoken words we are able to transmute literally tons of Humanity's negative thoughtforms and negative manifestations. If we invoke the 5th-Dimensional Violet Flame of God's Infinite Perfection to assist us in transmuting those negative thoughtforms and miscreations the effectiveness of our spoken words is instantly intensified to an even greater level.

The Beings of Light have said that comprehending the power of our spoken words is an imperative facet of the Divine Plan if we are going to fulfill the next phase in our evolutionary process. That phase of the plan involves anchoring the rest of the patterns of perfection for the New Earth into the mental and emotional strata of the planet so that they can be magnetized into the physical plane. In order for Mother Earth to complete her Ascension up the Spiral of Evolution into the 5th-Dimensional Realms of Infinite Perfection, the residue of our human miscreations on the old Earth must be transmuted back into Light. Using the power of our spoken words to accomplish this is an essential part of what we have all been preparing to do for lifetimes.

Pay attention to how you are using your Holy Breath through your spoken words. Think of your words as thought-forms, and see if your words correspond with what you want to create in your life. If they do not, then invoke the Violet Flame to transmute the negative thoughtform you unintentionally created and affirm with your spoken words what you want to create instead.

If you have the Heart Call to begin using your words to invoke the Violet Flame to transmute past and present miscreations, you can do so by affirming this simple, but extremely powerful, mantra which has been given to us by the Company of Heaven.

First of all, always begin any invocation, prayer or decree by saying:

I AM my I AM Presence and I AM One with the I AM Presence of every person on Earth and the entire Company of Heaven.

Then say this mantra throughout the day as often as you like.

Violet Flame Mantra

Transmute, transmute by the Violet Fire all causes and cores not of God's desire. I AM a Being of cause alone; that cause is Love, the Sacred Tone.

Transmute, transmute by the Violet Fire all causes and cores not of God's desire. I AM a Being of cause alone; that cause is Love, the Sacred Tone.

Transmute, transmute by the Violet Fire all causes and cores not of God's desire. I AM a Being of cause alone; that cause is Love, the Sacred Tone. And so it is.

33

WAYS TO EMPOWER YOUR LIGHTWORK

In our awakening process, we are beginning to understand the science of energy, vibration and consciousness in new ways. We are learning how very powerful our words are and we now know that our thoughts and feelings are creative. This means that whatever we focus our attention on with our thoughts, words, feelings and actions we cocreate, empower and sustain in our lives. There are well known statements that reflect this Truth.

"Where my attention is, there I AM"
"Where my thoughts go, my energy flows."

What the Company of Heaven wants to share with us at this time is how incredibly powerful our thoughts, words, feelings and actions are when they are empowered by other Lightworkers who are thinking, feeling, saying and doing the same thing. This is one of the reasons we are encouraged to gather together physically in groups for our Lightwork. When that is not available to us there is another way.

We are so blessed to be living in these times when in an instant technology enables us to connect with Lightworkers all over the world. Through the Internet, we have the awesome ability to join with fellow Lightworkers at specific times for Global Meditations and activities of Light. In our Weekly Vlogs for instance, every week thousands of people all over the world join with us to receive the sacred knowledge and to participate in the activities of Light the Company of Heaven leads us through.

In addition to events available on the Internet, we can also empower each other's Lightwork by sharing the same invocations, prayers, meditations and decrees. When we invoke the Light of God in any way, a permanent matrix is formed in the Realms of Cause. Then every time anyone else invokes the Light of God in the same way their Light is woven into that matrix, and they receive the full benefit of every other Lightworker who has recited that invocation or participated in that meditation.

That is why *"The Lord's Prayer"* is so very powerful. Every time we recite *"The Lord's Prayer"* our Light is woven into that thoughtform in the Realms of Cause. Then we receive the benefit from the Light of every person who has ever said that prayer from the moment it was first given to Humanity over 2,000 years ago.

For decades awakening Lightworkers have been aware of this fact and have been receiving invocations, meditations, prayers and decrees from the Company of Heaven that are designed to help us add to the Light of the world. By utilizing these Gifts from On High, we can empower our Lightwork no matter where we are or who we are with. The thoughtforms for these Gifts from the Company of Heaven have been building in momentum in the Realms of Cause and they are now incredibly powerful.

Because of the need of the hour, Lightworkers are being called to a higher octave of Divine Service. The Company of Heaven has asked us to make the invocations, meditations, prayers and decrees they have shared with us over the years available in an easily accessible form for anyone who is interested in empowering their own Lightwork in this way.

In response to the Beings of Light's request, we have produced a Book of Invocations titled "*I AM Cocreating the New Earth.*" This book is available as a physical book or an E-Book, and there is a set of three corresponding Mp3s or physical CDs that will help you easily empower your Lightwork. Both of these items are available on our website www.eraofpeace.org.

This sacred Book of Invocations and the corresponding Mp3s or CDs are a compilation of powerful decrees, visualizations, invocations and meditations that have been given to Humanity by our Father-Mother God and the Company of Heaven. The Divine Intent of these items is to give people all over the world a very easy way to join together either physically or in consciousness with other Lightworkers. This will greatly empower our Lightwork by unifying our invocations, prayers, meditations and visualizations.

Every time we use the power of the spoken word and the power of our thoughts and feelings to invoke these Gifts from On High, we are connecting with hundreds of thousands of Lightworkers who have been utilizing this information and cocreating the patterns of perfection for the New Earth in the Realms of Cause for decades. Now, due to the incredible shifts of energy, vibration and consciousness we have experienced over the past few years, our I AM Presence is able to empower our unified efforts in unfathomable ways.

When thousands of Lightworkers around the world are using the same decrees, invocations, visualizations and meditations we will reach a critical mass in no time. Then, Life on Planet Earth will be transformed into the wonders of the New Earth in what the seers in ancient times described as *"the twinkling of an eye"*.

The Mp3s and CDs are an effortless way to stay focused on the Light and to add to the Light of the world when you are doing other things. Play them softly as you go to sleep at night. Listen to them when you are exercising or doing housework or other things that do not need your full concentration. Use them with your meditation groups or any other time when you would like to add to the Light of the world.

These are wondrous but often challenging times. Whenever you can turn your attention to the exquisite patterns of the New Earth, instead of focusing on the negativity that is surfacing to be transmuted, Humanity, the planet and YOU will be infinitely better off.

Remember, where your attention is there you are. Every time you focus on the patterns for the New Earth, you are moving Humanity and ALL Life on this planet closer and closer to a critical mass in our Ascension process. When that happens, we will experience an unstoppable shift up the Spiral of Evolution for this sweet Earth and all her Life.

Dear One, if you are interested in purchasing the Book of Invocations and the three Mp3s or the three CDs that complement it, they are available on our website www.eraofpeace.org.

The Book of Invocations is titled: **I AM Cocreating the New Earth**

The three Mp3s and CDs are also titled: **I AM Cocreating the New Earth**

When you go to our website just click on the PRODUCTS tab at the top of our Home Page and you will be taken to the link where you can purchase these items at a reduced rate.

34

MANIFESTING CHANGE AND YOUR NEW LIFE PATH

The Beings of Light have been sharing with us ways in which we can fulfill our Divine Mission and enhance our ability to add to the Light of the world. I would like to share with you a Template they have given to us to empower our personal and collective transformation. I will share this with you as a guided visualization. If you feel the Heart Call to do so, please join with me now.

Breathe in deeply and go within to the Divinity of your Heart Flame. Listen carefully to these words which are stated in the 1st person so we will each experience them personally, but know that we are also cocreating this Template through the I AM Presence of every person on Earth in perfect alignment with their Divine Plan and their highest good. Please follow me through this visualization with the full power of your attention. In the Eternal Moment of NOW this activity of Light is God Victoriously accomplished the instant we Call.

Manifesting Change

I AM my I AM Presence and I AM One with the I AM Presence of every person on Earth. As One Unified Heart, and a consciousness of Pure Divine Love, we begin.

During this Cosmic Moment, I AM being held in the arms of God's Divine Grace. Within this forcefield of Infinite Light, I AM able to instantaneously manifest CHANGE in my life.

My I AM Presence is now pushing every facet of my life that I want and need to change to the surface of my conscious mind. As each of these things pass before my mind's eye, I acknowledge them and I cast them into the Violet Flame of God's Infinite Perfection. (pause)

Within the unfathomable frequencies of this Violet Flame every particle and wave of energy associated with the things I want and need to change are instantly transmuted back into Light. As this occurs, I forgive myself for any perceived transgression and I Love this precious Life energy free.

I AM grateful for this opportunity to change the things in my life that are no longer serving my highest good. As these changes take place within me instantaneously, I experience an inner calm and a deep sense of Peace. (pause)

The Divine Power to sustain these changes is now flowing through my Heart Flame from the very Heart of my Father-Mother God. This Gift of Divine Power will be daily and hourly intensified by my I AM Presence.

I AM now ready to cocreate a Template for my NEW Life Path. From this moment forth, I Consecrate my Life Force to a Life of Oneness, Divine Love, Reverence for ALL Life, Eternal Peace, God's Infinite Abundance, Vibrant Health,

Eternal Youth and everything else that supports my highest good and assists me in fulfilling my Divine Purpose and reason for Being.

I now raise my consciousness and I experience myself Ascending into the Realms of Illumined Truth. I cross over the Bridge to Freedom which is the highway of Light that connects Heaven and Earth. In deep humility and gratitude, I enter the Pure Land of Boundless Splendor and Infinite Light where the New Earth abides.

Within this exquisite Light, I see the entire Company of Heaven standing in readiness. They have come to help me cocreate my NEW Life Path. As One Unified Consciousness, the Beings of Light Breathe into their Heart Flames from the very Heart of my Father-Mother God the most intensified frequencies of 5th-Dimensional Crystalline Solar Light that I AM capable of receiving at a cellular level. On the Holy Breath, these selfless Messengers of God now Breathe this Divine Light into my Heart Flame. This is the Light I will use to cocreate the Template for my NEW Life Path which is being revealed to me now by my I AM Presence:

The Template for My NEW Life Path

With the Divine Intervention of my I AM Presence and the Company of Heaven, I now cocreate the Template for my NEW Life Path.

I AM a Beloved Child of God and I Love and respect who I AM.

As I sojourn through my Earthly experiences, I AM enveloped in the invincible protection of my Father-Mother God's Divine Love and Light.

I AM manifesting through Divine Alchemy my vibrantly healthy and eternally youthful 5th-Dimensional Crystalline

Physical, Etheric, Mental and Emotional Solar Light Bodies.

Divine Love perpetually flows through my Heart Flame blessing all Life and magnetizing wonderful, Loving relationships into every area of my existence.

I AM joyfully fulfilling my Divine Purpose and reason for Being, and I AM financially and creatively rewarded. Every day I AM open and receptive to the Infinite flow of God's Abundance.

I AM reaching my highest Divine Potential in all of my experiences as a daughter or son, a woman or man, a wife or husband, a mother or father, a grandmother or grandfather, as a relative, a friend, a coworker, a teacher, a way shower, a steward of this planet, a Lightworker and a cocreator of Heaven on Earth.

I communicate openly and honestly and I AM a compassionate and thoughtful listener.

My I AM Presence guides me unerringly, and I easily receive information and viable solutions to the various situations surfacing in my Life.

I AM a multidimensional Being of Light, and I abide simultaneously in both the Pure Land of Boundless Splendor and Infinite Light and in the physical world of form on Planet Earth.

With every breath, I AM the Open Door for the Light of God and the patterns of perfection I have called forth this day from the very Core of Creation.

I know and accept that through the unified efforts of Heaven and Earth this sacred and holy day, I have God Victoriously cocreated the Template for my NEW Life Path.

And so it is. Beloved I AM, Beloved I AM, Beloved I AM that I AM.

Thank you, Dear One. Spend some time contemplating the Template for your NEW Life Path. Pay attention to the changes you have made that are now being empowered with every breath you take through the Divine Intervention of your I AM Presence and the Company of Heaven.

35

BE A PEACE COMMANDING PRESENCE

During this confusing and often challenging time in Earth's Ascension process, the Company of Heaven is sending forth a Clarion Call to all who have ears to hear. As this Clarion Call reverberates through the Ethers, Humanity's I AM Presences are being alerted and inspired to awaken within our Heart Flames the inner knowing that we have been preparing for lifetimes to *BE a Peace Commanding Presence* during the unprecedented purging the Earth is experiencing at this time.

This inner knowing will remind each of us that we already have within the Divinity of our Heart Flame everything we need in order to be a Peace Commanding Presence. This knowing will also bring to the surface of our conscious mind the realization that when we respond to the adversity manifesting on Earth as a Peace Commanding Presence, we effectively dissipate the pain involved in the things manifesting around us.

Without remembering this profound Truth, it is very easy to look at outer-world appearances and come to the erroneous conclusion that Humanity and Planet Earth are spiraling into an abyss of negativity. As the residue of the old Earth is pushed to the surface to be transmuted back into Light, outer appearances create the illusion that everything that can go wrong is going wrong. We are witnessing catastrophic hurricanes, wildfires, earthquakes, floods, droughts, melting glaciers, wars, mass shootings and an increase of every other painful thing occurring on this planet. It is very easy to get pulled into the fear and anxiety being expressed by the masses. Unfortunately, that does not help at all. In fact, it is the worst thing that we can do.

Remember our thoughts and feelings are creative.

"Where my attention is there I AM."

Whatever we are thinking and feeling we are empowering. The Company of Heaven has revealed to us just how powerful our thoughts, words, feelings and actions are and how they are cocreating our everyday life experiences whether we are aware of it or not. When we focus on the horror of what is happening around the world and empower those terrible things with our fear and anxiety, we greatly complicate the problem. There is a philosophical statement that affirms that knowing. It is, *"When we grieve with someone, we water their garden of sorrow."*

This does not mean that we should put our head in the sand and pretend that the things we observe and experience are not happening. And it certainly does not mean that we do not care or have compassion for the people experiencing painful things or difficult situations. It simply means that when we become overwhelmed by another person's misery and wallow in their pain with them, we actually amplify their suffering. I know that is the very last thing any

caring person wants to do, but we often do it unintentionally. When we emotionally descend into another person's
pain and misery, we become part of the problem instead of
part of the solution. We cannot comfort or lift someone up
when we ourselves are writhing in agony or overwhelmed
with grief.

The Company of Heaven wants us to remember how we
can respond to the negative things occurring on Earth in
ways that will heal rather than exacerbate Humanity's pain
and suffering. First of all, we need to be aware of the things
that are happening around the world. Every day we need to
pay attention and we need to be informed about the negative things being pushed to the surface to be healed and
transmuted back into Light. However, instead of having the
reflex response of emotionally connecting with the shock
and horror of what is happening, we need to deliberately
stay centered in our Heart Flame. Then we can ask our I AM
Presence to help us detach from the pain, so that we can BE
a Peace Commanding Presence even in the face of the most
horrific adversity.

By affirming, *"I AM my I AM Presence and I AM One with
the I AM Presence of all Humanity"* we instantly alert the I
AM Presence of every person on Earth to stand in readiness to receive the Light of God being invoked on their
behalf. Once we align with the I AM Presence of every person in that way, we can greatly dissipate the suffering by
affirming:

*"I AM a Peace Commanding Presence and I ask the entire
Company of Heaven and the I AM Presence of every
person involved with this event to envelop him or her in
an invincible forcefield of God's Protection and Divine
Comfort."*

In order to BE a Peace Commanding Presence, we do not need to fully comprehend why something negative is happening or specifically understand what is surfacing to be healed in a particular event. This is a very complex time and literally lifetimes worth of Humanity's multifaceted miscreations from the old Earth are surfacing on a daily basis to be healed and transmuted back into Light. To be a Peace Commanding Presence, all we need to remember is that nothing is happening by accident.

As difficult as it is for us to reconcile this Truth with our finite minds, the Company of Heaven has told us that no one is a victim. No matter what we are experiencing, on a higher level of consciousness we have agreed to go through that particular ordeal in order to assist with the process of transmuting into Light our own and Humanity's miscreations from the old Earth. Pain and suffering of any kind are the result of the human miscreations associated with the fallen consciousness of our human egos. These miscreations must be transmuted back into Light before we can God Victoriously complete our Ascension into the 5th-Dimensional frequencies of the New Earth.

This inner knowing will help us to see the bigger picture and to realize that even the most horrific event can result in moving Humanity and the Earth forward in the Light. The most positive thing that occurs when Humanity becomes aware of any kind of tragedy is that people everywhere open their hearts and instantly feel compassion for the people involved in that negative event. This response allows even the most asleep people to experience the Oneness of ALL Life in profound ways. Amazingly, in the midst of the shock and horror, people forget their differences and begin reaching out to one another in the most Loving and helpful ways.

Precious Heart, practice being the Peace Commanding Presence you have been preparing to be for lifetimes. In the next chapter the Company of Heaven will help us remember how we can help Humanity to take advantage of their newly opened hearts and the compassion they are feeling toward their sisters and brothers in the Family of Humanity.

36

EXPANDING THE DIVINITY IN YOUR HEART FLAME

The Company of Heaven has reminded us of how important it is for each of us to be a Peace Commanding Presence in the face of the adversity surfacing all over the world. They pointed out the vitally important Truth that even the most horrific event can result in moving Humanity and the Earth forward in the Light.

This is possible because even if people are shocked or horrified, when they become aware of a tragedy that is adversely affecting their sisters and brothers they open their heart and experience a level of compassion and empathy for those involved in the negative event. This response allows even the most asleep people to get a glimpse of what the Oneness of ALL Life really feels like. In that moment, they forget their differences and they reach out to help one another in profound and Loving ways.

The Beings of Light are revealing to us the fact that when people open their heart, even if they do so temporarily during an unexpected negative event or situation, their I AM Presence has the ability to expand the Light of God flowing through their Heart Flame. This Divine Intervention has the potential of reversing one of the most tragic affects of Humanity's fall from Grace. What the Beings of Light want us to clearly understand, is that our I AM Presence can *only* expand our Heart Flame to its original size and Divine Potential if asked and given permission to do so.

The Beings of Light want to share some background about what happened to our Heart Flame when we fell from Grace. The Divine Intent of this sharing is to help us comprehend the magnitude of the opportunity that is being presented at this time to help us reverse the tragic results of our fall from Grace, so that we can once again expand the Threefold Flame within the hearts of ALL Humanity to their full Divine Potential.

Every Son and Daughter of God has a Divine Flame that pulsates within their heart. Prior to our fall from Grace our Heart Flame, which is known through all Creation as our Immortal Victorious Threefold Flame, completely enveloped our physical, etheric, mental and emotional bodies.

The Blue Flame of our Father God's Power activated our left-brain hemisphere, which is the rational, logical portion of our brain, and it also activated the Power Center within our Throat Chakra. The Blue Flame of our Father God's Power was then anchored within our heart and continually blazed through the entire left side of our Earthly Bodies.

The Pink Flame of our Mother God's Love activated our right-brain hemisphere which is the creative, intuitive portion of our brain. This Pink Flame then activated the Love Center within our Heart Chakra and was also anchored within our heart. Our Mother God's Pink Flame of Love continually blazed through the entire right side of our Earthly Bodies.

That may seem confusing since science tells us that on a physical level the right side of our brain controls the left side of our physical body and the left side of our brain controls the right side of our physical body which is true; but the Sacred Fire within our Threefold Heart Flame pulsates through our bodies differently.

Once the Masculine and the Feminine polarities of our Father-Mother God were perfectly balanced within our heart, they wove their frequencies together and formed the magnificent *Violet Flame of God's Infinite Perfection.* This perfectly balanced frequency of the Violet Flame blazed up into our physical brain structure and activated our spiritual brain centers. These centers are our pineal, pituitary and hypothalamus glands and the ganglionic centers at the base of our brain.

When these spiritual brain centers were activated, our Crown Chakra opened to full breadth. Once that occurred, our Father-Mother God breathed a Yellow-gold Flame of Christ Consciousness, which reflects the enlightenment and wisdom of every Son and Daughter of God, into our Crown Chakra and anchored this Sacred Fire between the Blue and Pink Flames in every person's heart. This completed the manifestation of our Immortal Victorious Threefold Flame. This Sacred Fire which pulsates in every single person's heart is the tangible manifestation of the Holy Trinity.

In the beginning, our physical, etheric, mental and emotional bodies lived, moved, breathed and had their Being within our Threefold Flame. At that time, we received our Life Force through a mighty shaft of Light that extended from the very Heart of our Father-Mother God, through our Crown Chakra and into our Heart Flame. This pillar of Light then passed through our spinal column and pulsated into our Chakras, which kept us directly connected to our I AM Presence and the entire Company of Heaven. The Life Force that passed through this shaft of Light was our Gift of

Life from our Father-Mother God. It was the unformed primal Light substance we were to use throughout our Earthly sojourn while we learned to become cocreators with our Father-Mother God.

Tragically, there was a point in time when we made the freewill choice to experiment with our thoughts and feelings in ways that were not based in Love. This fateful decision caused us to misqualify enormous amounts of our Life Force which literally wreaked havoc in our lives. In a merciful act of Divine Grace, our Father-Mother God issued a Cosmic Fiat with the intent of limiting the amount of Life Force we were able to misqualify with our thoughts and feelings. The intent of that Fiat was to prevent us from burying ourselves in such an overwhelming amount of negative energy that we would never be able to reclaim our Divine Birthright as Beloved Sons and Daughters of God.

Our God Parent's Cosmic Fiat directed the I AM Presence of every one of us to withdraw our Immortal Victorious Threefold Flame into a sacred chamber in our heart. That chamber is called our Heart's Permanent Seed Atom. Once our Threefold Flame was withdrawn into the Permanent Seed Atom in our heart it no longer enveloped our physical, etheric, mental and emotional bodies. It was reduced to a minuscule fraction of its original size which we now refer to as the "*Spark of Divinity*" in our heart. The mighty shaft of Light that used to flow through our Heart Flame was also reduced to a fraction of its original size. We now call, what used to be a powerful shaft of Light, our "*Silver Cord.*"

Now, during this unprecedented time, one of the most life-transforming things we can do is to expand our Immortal Victorious Threefold Flame back into to its original size and Divine Potential. This will assist each of us to permanently reconnect with our I AM Presence and the Company of Heaven. Once this occurs, our Father-Mother God will be able to restore our Silver Cord to the mighty shaft of Light it was in the beginning. This will greatly intensify the influx of our Life Force and catapult us, and the masses of Humanity, a quantum leap toward the enlightened state of Christ Consciousness.

The sacred knowledge and the activities of Light the Company of Heaven will reveal to us in the next few sharings are designed to teach all of us how to accomplish this vitally important step. We will learn how to restore our Heart Flames and the shaft of Light through which our Life Force will be greatly intensified.

We are being asked to focus on our Threefold Flame, and to visualize our I AM Presence breathing an intensified frequency of 5th-Dimensional Crystalline Solar Light into the Spark of Divinity which is the Permanent Seed Atom in our heart. We will accelerate this activity of Light by envisioning in our mind's eye the exquisite Blue Flame of our Father God's Power, the Pink Flame of our Mother God's Love and the Yellow-gold Flame of the Sons and Daughters of God's Wisdom being empowered with higher and higher frequencies of Divine Light as we progress through our day, breath by breath.

37

THE NEXT STEP IN EXPANDING YOUR HEART FLAME

The reason the selfless Messengers of God from the Realms of Illumined Truth are focusing so intently on helping us to reverse the adverse affects of our fall from Grace is because of the powerful opportunity being presented to us at this time. People everywhere, and the Earth herself, are experiencing a greatly intensified purging process that will probably not be complete for some time. This process is causing millions of people to experience extreme loss and pain in what often feels like unbearable circumstances.

This heartbreaking situation is causing billions of people around the world to open their heart with empathy and compassion for those who are suffering. When a person's heart is open, their I AM Presence has the ability to intervene and to flood them with Light in ways they cannot if the person's heart is closed. But before their I AM Presence is able to do that, the person or someone acting on the person's behalf must invoke their I AM Presence and give them permission to intervene.

The Beings of Light are sharing this important information with us now because we have the opportunity of assisting the I AM Presence of billions of people to expand the Immortal Victorious Threefold Flame in their heart. The Company of Heaven has assured us that returning the Threefold Flame within a person's heart to its original size and Divine Potential is one of the most life-transforming things One will experience in this Ascension process. When this expansion of the Heart Flame occurs, the Presence of God within the person is greatly amplified, which changes the way a person thinks, feels, speaks and acts.

Remember, a critical part of our purpose and reason for being on Earth during this momentous time is to help ease the pain and suffering that our precious brothers and sisters are experiencing. Only then will they be able to lift their heads above the chaos effectively enough to once again connect with their I AM Presence and the Company of Heaven.

Humanity reached a critical mass of Divine Love on December 21st and 22nd in 2012 that allowed *every single person* evolving on Earth to Ascend up the Spiral of Evolution into the initial embrace of the New Earth. The reason our Father-Mother God granted permission for even the most asleep or recalcitrant people on Earth to make it through the Shift of the Ages is because of the heart commitment you and I and the rest of awakening Humanity made through our I AM Presence on their behalf.

Our sisters and brothers were granted permission to move through the Shift of the Ages in spite of the human miscreations they were still responsible for transmuting back into Light. This was allowed by our Father-Mother God because *millions* of Lightworkers who are embodied on Earth made the heart commitment to hold the sacred space for our struggling sisters and brothers until they awakened.

Collectively, awakening Humanity promised to help our asleep and recalcitrant sisters and brothers to awaken as soon as possible. We agreed to do whatever is necessary in order to transmute the surfacing negativity from the old Earth. The Company of Heaven told us if we had not agreed to do that these souls would not have been allowed to Ascend into the initial impulse of the New Earth. That is because their surfacing negativity and the necessary purging that is taking place on Earth to clear their human miscreations would have been overwhelming and would have actually caused more harm than good.

In previous sharings the Beings of Light revealed the reason why Earth's purging process has gotten so intense. The difficult things that have taken place around the world recently have opened Humanity's hearts and initiated feelings of compassion and caring for our fellow Human Beings in extremely powerful ways. This has alerted the I AM Presence of billions of people and every one of them is now standing in readiness awaiting the opportunity to intervene in expanding Humanity's Heart Flames in Loving and effective ways.

The Company of Heaven has given us a powerful invocation that will allow us to join our unified hearts in this Holy Endeavor. Dear One, please join with me and the thousands of Lightworkers around the world who are empowering this activity of Light with us in this Eternal Moment of Now.

Expanding My Immortal
Victorious Threefold Flame

As One Voice, One Breath, One Heartbeat and One Consciousness of Pure Divine Love, we breathe in and out deeply and rhythmically as we enter the Divinity within our Heart Flame. And we begin.

I AM my I AM Presence and I AM One with the I AM Presence of ALL Humanity. What I invoke for myself I invoke on behalf of every man, woman, and child on Earth in perfect alignment with each person's Divine Plan and the highest good for all concerned.

The Holy Breath is the vehicle for the assimilation and the expansion of my Immortal Victorious Threefold Flame.

On every inbreath, I now assimilate into the Divinity of my heart greatly intensified frequencies of my Father God's Blue Flame of Power, my Mother God's Pink Flame of Love and the Sons and Daughters of God's Yellow-gold Flame of Wisdom.

On every outbreath, I now expand these greatly intensified Sacred Flames through my heart to bless all Life on Earth.

With every inbreath and every outbreath my Threefold Flame is expanding closer and closer to its original size and Divine Potential.

As my Heart Flame grows breath by breath, I realize that on every inbreath I AM passing through a portal into the Pure Land of Boundless Splendor and Infinite Light within the Heart of my Father-Mother God, and with every outbreath I AM the Open Door through which the Gifts and Divine Blessings from my Father-Mother God flow into the physical plane to bless Humanity and ALL Life on Earth.

My I AM Presence is now encoding this knowing within my heart and mind, so that I will be consciously and intuitively aware of this profound Truth with every breath I take. And so it is. Beloved I AM That I AM.

Precious Heart, focus on the expansion of your and Humanity's Threefold Flames. As you go about your day.

38

OUR LIGHTWORK IS
MAKING A DIFFERENCE

There are thousands of Lightworkers around the world who have selflessly participated in the activities of Light that have been given to us by the Company of Heaven through our Weekly Vlogs. These selfless Beings of Light want to remind us that our Father-Mother God have granted a Cosmic Dispensation that gives the Company of Heaven permission to amplify our unified efforts. Just imagine how that Gift from On High is increasing our ability to make a positive difference!

The Company of Heaven told us that the Divine Intent of the Celestial Sharings we have been blessed with is to inspire you and me and the rest of awakening Humanity to take advantage of a unique opportunity to expand Humanity's Heart Flames. The compassion and empathy people are feeling, due to the painful things they are witnessing as Earth's unprecedented purging continues, have caused billions of people to open their hearts in profound ways as they reach out to help one another.

In spite of the chaos surfacing in the outer-world to be healed and transmuted back into Light, every single day miracles are taking place on this planet. This is the result of the dedicated efforts that the Company of Heaven and you and I and the rest of awakening Humanity have made as we worked in unison with each other and added to the Light of the world.

Positive changes are taking place within the hearts and minds of even the most asleep people. From the Higher Realms of Consciousness and the New Earth these changes are quite obvious. It is only in the dense physical plane of the old Earth that it is difficult to perceive the miracles taking place on this planet.

When we raise our consciousness, it is easy to see the wonders unfolding on Earth as the masses of Humanity awaken and once again respond from a heart-based space of Love and Reverence for ALL Life. From this higher perspective, we clearly know that the havoc being instigated in the outer-world involves a minuscule fraction of the seven billion people evolving on this planet. In the Realms of Truth it is clear that Earth's Ascension process has already been God Victoriously accomplished in the Realms of Cause. There is no turning back.

It is this Glorious perspective that the Company of Heaven wants us to have access to while we are fulfilling the remainder of our Divine Plans, and assisting the Earth and all her Life through the final stages of our Ascension into the Light.

No one knows exactly how long this final stage which involves purging the residue of the old Earth will take. That is up to Humanity and how we choose to use our free will and our creative faculties of thought and feeling during the next few years. But if we raise our consciousness, and walk through the times ahead while functioning from the perspective of the New Earth, this final phase of our Ascension process will be a wondrous experience.

The Company of Heaven is dedicated to helping each and every one of us return to Christ Consciousness. Once that is accomplished, never again will we doubt the profound Truth that this blessed planet and ALL her Life are victoriously Ascending into the 5th-Dimensional Realms of Crystalline Solar Light where the New Earth abides. We will know that *VICTORY IS OURS!*

Today, our Beloved Company of Heaven has given us an activity of Light that will assist us in returning to Christ Consciousness. If you have the Heart Call to participate with me on behalf of yourself and all Humanity, please go within to the Divinity of your expanding Immortal Victorious Threefold Flame and be here now. And we begin.

I AM Returning to Christ Consciousness

I AM my I AM Presence and I AM One with the I AM Presence of ALL Humanity. What I invoke for myself this sacred and holy day I invoke on behalf of every man, woman and child on Earth. I do this in perfect alignment with each person's Divine Plan and the highest good for all concerned. This is possible because WE ARE ONE and there is no separation.

On the Holy Breath, I now breathe in and out deeply and rhythmically through my newly-expanded Heart Flame. With every inbreath, I Ascend into the Power, Love and Wisdom within the Heart and Mind of my Father-Mother God.

With every outbreath, I expand the Power, Love and Wisdom from within the Heart and Mind of my Father-Mother God through my Heart Flame to bless all Life on Earth.

On every inbreath my expanded Heart Flame Ascends into new heights of Divinity, and on each outbreath my expanded Heart Flame becomes a stronger pulsation of my Father-Mother God's Blessings into the world of form.

My Heart Flame is the inward portal for my return to Christ Consciousness, as well as the connection with my I AM Presence and the Company of Heaven. Through the Holy Breath, my return to Christ Consciousness and my inner journey back to God are balanced with my outer service to Humanity and all Life. It is within this balance that I expand my Threefold Flame and once again return to the elevated state of Christ Consciousness.

The full Divine Momentum of Christ Consciousness now flows from the Heart of my Father-Mother God through my Crown Chakra and my pineal gland into my mental and emotional bodies. As I return to the enlightened state of Christ Consciousness, my I AM Presence recalibrates my heart and mind to withstand higher frequencies of the Divine Consciousness of Oneness and Reverence for ALL Life.

In the enlightened state of Christ Consciousness, I AM able to easily communicate with my I AM Presence, my Father-Mother God and the entire Company of Heaven. This is accomplished through the natural process of open heart and mind telepathic communication.

I realize now, as never before, that Christ Consciousness is my Divine Birthright, for I AM a Beloved Daughter or Son of God. In this elevated level of consciousness, I clearly know that I AM One with my Father-Mother God and every particle and wave of Life throughout the whole of Creation. Now that I AM living, moving, breathing, and being within the elevated state of Christ Consciousness, I also know all that my Father-Mother God have is mine. I now comprehend in new and profound ways that the Path of Divine Love is the Way, the Truth and the Life for every Daughter and Son of God.

From this moment forth, Light that is flowing through my newly-expanded Heart Flame is creating an environment of Divine Love that is flooding the planet. The illusions of separation and duality are being transmuted into Light. My heart is unified with the hearts of all of the Daughters and Sons of God evolving on Earth. At long last, I experience the bliss of knowing that I AM One with ALL Life, and that LOVE IS ALL THERE IS.

Knowing this profound Truth evokes from within the deepest recesses of my Being a reverent feeling of Infinite Gratitude. And so it is.

Thank you, Dear One. Ask your I AM Presence to help you ACCEPT and KNOW that Christ Consciousness is your Divine Birthright and that through your expanding Threefold Flame, you are daily and hourly returning to that enlightened state of Divine Consciousness.

39

I Am Ascending Into
My I am Presence

For the past few sharings we have been working with the Company of Heaven and the I AM Presence of every person on Earth to help expand Humanity's Heart Flames to the size and Divine Potential we experienced prior to our fall from Grace. The Company of Heaven has revealed that there have been many positive shifts during this time. They say that these shifts have prepared Humanity's I AM Presences for a collective Ascension into a higher frequency of energy, vibration and consciousness.

Now the Beings of Light in the Realms of Illumined Truth are asking us to join our unified hearts with theirs. They have given us an activity of Light which they affirm will help to move Humanity forward in the Light a quantum leap. Thousands of people all over the world are joining with us this moment, and together we will encode this activity of Light in the Eternal Moment of NOW. This means that no matter when you are reading these words and participating in this Gift from On High, your magnificent Light is being woven into this thoughtform for the benefit of ALL Humanity. YOU are receiving the full benefit of the collective efforts of the Company of Heaven and every person who has participated in this activity of Light.

Please join me now with the full power of your attention. And we begin.

I AM Ascending Into My I AM Presence

I AM my I AM Presence and I AM One with the I AM Presence of ALL Humanity. As this wondrous Ascension in the Light occurs within me, it occurs within every person in perfect alignment with his or her Divine Plan.

I breathe in deeply and as I do I go within to the Divinity of my heart where I focus my attention on my Immortal Victorious Threefold Flame. Within the full embrace of my newly expanded Threefold Flame, I realize that I have transcended the old Earth and crossed the threshold into the 5th-Dimensional Crystalline Solar frequencies of the New Earth. I have truly entered a New Day filled with the full-gathered momentum of Heaven on Earth.

Victory is mine! Victory is mine! Victory is mine!

With this inner knowing, I realize that I have the awesome responsibility of becoming the full manifestation of my I AM Presence while I AM still embodied on Earth. This literally means Transfiguring my physical, etheric, mental, and emotional bodies into the 5th-Dimensional Crystalline Solar Light Bodies of my I AM Presence.

This Divine Alchemy is occurring within me now at an atomic, cellular level. Every electron, every atom, every subatomic particle and wave of my Earthly Bodies and all of the spaces in between the atoms and molecules of my bodies are being filled with multifaceted 5th-Dimensional Crystalline Solar Light.

My I AM Presence is now able to take full dominion of my Earthly Bodies. As this occurs, my thoughts, feelings, words, actions, memories and beliefs begin to reflect the Transfiguring Divine Love, the Infinite Abundance, Eternal Peace, Bliss, Harmony and Oneness of my Father-Mother God. My physical reality is being transformed, and I now experience at every level the Infinite Physical Perfection of the New Earth.

My I AM Presence now claims full dominion and authority within my Earthly Bodies. I stand forth now as a complete God Being pulsating within the glorious multi-colored, multidimensional radiance of my I AM Presence.

My feet are planted firmly on the New Earth, and simultaneously I AM One with all of the Ascended Realms of Infinite Perfection. I AM a Divine Being of resplendent Light, now realizing the fullness of that Light on every level of my Being. As I AM lifted up, all Life is lifted up with me. Therefore, I know that within my I AM Presence, I AM now ALL of Humanity standing forth and realizing that we are Divine Beings—Sons and Daughters of God—on every realm associated with the New Earth.

Within my I AM Presence, I AM the Crystalline White Ascension Flame blazing in, through, and around every particle and wave of Life. I AM liberating every physical and chemical interaction within the Earthly Bodies of ALL Humanity, the Elemental Kingdom, and the physical, etheric, mental, and emotional strata of Mother Earth. The Ascension Flame is raising all of the energy bonds between atoms and within atoms into the 5th-Dimensional Crystalline Solar Frequencies of God's Infinite Perfection and the New Earth.

I KNOW and ACCEPT that contained within this flowing electronic pattern of Light is everything necessary to

Transfigure the entire physical realm into the patterns of perfection for the New Earth. This unfathomable Light contains everything necessary to set straight the orbit, spin, and electronic charge of every cell, atom, and electron of Life on the old Earth. I feel all energy bonds within the atomic realm now Ascending in vibration toward the frequency of Infinite Physical Perfection. Every cell of Life is now blazing with the full perfection of 5th-Dimensional Crystalline Solar Light.

Within my I AM Presence, I AM the Ascension Flame and the 5th-Dimensional Crystalline Solar Frequencies of Light blazing through every interaction within Humanity and all of the energy bonds therein—this includes the relationships of all people, organizations, races, religions and nations—liberating these interactions into the Harmony of a Higher Order of Being, Ascending the influence of Humanity's I AM Presence on Earth.

Within the embrace of the Ascension Flame, I AM now clearly receiving Divine Promptings, Ideas and Concepts from my I AM Presence. I realize that I AM a Living and Light-filled Temple of Vibrant Health, Eternal Youth, God's Infinite Abundance, Eternal Peace, Harmony, Balance, Happiness and Abounding Joy.

Daily and hourly, the Ascension Flame is lifting me into the Higher Reality of the New Earth. Within this octave of Light, I AM Ascending into the 5th-Dimensional Crystalline Solar Light Bodies of my I AM Presence. Through a process of Divine Alchemy, these perfected vehicles will manifest through my Earthly Bodies in the physical world of form where they will be permanently sustained by God's Divine Grace.

I now return my consciousness to the room, and I become aware of my Earthly Bodies. My I AM Presence now *assimilates my 5th-Dimensional Crystalline Solar Light Bodies into my physical, etheric, mental and emotional Earthly Bodies. This occurs at a cellular level, as I breathe in and out deeply and rhythmically.*

With every breath, I absorb the bliss of this moment and I AM Grateful, I AM Grateful, I AM Eternally Grateful.

And so it is, Beloved Father-Mother God—ALL That Is—I AM.

Dear One, please hold the sacred space for this powerful activity of Light and repeat it as often as you are inspired to do so.

40

WE ARE BEING CALLED TO A HIGHER SERVICE

When we focus on the many traditions of this Holy Season, we are given lots of opportunities to open our hearts and to feel grateful for our families and the many blessings in our lives. Every time we have a Loving thought or express Gratitude for something, we add to the Light of the world. Our Father-Mother God and the Company of Heaven want us to know how important those Light-filled thoughts and feelings are for not only ourselves and our families, but also for the Earth and all Life evolving upon her. The intent of this message is to inspire all of us to increase our positive thoughts and feelings as we go about our day. If we pay attention and stay focused in the moment, we can add to the Light of the world with every breath we take.

This is a wondrous but often confusing and challenging time. We are being told from On High that the need of the hour is great, but that the positive effects of our heart-based thoughts, words, actions and feelings will be life-transforming for both Humanity and Mother Earth. As a word of encouragement, our God Parents are reminding us once again that the Light of God is infinitely more powerful than the fragmented and fear-based things being miscreated by an unawakened Humanity.

During this Cosmic Moment, on behalf of you and me and every single person, group, organization, company and activity of Light that is in any way striving to add to the Light of the world, our God Parents and the Company of Heaven are orchestrating a NEW Divine Plan that will allow us to unify our hearts and effectively expand *every* person's Lightwork.

I will share with you that I have been responding to the requests of our Father-Mother God and the Company of Heaven for 50 years. Beginning with the classes I had in my home, I have been offering free meditations, classes and seminars around the world since 1968. In all of these years, I have never felt such an urgent, yet *hopeful*, request from On High.

The Divine Intent of this Clarion Call from our Father-Mother God is to trigger, within each of our Heart Flames, the remembrance of what we volunteered to do individually and collectively to add to the Light of the world during this particular lifetime. For millennia our I AM Presence has guided us through powerful and often difficult experiences designed to strengthen us and prepare us for this moment. The intent of this preparation was to temper our resolve so that no matter what our recalcitrant sisters and brothers or Mother Nature confront us with during Earth's imperative purging process, we will be able to fulfill our mission by staying focused on the Light.

This is the moment for which we have all been preparing. It is through our individual and collective efforts that Humanity and Mother Earth will transcend the surfacing negativity and the chaos we are witnessing in the outerworld. Each and every one of us already has everything we need within us to accomplish what we have been uniquely prepared to do. Now it is time for us to act.

To help us grasp the critical need of our individual and collective contributions to the facet of Earth's Divine Plan that we are now in the midst of, the Beings of Light have given us a metaphor to contemplate. They asked us to think of the myriad lifetimes we have experienced since we were first breathed forth from the Heart of our Father-Mother God. Now, envision that the Life Force we expended during each of those lifetimes, as well as the Life Force we expended between lifetimes, has been woven into an exquisite Golden Thread of Light that we have volunteered to weave into the Tapestry of Life that will form the New Earth.

Our Father-Mother God revealed that billions of additional souls also volunteered to weave their Golden Thread into this particular Tapestry for the New Earth, but they were not selected. Our God Parents chose us, because they felt that our individual and collective experiences had a better chance of succeeding in the unprecedented experiment unfolding on Earth. This has nothing to do with ego or the erroneous impression that we are more special than our sisters and brothers who were turned away. It simply means that our Father-Mother God felt that with our *willingness* and our *tenacity*, we had a better chance of staying focused on the Light during the necessary purging process the Earth was destined to go through.

What the Company of Heaven wants each and every one of us to clearly understand is that the Tapestry of Life for the New Earth will be incomplete without ALL of our Golden Threads. In spite of what you may believe about yourself, or how inadequate you may feel when it comes to being a Lightworker, no one's Golden Thread is any more important than another person's Golden Thread. Every person's

Golden Thread is critical to the success of Earth's Ascension in the Light. It is for this very reason that our Father-Mother God and the Company of Heaven are orchestrating a NEW Divine Plan that will empower and effectively expand every person's Lightwork a thousand fold.

Now, listen carefully and let the following words from our Father-Mother God resonate in your Heart Flame as they share with you the Truth of who you are:

The Truth About YOU

"You are a precious and Beloved Child of God. Your unique Golden Thread of Life confirms your Divinity and reveals the reality that you are an essential part of Earth's Ascension in the Light. This knowing will renew your faith in yourself and will remind you that you are a priceless Human Being. Once this realization truly registers in your heart and your conscious mind you will never again say, 'What good could I possibly achieve' 'What value am I?' 'What difference will one soul make?' You will recognize those words to be a sacrilege.

"We are your Father-Mother God. We created you and we have chosen to express some beautiful manifestation of Life through you. You are destined to fulfill a portion of the glorious Divine Plan unfolding on Planet Earth. Now is the time for you to release the unique perfume and music of your Being to bless all Life. The purity of your individual fragrance and keynote is unlike any other ever released by the evolving Sons and Daughters of God. Something sacred is hidden within your Being that has never been known by another. It is an exquisite expression of Life which your I AM Presence alone can externalize. It is time for you to accept this Divine Truth. It is time for you to stand revealed as your mighty I AM Presence grown to full stature.

And so it is."

Dear One, contemplate your Golden Thread of Life. Think of it as an exquisite stream of Golden Light that extends from the very Heart of our Father-Mother God into your Heart Flame. This Golden Thread of Life is pulsating with all of the sacred knowledge, wisdom, strength, courage, skill, willingness and tenacity you have developed during your many sojourns through various time frames and dimensions since you were first breathed forth from the Heart of our Father-Mother God.

41

REMEMBERING OUR HEART COMMITMENT

Due to the need of the hour, our Father-Mother God and the Company of Heaven have been revealing to us the fact that they are initiating a NEW facet of the Divine Plan. We have been told many times that in order for Humanity and Mother Earth to receive the full benefit of the Gifts pouring forth from the Heavenly Realms, those of us embodied on Earth must offer to be the Open Door through which the Light of God will flow to accomplish that portion of the Divine Plan. The Company of Heaven is sharing information with us today with the Divine Intent of inspiring us to be the Open Door for this new Divine Plan.

A critical part of our purpose and reason for being on Earth during this momentous time is to help ease the pain and suffering that our sisters and brothers are experiencing. Only then will they be able to lift their heads above the chaos effectively enough to once again reconnect with their I AM Presence and complete their Ascension onto the New Earth.

Here is a brief reminder of the Heart Commitment we all made through our I AM Presence, whether we are consciously aware of it or not. Humanity reached a critical mass of Divine Love on December 21st and 22nd in 2012. This allowed *every single person* evolving on Earth to Ascend up the Spiral of Evolution into the initial frequencies of the New Earth. The reason our Father-Mother God granted permission for even the most asleep or recalcitrant people on Earth to make it through the Shift of the Ages is because of the heart commitment you and I and the rest of awakening Humanity made on their behalf.

Our sisters and brothers were granted permission to move through the Shift of the Ages in spite of the human miscreations they were still responsible for transmuting back into Light. This was allowed by our Father-Mother God because millions of Lightworkers compassionately agreed to hold the sacred space for our struggling sisters and brothers, so they would not be left behind.

Awakening Humanity promised to help our asleep and recalcitrant sisters and brothers to awaken as soon as possible. We also agreed to do whatever is necessary in order to help them quickly transmute their surfacing negativity from the old Earth. The Company of Heaven told us that *if we had not agreed to do that*, these souls would not have been allowed to Ascend into the initial impulse of the New Earth. That is because their surfacing negativity and the necessary purging that is taking place on Earth to clear their human miscreations would have been overwhelming and would have actually caused more harm than good.

As we monitor the surfacing negativity, we are witnessing deplorable and appalling decisions that are being made by those in power around the world. The results of those seemingly mindless and heartless actions will definitely affect people and the Earth in extremely adverse ways. When we see such things taking place, *in spite of all of the*

Lightwork we are doing, it is easy to come to the conclusion that our efforts are in vain. Our Father-Mother God and the Company of Heaven have revealed that this is causing many Lightworkers to feel overwhelmed and even hopeless. Consequently, many of them are giving up and making the fateful decision to stop invoking the Light. People are afraid that we made a mistake. They fear that in spite of our eart commitments, the surfacing negativity is causing more harm than good.

The reality is, if Lightworkers do nothing to intervene in the current situation, the actions of our recalcitrant sisters and brothers could indeed cause more harm than good. Fortunately, our Father-Mother God and the Beings of Light also see the potential of that horrific unintended consequence. That is precisely why they are orchestrating this vitally important NEW facet of the Divine Plan, and why they are sending forth a Clarion Call invoking the assistance of every Lightworker on Earth.

When our Father-Mother God granted permission for every single person on Earth to Ascend through the Shift of the Ages, which was an unfathomable act of Divine Grace, they knew this would only work if the Lightworkers fulfilled our heart commitment to hold the sacred space for the awakening of these recalcitrant souls. There are millions of Lightworkers who add to the Light of the world in their own way every single day. These dedicated Beings are making a tremendous difference. However, in order to transmute the hundreds of lifetimes worth of negativity surfacing now in the outer world, our God Parents have come to the conclusion that much more Light is needed.

The NEW facet of the Divine Plan that our Father-Mother God and the Company of Heaven are setting into motion is designed to exponentially expand the Lightwork that every single person on Earth has volunteered to accomplish in this lifetime. Today we are being asked to encode the Template for this NEW facet of the Divine Plan into the mental and emotional strata of Earth. This is being accomplished in the Eternal Moment of NOW, so no matter when you are reading these words your magnificent Light is being woven into this Template.

The Template for Our Father-Mother God's NEW Facet of the Divine Plan

Our Father-Mother God have revealed to us at *Era of Peace* that the work we have been doing over the past 50 years in cooperation with the Company of Heaven has resulted in the tangible manifestation of an ever-expanding Planetary Grid of Transfiguring Divine Love. This Grid of Divine Love envelops Mother Earth in exquisite sacred geometric patterns of multicolored and multifaceted 5th-Dimensional Crystalline Solar Light that has been expanding in a rhythmic momentum for five decades. They said that this expansion occurs every time Humanity joins us either physically or in consciousness during one of our Free Seminars, or any of the other activities of Light we offer that add to the Light of the world, such as our YouTube Meditations, our Internet Broadcasts, our Weekly Vlogs, our Monthly Newsletters and our Annual World Congress on Illumination.

Due to what is being referred to as *"the urgency of the hour"*, our Father-Mother God and the Legions of Light in the Realms of Illumined Truth have decided to use our Planetary Grid of Transfiguring Divine Love as the vehicle through which they will implement this NEW facet of the Divine Plan. In spite of our Father-Mother God's and the Company of Heaven's desire to quickly complete Earth's painful purging process, they cannot do this without

209

our help. We have free will which means we must ask for assistance from On High and offer to be the Open Door through which the Light of God will flow to accomplish this Divine Plan. Fortunately, what this plan requires is incredibly simple and can be easily integrated into our individual and collective Lightwork.

The Divine Intent of this NEW facet of the Divine Plan is for the Company of Heaven and the I AM Presences of awakening Humanity to expand a thousand fold the Lightwork that you and I and every single person, group, organization, company and activity of Light on Earth is participating in. This unfathomable influx of Light will be breathed into the Grid of Transfiguring Divine Love by our Father-Mother God in a rhythmic momentum during the Free Seminars being offered every month by *Era of Peace.* This Gift of Light will then bathe the Earth for the entire month and amplify a thousand fold every single thing any person does that adds to the Light of the world in any way.

Each month I will announce where the Free Seminar will be. These Seminars are always free and open to the public. Our NEW Free Seminars are titled, *"It Is Time To Take The Next Step."* Hopefully, hundreds of people in and around the area will have the Heart Call to physically attend the seminar and weave their Golden Thread of Light into the Chalice of Light we will all form through our unified Heart Flames. If you are not on our mailing list to receive our free monthly Online Newsletter or our free Weekly Vlogs you may sign up on our website www.eraofpeace.org.

In addition to those who will be physically present, our Father-Mother God are invoking Lightworkers around the world who are aware of the Free Seminars to take a moment that day to weave their Golden Thread of Light into our Chalice of Light. This will greatly increase the amount of

Light our Father-Mother God will be able to breathe into the Grid of Transfiguring Divine Love.

There is a Second Phase to this Divine Plan

During the Free Seminar, the Beings of Light will help us to take even greater advantage of this collective Cup of Humanity's Consciousness. Every month our God Parents and the Company of Heaven will evaluate how the expansion of our Lightwork through the Grid of Transfiguring Divine Love has benefited Humanity and the Earth. They will then determine what additional assistance can be accomplished that day through our unified efforts. I will not know what that facet of the Divine Mission is prior to the Free Seminar, but I will share that information with you in our free monthly Online Newsletter following the seminar.

Once you start benefiting from this monumental influx of Light and realize the incredible assistance Humanity is receiving from On High, you will no longer feel afraid, helpless or hopeless. On the contrary, you will feel greatly motivated to *"Keep on keeping on."*

During this momentous time it will help to keep affirming to yourself:

"The Light of God is ALWAYS Victorious and I AM that Light."

Dear One, listen to your heart and respond to our Father-Mother God's Clarion Call. Your Light, your Love and YOUR Divine Intervention are needed NOW!

42

WHAT IS TRANSFIGURING DIVINE LOVE?

Outer appearances are often deceiving and can be very discouraging if we take them at face value. That is why our Father-Mother God want to share more sacred knowledge about their Transfiguring Divine Love and the incredible assistance we are receiving through our newly empowered Planetary Grid of Transfiguring Divine Love.

Awakening Humanity is beginning to realize that we can no longer rely on our mental perceptions or our logical thinking alone. People are beginning to clearly understand that we must now reach into the wisdom of our hearts and tap into the sacred knowledge that holds the vision of who we are and why we are here during this Cosmic Moment of Earth's Ascension. Within that vision reverberates the knowing that we are receiving more assistance from the Heavenly Realms than ever before in the history of time.

According to our Father-Mother God, the most powerful assistance ever given to Humanity is the Flame of Transfiguring Divine Love. This miraculous Gift of Light is the mightiest force in the Universe. It is an unfathomable frequency of God's Love that has been relatively dormant on Earth for aeons of time. For billions of years this unparalleled Divine Love has been held within the Heart of our God Parents awaiting the moment when it would be activated by the collective invocation and Heart Call of the Sons and Daughters of God.

During the dawn of the New Millennium in 2000, the Solar Logos from our Central Sun, Alpha and Omega, evaluated Earth's progress and determined the greatest need of the hour for this planet. At that time, it was clear that without superhuman Divine Intervention there would be millions of souls who would not be ready in time to make it through the Shift of the Ages which was destined to occur in 2012. With that heart-knowing, Alpha and Omega sent forth a Clarion Call to our Father-Mother God and the Legions of Light throughout Infinity asking for assistance to activate the Flame of Transfiguring Divine Love on Earth. The response came on celestial wings of Love and compassion from the far reaches of the Cosmos. Literally billions and billions of Light Beings volunteered to assist Alpha and Omega in this Divine Mission.

When all was in readiness, the illumined souls joined together in perfect unison with the I AM Presences of awakening Humanity. As One Breath, One Voice, One Heartbeat, One Energy, Vibration and Consciousness of Pure Divine Love this collective body of the Sons and Daughters of God throughout Infinity invoked the Flame of Transfiguring Divine Love into action on Earth.

For several months, Lightworkers magnetized the Flame of Transfiguring Divine Love from the Heart of God and breathed it into the physical plane through the Open Door of their collective consciousness. Day by day, this Sacred Flame built in momentum and might until it was powerful enough to be sustained in the Heart Flame of every person evolving on this planet. On August 17, 2001, the I AM Presence of every man, woman and child on Earth secured the Flame of Transfiguring Divine Love within their Heart Flame. That miraculous activity of Light occurred during the 14th anniversary of Harmonic Convergence.

The Flame of Transfiguring Divine Love is a deep rose color with an aquamarine aura of Clarity. Within the center of the Flame is a resplendent, opalescent Sun of Transfiguration. This magnificent Gift from God contains within its frequencies patterns of Divine Love beyond anything we have ever known or even dared to dream about. Once anchored within the Heart Flame this Love sends forth a beacon of Light that magnetizes unto itself the full spectrum of the 5th-Dimensional Crystalline Solar Light that is pulsating in the Causal Body of God.

As Transfiguring Divine Love permeates every cell, organ, gland, muscle, electron, atom and subatomic particle and wave of our physical, etheric, mental and emotional bodies, an environment is created in which the I AM Presence is quickened and exalted to take full dominion. As this occurs, our Earthly Bodies are gradually Transfigured into the limitless physical perfection of our 5th-Dimensional Crystalline Solar Light Bodies. This is an individual process that will take place within each person according to each person's ability to assimilate and integrate the unprecedented frequencies of this Divine Light.

Encoded within the frequencies of Transfiguring Divine Love is a *Divine Intelligence* that is capable of discerning and revealing to each of us the erroneous experiences, beliefs, attitudes, fears, thoughts, words, actions and feelings we are utilizing to deceive ourselves and to support belief systems that conflict with the Truth of our Oneness with all Life. This Divine Intelligence exposes the illusion of our separation from God and any other beliefs or actions that reflect separation, duality or a lack of Reverence for ALL Life.

As the Clarity of the Flame of Transfiguring Divine Love enters our conscious minds we begin to truly *know* that every Human Being is Divine, regardless of how far his or her behavior patterns and life experiences may be from reflecting that Truth. This is a vitally important realization in Humanity's healing process. Our thoughts and feelings are creative, and whatever we focus our attention on we empower and bring into form. If we are constantly thinking and talking about the negative behavior patterns people are participating in, or the things we don't like about the people themselves, we simply add our energy and power to the very things we dislike. This is true whether we are talking about our loved ones, our friends and coworkers, our associates and acquaintances or our governmental officials and world leaders. Actually, the more powerful and influential a person is the more crucial it is for us to empower their I AM Presence instead of the mistakes they are making through their fallen consciousness.

We can empower and energize every person's Divine Potential by focusing our attention on their Heart Flame and by asking their I AM Presence to take control of their thoughts, words, actions and feelings. Every person's I AM Presence will guide them to respond and behave in ways that reflect the highest good for all concerned. We can empower people's Divine Potential even further by asking their I AM Presence to expand the Divine Intelligence within the Flame of Transfiguring Divine Love which is now anchored in every person's heart. This expansion will accelerate the process of exposing people's erroneous belief systems, and it will enhance their ability to remember that they are One with all Life.

This may seem like a very simple antidote for the atrocities people are inflicting on each other throughout the world, but it is one of the most powerful things we can do to hasten Humanity's awakening.

Dear Heart, contemplate the information being shared by the Company of Heaven in this sharing and you will begin to get a glimpse of the significance of the Divine Intervention we are receiving from our Father-Mother God through the NEW facet of their Divine Plan and the empowerment of our Planetary Grid of Transfiguring Divine Love.

43

INVOKING THE NEWLY EMPOWERED FLAME OF TRANSFIGURING DIVINE LOVE

Our Father-Mother God's newly implemented facet of the Divine Plan is giving us a powerful opportunity to help our sisters and brothers who are still asleep. Those of you, who are reading these words, have been prepared, probably for aeons of time, to assist with the Divine Mission of helping unawakened Humanity transmute their misqualified energy, so that they can complete their Ascension onto the New Earth. If that were not the case, your I AM Presence would not have drawn this information into your sphere of awareness. This is a vitally important service and the entire Company of Heaven is standing in readiness to help you. These Beings of Light will joyously support your every effort in this essential endeavor.

Many people are so buried in the effluvia of their negative belief systems that they cannot raise their heads above the chaos and confusion effectively enough to reunite with their I AM Presence. These people have no concept of the Oneness of Life and they truly believe that they must lie, steal, cheat and kill for their survival. Those of us who have awakened from that nightmare and remember that we are all One have the responsibility of being our brothers' and sisters' keepers until they can awaken to that Divine Truth themselves. This does not mean that we are to just passively wait and watch for their awakening. It means that we are to actively be the Instrument of God we have volunteered to be.

To begin the process, we need to open our hearts to every evolving soul on Earth. This is not easy when we observe some of the terrible things people are doing to each other and to the other life forms on the planet, but it is a necessary step in becoming an Instrument of God.

The most powerful awakening force in the Universe is the power of God's Transfiguring Divine Love flowing from your sacred Heart Flame into the Heart Flame of another Human Being.

We never know what set of circumstances compels people to choose the negative paths they have chosen or what causes them to make the self-destructive decisions they make, but in order to shift our feelings from anger and disappointment to Love and understanding, we need to step back and contemplate the bigger picture. First of all, we must remember that *everyone* is doing the best they can according to their wisdom, their understanding and their belief systems. This is true regardless of whether or not we think they should know better or whether it is obvious to everyone else in the world that what the person is doing is wrong. If the person fully understood the principle of the Oneness of all Life, and the ramifications of their negative actions in the face of the fundamental Law of the Circle, they would not behave in the negative manner in which they are behaving.

When we grasp the Truth that everyone is doing the best they can our thinking changes. We no longer think of people as bad or evil. Rather, we think of them in the same way we think of unaware children who are not able to comprehend the results of their behavior. Sometimes children do terrible things without any idea of what the end result of their actions will be. However, instead of hating them and wishing them harm, we embrace them with Love and we patiently demonstrate to them better ways of behaving.

the Oneness of ALL Life resonates in the deepest recesses of our hearts, the validity of war and all of the other atrocities we inflict on each other and Mother Earth are impossible to justify.

As our newly empowered Grid of Transfiguring Divine Love bathes the Earth, more and more people are awakening and remembering who they are and why they are here. This is opening the door for the Light of God to increase on Earth in powerful ways. The Company of Heaven has blessed us with an invocation that will help us to join our hearts in a collective activity of Light. If you have the Heart Call to do so please join with me now.

And we begin.

INVOKING THE FLAME OF
TRANSFIGURING DIVINE LOVE

I AM my I AM Presence and I AM One with my Father-Mother God and the I AM Presence of every person on Earth. As One unified force of Light, we breathe in deeply, and on the Holy Breath we collectively Ascend in consciousness into the very Heart of our Father-Mother God.

Instantly, we are enveloped in the full embrace of God's Transfiguring Diving Love. We hear the melodious tones and absorb the celestial fragrance of this Sacred Fire. The splendor of this Divine Love permeates our Beings and lifts us into the Realms of Illumined Truth. Within this forcefield of Light, we accept our Oneness with ALL Life in a new and profound way. We experience a Love and Reverence for Life beyond anything we ever dreamed possible.

Divine Wisdom is awakening within our hearts, and in a flash of enlightenment we know, and fully understand, how we are to demonstrate this Reverence for ALL Life to the masses of Humanity. This realization is recorded in our conscious minds and encoded within our DNA structures. It will now be tangibly available whenever we need to recall this sacred knowledge in our service to Humanity and all Life.

The Flame of Transfiguring Divine Love's aquamarine aura of Clarity now begins to gently bathe us in the radiance of Divine Intelligence. We are all being lifted into new levels of lucidity, comprehension, knowing, wisdom, insight and understanding. As we revel in the wonder of this magnificent frequency of Clarity, we begin to grasp the magnitude of the opportunities contained within our newly empowered Planetary Grid of Transfiguring Divine Love.

In deep humility and gratitude, we accept the opportunities that are being presented to us within the Heart of God, and we volunteer to be the Open Door for the intensified frequencies of our Father-Mother God's Transfiguring Divine Love.

For a sublime moment, we assimilate this experience as we breathe in and breathe out, slowly and rhythmically.

We now return our attention to the room and we prepare to go about the business of our Father-Mother God in a state of sublime Harmony and Peace. And so it is.

Dear One, please hold the sacred space for this power-ful activity of Light and allow yourself to become familiar with the wondrous frequencies of our newly empowered Planetary Grid of Transfiguring Divine Love.

44

EMPOWERING OUR PLANETARY GRID OF DIVINE LOVE

Due to the unprecedented influx of Light that has taken place over the past several years, the I AM Presence, which is the Divinity within every person's Heart Flame, is at long last reclaiming dominion of our Earthly experiences. The Divine Intervention of our I AM Presence is allowing the entire Company of Heaven to work more closely with us than ever before.

These selfless Messengers of our Father-Mother God are asking us to join with them now, in unified consciousness, to empower the Planetary Grid of Transfiguring Divine Love that Lightworkers have been cocreating on behalf of Humanity and Mother Earth over the past 50 years.

This activity of Light will enable the Grid of Transfiguring Divine Love to assimilate the unfathomable influx of Light our Father-Mother God will breathe into it, in a rhythmic momentum, during Humanity's Global participation in the monthly Free Seminars being offered by *Era of Peace*. The Divine Intent of this influx of Light is to expand the Lightwork of every person on Earth a thousand fold every single day.

In deep Gratitude for our ability to serve Life in this way, let's join together in consciousness now with the I AM Presence of every man, woman and child on Earth, as we unify our hearts with the hearts of our Father-Mother God and the entire Company of Heaven. Together we will magnetize from the Core of Creation the most intensified frequencies of the 5th-Dimensional Crystalline Flame of Transfiguring Diving Love that Humanity and the Earth are capable of withstanding at a cellular level. Breathe in deeply and go within to the Divinity of your Heart Flame. Please join me now with the full power of your attention and your Divine Intentions. And we begin.

Empowering Our Planetary Grid of Transfiguring Divine Love

I AM my I AM Presence and I AM One with the I AM Presence of ALL Humanity. As One Voice, One Breath, One Heartbeat, and One Energy, Vibration and Consciousness of Pure Divine Love we invoke our Father-Mother God and the Legions of Light throughout Infinity. Beloved Ones, come forth NOW!

We are One with ALL of these magnificent Forces of Light. Through our sincere Heart Call, they have joyously come to help Humanity's I AM Presence empower and sustain the Lightwork of every man, woman and child on Earth a thousand fold every day.

Beloved Legions of Light, we ask that you gather up every electron of precious Life energy being expended by Humanity during this sacred and holy time. Purify this energy with the power and might of a thousand Suns using the NEW 5th-Dimensional Solar Frequencies of the Violet Flame of God's Infinite Perfection. Weave this purified energy into the collective Cup of Humanity's Consciousness, so that every electron of precious Life energy released by the Sons and Daughters of God at this time will be used to exponentially expand the Light of God through the Planetary Grid of Transfiguring Divine Love that is now enveloping Mother Earth and ALL her Life.

We accept that this activity of Light is being God Victoriously accomplished right here and right now. We also accept that through Humanity's I AM Presence this activity of Light will be permanently sustained, increasing daily and hourly the maximum that Cosmic Law will allow with every breath we take.

Beloved Father-Mother God, we ask that you now breathe the highest possible frequencies of Divine Love, Oneness and Reverence for All Life into every person's Heart Flame.

In Oneness with the I AM Presence of every person on Earth and the entire Company of Heaven, we now affirm within the Divinity of our Heart Flame:

"I AM the Cup, the Holy Grail, through which the Light of God now flows to bless every particle and wave of Life evolving on this precious planet.

"I AM my I AM Presence, and I now invoke my Father-Mother God to breathe their Infinite Light into our Planetary Grid of Transfiguring Divine Love. As this exquisite Light blazes through the Grid of Divine Love it bathes the Earth and expands every person's Lightwork a thousand fold every day."

Now, this unfathomable influx of our Father-Mother God's Infinite Light lifts every atomic and subatomic particle and wave of Life on Earth into a Higher Order of Being.

As this wondrous Light is anchored within the Divinity of every person's Heart Flame, it expands into the Heart Flame of every other person on Earth unifying Heart Flame with Heart Flame. Through this amazing activity of Light, the I AM Presence of every person becomes a power point of Divine Love and Oneness unified in consciousness with the I AM Presence of every other person.

*Through the unified efforts of Heaven and Earth, we are empowering our Planetary Grid of Transfiguring Divine Love. This Forcefield of Light is extending from the very depths of Humanity's pain and suffering into highest frequencies of the 5th-Dimensional Realms of God's Infinite Light. This Grid of Divine Love is the **Bridge to Freedom** over which this blessed planet and ALL her Life are now Ascending into the 5th-Dimensional Realms of Perfection on the New Earth.*

Through this activity of Light, we are reclaiming our Divine Birthright as Sons and Daughters of God as we become Love in action. We are collectively changing the core vibration of the primal Light substance, which has gone into creating the present negative conditions that are surfacing all over the planet to be healed and transmuted into Light.

This activity of Light is bringing into tangible form the archetypes for the patterns of perfection for the New Earth. These patterns are now flowing into the heart and mind of every man, woman and child through the mental and emotional strata of this planet.

The I AM Presence within every person is the Open Door for these resplendent patterns of Divine Love. We are the CAUSE of Divine Love now being re-established on Earth. Together we are setting in place the basic Spiritual Forces of Divine Love over which the Earth and ALL her Life are at last Ascending out of our long exile in darkness into the 5th-Dimensional Realms of Light associated with the New Earth. The Love of God is now thriving on Earth through each us, and through the I AM Presence of every person on the planet.

Through this activity of Light, Humanity is being raised into a profound awakening of Supreme Love Consciousness. We are, here and now, the Masters of Love we were always destined to be. We are Beings of Love, accepting responsibility for Loving this sweet Earth and ALL her Life free. We are One with this blessed planet, and the planet is One with us.

Our Father-Mother God and the Company of Heaven are now intensifying their Light through every person's Heart Flame. This influx of Light is lifting ALL Humanity into a higher octave of Divine Service. Every person on Earth is being permanently invested with a Cosmic Forcefield of Divine Love. This forcefield is initiating each of us into a Higher Order of Service to Humanity and the Light. Our Lightwork is being intensified a thousand fold every day through the Planetary Grid of Transfiguring Divine Love.

Beloved Father-Mother God, we accept that this activity of Light is being God Victoriously Accomplished, even as we Call. And so it is!

Beloved I AM, Beloved I AM, Beloved I AM That I AM.

Dear One, please hold the sacred space for this powerful activity of Light and repeat it as often as you are inspired to do so.

45

A QUANTUM SHIFT TOWARD CHRIST CONSCIOUSNESS

We have been preparing for lifetimes to be the stabilizing Force of Light during the unprecedented purging process the Earth is now going through. In order to accomplish this monumental task, we are receiving more assistance from the Company of Heaven than has ever been rendered to the Sons and Daughters of God in any system of worlds.

In the new facet of the Divine Plan that our Father-Mother God recently initiated, the Planetary Grid of Transfiguring Divine Love which Lightworkers have been cocreating for the past 50 years is being greatly empowered. The Company of Heaven has been granted permission to encode within this Grid of Divine Love the highest frequencies of Christ Consciousness that Humanity's I AM Presences have ever received.

The Divine Intent of this facet of our Father-Mother God's plan is to greatly accelerate the awakening taking place within the masses of Humanity. This influx of Christ Consciousness will benefit everyone. And in even more powerful ways, it will affect the Millennials and the children who have been uniquely prepared to reach into the Realms of Cause where they will tap into the viable solutions for every single malady manifesting on Earth.

I have been shown the Divine Potential for this new facet of the Divine Plan and it is glorious to behold. The Company of Heaven said that in order for this plan to succeed God Victoriously, it is essential that Lightworkers embodied on Earth participate. In this book, and in our Weekly Vlogs and our Monthly Newsletters, we will share the ongoing sacred knowledge being given to Humanity by the Company of Heaven. This will allow you to have access to each phase of the Divine Plan as it is revealed to us step-by-step.

During this critical moment, all of us are being asked to serve as surrogates on behalf of every man, woman and child on Earth. The activity of Light we will participate in during this sharing has been given to us by the Company of Heaven. Together we will help every person's I AM Presence integrate brand new frequencies of Christ Consciousness into their heart and mind. This is being accomplished in the *Eternal Moment of Now,* so no matter when you are participating in this activity your magnificent Light is being woven into this phase of the Divine Plan and will greatly benefit you and the rest of Humanity.

In addition to every person receiving brand new frequencies of Christ Consciousness, during this guided meditation a concentrated influx of Light will flow through the RNA and DNA genetic codes of the Millennials and the children. The Millennials are the young men and women who range from 18 to 32 years old. The children are those precious Ones who are being born now and those through the age of 17 years old who have followed the Millennials into embodiment to assist them with the final stages of Earth's Ascension process.

In the Inner Realms the Millennials and the children are known as the Holy Innocents. Under the guidance of each one's I AM Presence these NEW frequencies of Christ Consciousness will help them to prepare for the eventual activation of the special *consciousness codes* they brought with them into embodiment. These codes are designed to help the Holy Innocents fulfill the vital facet of the Divine Plan they have been preparing for a very long time to accomplish during this Cosmic Moment in Earth's Ascension process. The Beings of Light will reveal much more about the Divine Mission of the Millennials in the next few sharings.

Now let's focus on this activity of Light. Christ Consciousness is the enlightened state of consciousness we were invested with by our Father-Mother God when we were first breathed forth from the Core of Creation. After we fell into the abyss of separation and duality we lost Christ Consciousness and the ability to communicate with our I AM Presence. Since that fateful time, we have been struggling to reverse the adverse effects of our fall from Grace and to reclaim our Divine Birthright as Sons and Daughters of God by returning to Christ Consciousness.

Please join with me now as we participate in this activity of Light, which is designed to move Humanity en masse a quantum leap forward in our endeavors to return to Christ Consciousness. Breathe in deeply and go within to the Divinity of your Heart Flame. Follow me through this guided meditation with the full power of your attention and be here now. And we begin.

Return to Christ Consciousness

I AM my I AM Presence and I AM One with the I AM Presence of ALL Humanity. What I invoke for myself I invoke on behalf of every man, woman and child on Earth in perfect alignment with each person's Divine Plan and the highest good for all concerned. This is possible because WE ARE ONE and there is no separation.

On the Holy Breath I now breathe in and out, through my Heart Chakra, deeply and rhythmically. With every inbreath, I align with the Love of my Father-Mother God and the Sacred Breath of the Holy Spirit.

With every outbreath, my God Parents open my Heart Chakra to new breadths and project their Divine Love and Power into the physical plane of Earth.

Through this activity of Light, the portal within my right-brain hemisphere and my Heart Chakra, through which the Love of my Mother God originally flowed to bless all Life on Earth, is once again opening to full breadth.

As the full Divine Potential of my Mother God's Pink Flame of Divine Love pulsates through my Heart Chakra, it is brought into perfect balance with my Father God's Blue Flame of Divine Power which is also pulsating within the Divinity of my heart.

My newly balanced Heart Flame has a dual pulsation. The first pulsation is the inbreath—assimilating and absorbing the Power and Love of my Father-Mother God. The second pulsation is the outbreath—expanding and radiating out the Power and Love of my Father-Mother God.

My Heart Flame is the inward portal for my return to Christ Consciousness. It is also the Open Door that will allow me to once again communicate with my I AM Presence and the Company of Heaven. It is through this Open Door that the blessings from my Father-Mother God and the Realms of Illumined Truth radiate outward into my daily life.

On the Holy Breath, my return to Christ Consciousness and my inner journey back to my Father-Mother God are balanced with my outer service to Humanity and all Life. It is within this balance that I open my Heart Chakra once again to the perpetual flow of my Mother God's Transfiguring Divine Love.

My Father God's Blue Flame of Power and my Mother God's Pink Flame of Divine Love are now balanced within my Heart Flame. These two aspects of my Father-Mother God now merge into the magnificent Violet Flame of God's Infinite Perfection. This Sacred Fire blazes up from my Heart Chakra and expands into my physical brain structure activating my pineal, pituitary and hypothalamus glands, and the ganglionic center at the base of my brain.

The activation of my spiritual brain centers creates the sacred space for the opening of my Crown Chakra. As this occurs, a greatly intensified frequency of the Yellow-gold Flame of Christ Consciousness begins flowing from the very Heart of God into the Planetary Grid of Transfiguring Divine Love. These brand new frequencies of Christ Consciousness now flow through my I AM Presence and my Crown Chakra into my pineal gland.

With this influx of Light, the highest frequencies of Christ Consciousness that I AM capable of integrating, flow through my pineal gland into my mental and emotional bodies. As I return to Christ Consciousness, my heart and mind are recalibrated to higher frequencies of Divine Love, Oneness and Reverence for All Life than I have experienced since Humanity's fall from Grace aeons ago.

The illusions of separation and duality are shattered. And I now know that I AM One with all of the Sons and Daughters of God evolving on Earth. At long last, I experience the bliss of knowing that LOVE IS ALL THERE IS and I AM that Love. And so it is.

Dear One, please hold the sacred space for this powerful activity of Light and repeat it as often as you are inspired to do so. This is a multidimensional activity of Light that is accomplishing far more than we are able to perceive with our finite minds.

46

WHO ARE OUR ASLEEP AND RECALCITRANT SISTERS AND BROTHERS?

The Beings of Light have been reminding us of the heart commitment we made to hold the sacred space for the awakening of our asleep and recalcitrant sisters and brothers. We volunteered to do this in order to help them complete the process of transmuting their past karmic liabilities, so they can move forward in the Light with the rest of the Earth.

People all over the world are awakening in record numbers, but there are still many people who are so overwhelmed with their challenging life experiences that they are having difficulty hearing the inner voice of their I AM Presence and remembering their purpose and reason for being on Earth during this auspicious time. These are the people our Father-Mother God are trying to assist with the influx of Light that is now flowing through our newly empowered Planetary Grid of Transfiguring Divine Love. This new facet of the Divine Plan is also designed to awaken the Millennials and the children who have come to assist us in cocreating the patterns of perfection for the New Earth.

In order to help us perceive the bigger picture, the Company of Heaven is revealing the difference between what they refer to as our asleep and our recalcitrant sisters and brothers. First of all, they want to make it perfectly clear that this is not a judgment. We are One with these souls and there is no separation. The Company of Heaven also wants to caution us against using this information to try to figure out if the people we know or those we observe are either asleep or recalcitrant. There is absolutely no way for us to know that without knowing about all of their lifetimes and what their specific mission is in this lifetime. Only their I AM Presence has that knowledge, and it is actually none of our business.

The reason the Beings of Light want us to have this information is so we will understand why things are happening the way they are and the different levels of consciousness that are creating the outer-world appearances that seem so challenging. Being informed helps us to evaluate where our Light is needed the most.

The people who are considered *asleep* are good people, but they are so overwhelmed with their painful life experiences and struggling so hard to survive that they cannot seem to raise their heads above the negativity. They would love to see the Light and remember their I AM Presence, but they are so discouraged and beaten down by the negativity around them that they no longer believe that is even possible.

The new Divine Plan that has been initiated by our Father-Mother God is specifically designed to awaken our asleep sisters and brothers. The Lightwork of every person on Earth is now being amplified a thousand fold every day through our newly empowered Planetary Grid of Transfiguring Divine Love. This is allowing the I AM Presences of our asleep sisters and brothers to gradually lift their heads above the negativity, so they will once again remember that they are Beloved Sons and Daughters of God and that ALL our Father-Mother God have is theirs.

The people who are considered *recalcitrant* have a very different consciousness than those who are merely asleep. These are our sisters and brothers who need much more assistance if they are going to be awakened from their fear-based and manipulative consciousness. The people who are referred to as recalcitrant by the Beings of Light are people who have deliberately chosen to oppose the Light for their own personal gain.

In the Realms of Illumined Truth, prior to the Shift of the Ages, the I AM Presence of every one of these recalcitrant souls helped to convince them to make the decision to do whatever is necessary to clear up their karmic liabilities, so they would not be left behind. Unfortunately, they are now resisting that agreement. Out of fear, these sisters and brothers are fighting tooth and nail to keep the Earth from completing her Ascension process. They desperately want to maintain their power and wealth and they are terrified that if they lose their ability to control and manipulate the masses of Humanity they will not be able to do so, which is true.

This faction of our sisters and brothers has fallen to the depths of separation and duality. Their ego has manipulated them into believing that their purpose and reason for being is to accumulate power and wealth for their personal gratification. They think whatever pain they happen to inflict on people or the Earth in order to get what they want is justified. The recalcitrant souls have been manipulated and controlled by their fear-based and fragmented human egos for so long that they willingly overlook the fact that their actions are wreaking havoc everywhere.

They do not seem to care if they pollute the water we drink or the air we breathe or the food we eat as long as they are able to continue accumulating the obscene amounts of wealth and power they crave. They have found that the best way for them to maintain control over the masses is to perpetuate fear, hate and suspicion between people of different genders, races, religions, nationalities, socioeconomic classes and lifestyles. We can see evidence of this surfacing all over the world at this time.

The Company of Heaven knows it is difficult for awakening Humanity to fathom that there is still so much resistance from our recalcitrant sisters and brothers, but there is a reason why they are bringing this to our attention now. Monumental changes have taken place over the past few decades and we have finally reached the point where this level of self-obsessed and narcissistic consciousness will no longer be allowed to interfere with Humanity's awakening or Earth's Ascension process. This is one of the main reasons our Father-Mother God have initiated the new phase of their Divine Plan.

With every person's Lightwork being amplified a thousand fold every day, the I AM Presences of even the most recalcitrant souls are being given powerful opportunities to help them awaken and reclaim their Divine Birthrights as Sons and Daughters of God. The hope is that every single recalcitrant person will respond positively to this influx of Light as soon as possible. Our Father-Mother God, the Company of Heaven and awakened Humanity are all holding the sacred space for this to happen. However, if the recalcitrant souls choose to not correct their behavior patterns a contingency plan has been set into motion.

Our Father-Mother God have encoded in their new Divine Plan a process for this depth of fallen consciousness to be cleansed from the mental and emotional strata of the planet. The Company of Heaven is assuring us that recalcitrant people still have time to awaken and to fulfill their agreement to transmute their karmic liabilities, but if they choose to continue on the destructive path they are on things will definitely change for them.

These recalcitrant souls will not be allowed to delay the Earth's Ascension process any longer. Once their I AM Presence knows for sure they are not going to change their behavior in this lifetime, a merciful plan has been set into motion that will allow them to continue their learning experiences in another time and place.

When it is time for the recalcitrant people to pass through the natural transition we call death, they will be transferred to special schools in the inner planes. This will be an individual process and will occur for each person in Divine Timing. There will not be a mass exodus. Each person will stay in the inner schools for however long it takes to complete their lessons and transmute their human miscreations back into Light. Only after that process is complete and he or she has returned to Christ Consciousness will they be allowed to embody on the New Earth where they will continue learning how to become cocreators with our Father-Mother God. This will be a long road for them, but it is infinitely better than being left behind during the Shift of the Ages. This merciful plan is truly a gift of Divine Grace.

As a word of encouragement, the Beings of Light want us to know that our Father-Mother God's new Divine Plan is already making a positive difference. They said the amplification of Humanity's Lightwork is accelerating the Earth's purging process. This is causing both asleep and recalcitrant souls to awaken in record numbers which is expediting Earth's Ascension in the Light. So let's keep on keeping on.

The next phase of our Father-Mother God's new plan involves the awakening of the Millennials and the children who are embodying on Earth now and those who are already embodied. These precious Ones were held in the Realms of Illumined Truth for a very long time where they prepared for the moment when Humanity would finally free ourselves from trap of the wheel of karma we inadvertently created when we fell into separation and duality.

In the next sharing, the Company of Heaven will reveal information about the events that allowed the Earth to Ascend off of the wheel of karma. Those events paved the way for the birth of the Holy Innocents who have come to help through the final stages of Earth's Ascension process.

47

ASCENDING OFF OF THE
WHEEL OF KARMA

Today the Company of Heaven wants to share some information about the events that allowed the Earth to Ascend off of the wheel of karma which we had been trapped on since our fall from Grace. That monumental event paved the way for the birth of the Millennials and the children and brought us to this miraculous point in time. Once you are aware on a conscious level of the preparation that has taken place through the unified efforts of Heaven and Earth, the significance of the opportunity manifesting for us now will be obvious.

The Shift of the Ages

We have talked about the Shift of the Ages several times, but the Company of Heaven wants us to have a cohesive context for the Divine Mission we are embarking on now. The Shift of the Ages is a rare moment in time that occurs only once in several million years. This event involves a unique alignment during which celestial and galactic cycles, within cycles, within cycles throughout the whole of Creation dovetail into one synchronized pulsation. This event rhythmically unifies all Life everywhere for one Cosmic Moment. During that awesome moment, every particle and wave of Life pulsates in unison with the Heartbeat of our omniscient, omnipresent, omnipotent Father-Mother God—The Cosmic I AM—All That Is. In that instant, our Father-Mother God inbreathe all Life up the Spiral of Evolution into the next phase of our evolutionary process.

The Shift of the Ages was God Victoriously accomplished on December 21st and 22nd in 2012. During that Cosmic Moment, the Earth and our Solar System aligned with the Galactic Core of the Milky Way and our Father-Mother God inbreathed the Earth and ALL Life evolving upon her up the Spiral of Evolution into the initial impulse of the timeless, spaceless frequencies of the 5th-Dimensional New Earth.

The miracle that allowed every single person on Earth to move through the Shift of the Ages did not happen by chance. It happened through the unified efforts of millions of awakened Lightworkers and the Company of Heaven. This collaboration took place over a 25-year period that began with a global event called Harmonic Convergence.

Harmonic Convergence

Harmonic Convergence was an amazing event that took place August 15th, 16th, 17th and 18th in 1987. Prior to that event, hundreds of thousands of Lightworkers all over the world became aware of a rare celestial alignment that would occur during those specific days. People intuitively recognized the powerful opportunity that alignment would provide for them to add to the Light of the world, and they selflessly responded to their Heart's Call. Lightworkers traveled to sacred sites all over the planet and volunteered to serve as the Open Door through which the Light of God that was destined to bless the Earth on those days would flow.

There was obviously Divine Intervention involved in the Lightworkers' global response. Harmonic Convergence occurred before the existence of the internet and social media. In spite of that fact, Lightworkers around the world found out about this impending opportunity and intuitively realized the need for their deliberate participation. Some of the people were consciously aware of what was taking place, but many were just responding to a subtle inner knowing. The various sacred sites Lightworkers were drawn to were actually acupuncture points along the meridians in Mother Earth's *Crystal Grid System*. This system is identical to the acupuncture meridians and pressure points within our own physical bodies.

The Company of Heaven asked those of us associated with *Era of Peace* to organize a global gathering of Lightworkers within the sacred forcefield of *"Diamond Head"* in Honolulu, Hawaii. The Beings of Light revealed that Diamond Head represents the Crown Chakra for Mother Earth. They said that the Hawaiian Islands are remnants of the massive continent of Lemuria where the initial impetus for Humanity's fall from Grace took place. We were deeply honored to be able to serve the Earth and all her Life in that way, so we gratefully agreed to organize the gathering of Lightworkers. That sacred conclave initiated the *First Annual World Congress on Illumination*.

Approximately 500 people from all over the world came to the first World Congress on Illumination to serve on behalf of Humanity and all Life on Earth. During the four days of Harmonic Convergence, the Light of God flowed through the Portal of Light at Diamond Head and blazed through the Chalice of our unified Heart Flames into the

Sun of Even Pressure in the center of the Earth. Once the Light was anchored in the Divine Momentum in the heart of Mother Earth, it expanded as a tremendous starburst out through Earth's Crystal Grid System. This unfathomable Light was then anchored permanently into the physical, etheric, mental and emotional strata of Mother Earth through the Heart Flames of the myriad Lightworkers who were stationed at Earth's acupuncture points around the world.

That influx of Light infused Mother Earth and all Life evolving upon her with unprecedented frequencies of primal Light substance from the very Core of Creation. That miraculous event allowed the Mighty Elohim, who are the Builders of Form, to raise Humanity and the Earth off of the *wheel of karma* which we had been trapped on since our fall from Grace aeons ago. Once the Earth and all her Life Ascended off of the wheel of karma, the Elohim placed us back on the Spiral of Evolution where we were able to finally reclaim our rightful place in our evolutionary process. This allowed the Sons and Daughters of God on Earth to begin in earnest our journey back to the Heart of our Father-Mother God and our return to Christ Consciousness.

We were trapped on the wheel of karma for so long that many people came to the erroneous conclusion that the wheel of karma is a natural part of our evolutionary process. On the contrary, the wheel of karma was a horrific human miscreation that was inadvertently created by Humanity's fragmented and fear-based human egos when we fell into the abyss of separation and duality.

For literally thousands of lifetimes we have been trapped on the wheel of karma experiencing cycles of birth and death with painfully little progress. No matter how hard we tried to reclaim our Divine Birthright by returning to

Christ Consciousness our efforts seemed to be in vain. Each lifetime felt like we were stepping on the gas with our car in neutral, but that is no longer the case. Since Harmonic Convergence, everything has changed.

We are no longer trapped on the wheel of karma where progress was virtually at a standstill. We are now back on the Spiral of Evolution and we are functioning within the Universal Law of the Circle. This is what our Father-Mother God intended in the beginning and where we were always supposed to be. Now our karmic miscreations and liabilities from the past can surface at a greatly accelerated pace. This is allowing us to transmute into Light literally hundreds of lifetimes worth of negativity in *"the twinkling of an eye."* This purging is reflected in the challenges we are witnessing all over the world. Fortunately, this difficult situation will be temporary. Our Father-Mother God's newly initiated Divine Plan is making a big difference in completing Earth's purging process.

Our Father-Mother God are now focusing their new Divine Plan on awakening the Millennials and the children who are now embodied on Earth. These precious souls have been waiting in the inner planes for the time when the Earth would Ascend off of the wheel of karma and begin her ascent up the Spiral of Evolution. That Cosmic Moment has arrived and the Millennials and the children are now ready to fulfill the vitally important missions they came to Earth to accomplish during these wondrous but often tumultuous times.

The Beings of Light are revealing enlightening information about the Divine Missions for which the Millennials and the children have been preparing. I believe this knowing will sooth your heart and inspire new levels of Divine Purpose, Enthusiasm and Joy within you.

48

WHO ARE THE MILLENNIALS AND THE CHILDREN?

The Company of Heaven wants to reveal to us who the Millennials and the children are in relationship to the magical Divine Plan unfolding on Earth. In the last sharing we learned about Earth's Ascension off of the wheel of karma which took place during Harmonic Convergence in 1987. That event not only freed Humanity from the oppressive wheel of karma which blocked our evolutionary progress for aeons of time, it cleared the way for the coming of the Millennials who are now 18 to 32 years old and the children who have followed them into embodiment.

All of these precious souls have come to help us transmute into Light the atrocities Humanity has inflicted on Mother Earth and all Life evolving upon her since our fall from Grace. Once that purging is complete, the Millennials and the children will help us to easily cocreate the patterns of perfection for the New Earth. The Company of Heaven said that this will occur in wondrous ways we have not yet imagined.

The patterns for the New Earth are formed from 5th-Dimensional Crystalline Solar Light which reverberates with frequencies of Divine Love, Oneness, Reverence for ALL Life and the Divine Intention of always manifesting the highest good of all concerned.

If you are over 32 years old, a critical part of your reason for being on Earth has been to prepare the way for the Millennials and the children who would be born once the Earth was freed from the entrapment of the wheel of karma. Whether you were consciously aware of this facet of your Divine Mission or not, our Father-Mother God want you to know that through your I AM Presence you have succeeded God Victoriously. Now it is time for you and me and the rest of awakening Humanity to fulfill the next miraculous phase of Earth's Ascension process.

The Holy Innocents

The Company of Heaven is revealing to us that since the Earth Ascended off of the wheel of karma in 1987, every Son and Daughter of God who has embodied on Earth has been born *karma free*. The Earth has reclaimed her rightful place on the Spiral of Evolution, and Humanity is once again evolving within the Universal Law of the Circle. This is where we were prior to our fall from Grace. It is where Humanity and the Earth absolutely had to be in order to make it through the Shift of the Ages which occurred during the December Solstice in 2012.

The Millennials and the children who have embodied on Earth since 1987 are known in the Inner Realms as the Holy Innocents. These are Sons and Daughters of God who had not begun their evolutionary journey on Earth when we tragically fell from Grace. When the horrific results of our descent into separation and duality became clear, our Father-Mother God issued a Cosmic Edict to protect the Holy Innocents from being trapped on the wheel of karma.

Our God Parents directed the Solar Logos, Alpha and Omega, from our Central Sun, to prevent the Holy Innocents from embodying on Earth until Humanity was able to transcend the wheel of karma and return to the Spiral of Evolution and the Law of the Circle. Alpha and Omega agreed and since that time aeons ago, the Holy Innocents have been studying and evolving in the Temples within the electronic belt around the Central Sun. This took much longer than anyone imagined and as a result the souls who have been born since 1987 are much more evolved than the rest of us were when we embodied on Earth for the first time.

While waiting in the Inner Realms, the Millennials and the children were trained in unique and powerful ways to help the rest of us transcend the pain and suffering of the old Earth. These souls were not only born karma free, their I AM Presence encoded unique *consciousness codes* within their DNA prior to this embodiment. The Divine Intent of the *consciousness codes* is to provide these enlightened souls with easy access to the sacred knowledge they accumulated while they were waiting in the Temples in the electronic belt around the Central Sun of Alpha and Omega.

This sacred knowledge resonates with the knowing that *"We are One"* and that *"Love is ALL there is."* This is the consciousness of the New Earth, and it reflects the *Reverence for ALL Life* that is necessary in order for the Millennials and the children to connect with their I AM Presence. Once this occurs, they will easily reach into the *Realms of Cause* where the viable solutions for every single malady on Earth exist.

When we observe the outer appearances of what is occurring on Earth at this time, it is easy to think this information cannot possibly be true. There are many examples of the Millennials and the children awakening and doing amazing things to improve the quality of life for Humanity and the

Earth. Unfortunately, there are also many instances where these precious Ones are suffering and do not seem to be any more awake than the masses of Humanity. It is now time for all of them to awaken, so they can accomplish what they have come to Earth to do. The Beings of Light are stressing to awakening Humanity that in order for the asleep Millennials and children to awaken, they desperately need our help. They must transcend the dense frequencies of the carbon-based old Earth and integrate into the 5th-Dimensional Crystalline-based Solar frequencies of Light associated with the New Earth. You and I can help them do that.

With the birth of 2018 and the initiation of our Father-Mother God's new Divine Plan, everything has changed. Our Lightwork is being amplified a thousand fold every day through our newly empowered Planetary Grid of Transfiguring Divine Love. This is truly unprecedented Divine Intervention and as a result the Legions of Light are heralding *"a New Day"* on Planet Earth.

Now on behalf of the Millennials and the children, we are being asked to redouble our efforts. We are being told from On High that through the unified efforts of Heaven and Earth, activities of Light are being orchestrated this year that will help us to awaken the Millennials and the children in ways we did not have access to in the past. The Company of Heaven said these activities of Light will also enhance our ability to help awaken the asleep and recalcitrant souls.

Dear One, the Beings of Light will begin sharing information about these powerful activities of Light in the next few sharings. As we begin this process we are being asked to invoke the I AM Presence of every Millennial and every child. As we hold them in our heart and prayers, Archangel Michael will envelop them in an invincible forcefield of Infinite Protection.

49

WHAT AWAKENING THE MILLENNIALS AND THE CHILDREN WILL MEAN FOR ALL OF US

With the birth of 2018 and the initiation of our Father-Mother God's new Divine Plan, everything changed. Our Lightwork is being amplified a thousand fold every day through our newly empowered Planetary Grid of Transfiguring Divine Love. This is truly unprecedented Divine Intervention. As a result, the Legions of Light are heralding "*a New Day*" on Planet Earth.

Now, on behalf of the Millennials and the children, we are being asked to redouble our efforts. We are being told from On High that through the unified efforts of Heaven and Earth, activities of Light are being orchestrated that will help us to awaken the Millennials and the children in ways we did not have access to in the past. The Company of Heaven said these activities of Light will also enhance our ability to help awaken the remaining asleep and recalcitrant souls. So what will this mean for the Earth and all Life evolving upon her?

The Company of Heaven said in order for us to get a glimpse of what the awakening of the Millennials and the children will do for Humanity and the Earth, they would like to share some information about what the Millennials and children who are already awake are doing to assist with Earth's Ascension process.

At some level the recalcitrant souls know their reign of power and greed is in jeopardy, and they are doing everything they can to interfere with the awakening of the Millennials and the children. Their efforts are now in vain, but the atrocities they have inflicted on Humanity and the Earth over aeons of time have wreaked havoc. The things these wayward souls have been able to accomplish in this lifetime alone are astonishing. Fortunately, the awakened Millennials are aware of their nefarious efforts and they are actively involved with transmuting the recalcitrant souls' human miscreations. The awakened Millennials and children are cocreating new paradigms that will make the old models of separation and duality obsolete.

The Company of Heaven has pointed out a few things that awakened Millennials are aware of and are working to change. As we identify these things, know that the 5th-Dimensional Crystalline Solar Violet Flame of God's Infinite Perfection is blazing in through and around these miscreations. This Sacred Fire is transmuting them cause, core, effect, record and memory the maximum that Cosmic Law will allow.

As these miscreations are pushed to the surface of our conscious minds, viable solutions from the Realms of Cause are simultaneously flowing into the mental and emotional strata of Mother Earth. The Millennials and children are able to tap into this information to some degree, but once the *consciousness codes* within their DNA are activated they will be uniquely prepared to intervene in ways that will solve every malady on Earth.

For decades recalcitrant souls have developed ways to block the awakening of the Millennials and the children. In order to do that they had to prevent the I AM Presences of these precious Ones from activating the *consciousness codes* within their DNA. It seems as though the most effective way of blocking this activation was by polluting the Earth and contaminating the physical, etheric, mental and emotional bodies of the Millennials and the children with toxic substances. Here are a few of the blatantly obvious results of Earth's deliberate contamination.

- Forty years ago in the United States of America the statistics for children born with Autism was one in 10,000. Today, one out of every 35 children born in the United States is diagnosed with Autism.
- In the past 40 years the manipulation of the food industry has resulted in obesity reaching epidemic levels.
- Within the same 40-year period cancer, diabetes, asthma, lung disease, hepatitis, heart disease, dementia, Alzheimer's, depression, drug and alcohol addiction, and colon cancer in people under 50 years of age have also sky rocketed into epidemic proportions.

It is the general consensus that all of these dramatic changes are environmental and have been caused by toxic substances that have polluted the air we breathe, the water we drink and the food we eat. This has all been allowed by governments and corporations under the guise of improving life and the advancement of science. But the vast majority of people involved with polluting the Earth in this destructive and seemingly heartless way are doing it for money, power and personal gain. It appears that their self-obsessed and narcissistic actions are being done with utter and total disregard for both Humanity and the Earth.

At the present time 663,000,000 people on this planet do not have access to clean drinking water. That is twice the population of the United States of America. Every year there are more deaths in the world from dirty water than there are from all forms of violence combined, even war. The appalling thing about these statistics is that we have all of the knowledge, all of the technology and all of the skill necessary to correct this situation right here and right now. It is only the greed and corruption of governments and corporations that are preventing every person on Earth from having clean drinking water.

The Millennials around the world are awakening to this horrific problem. They are cocreating conscious corporations and nonprofit organizations with the goal of bringing clean water to every person on Earth. One of the most heart-based and effective global nonprofit organizations working in this area is called *"Charity Water."*

Another heart-based organization involving Millennials and children around world is called *"Global Citizens."* These precious ones are working with the United Nations in an effort to eliminate extreme poverty on Earth by the year 2030.

The Millennials are also committed to creating a healthy food industry. One of the most globally known organizations is involved in educating people and making healthy food available to everyone on the planet. This organization is known as *"The Food Revolution."* They are cocreating new models that help people navigate through the toxic foods being promoted around the world. They also inform people about the deadly toxic chemicals that are being used to grow and to genetically modify our food.

Many other Millennials are confronting the recalcitrant consciousness of greed and corruption by becoming active in various fields of government, politics, the judicial system, science, technology, education, agriculture, the food industry, medicine, the pharmaceutical industry, the environment, renewable energy, socially responsible banking and investments, harmonious family life and spiritual awakening.

This list is just the beginning. Amazingly, in most instances, the *consciousness codes* within the DNA of the Millennials and the children have not even been activated yet. The Divine Intent of the *consciousness codes* is to provide these enlightened souls with easy access to the sacred knowledge they accumulated while they were waiting in the Temples in the electronic belt around the Central Sun of Alpha and Omega. This sacred knowledge resonates with the knowing that "*We are One*" and that "*Love is ALL there is.*"

Imagine what the Millennials and the children will be able to accomplish once their *consciousness codes* are activated and they are able to remember everything they learned prior to this embodiment. The Company of Heaven said that when their *consciousness codes* are activated these enlightened Ones will be able to tap into sacred knowledge in the Realms of Cause that will transcend anything the evolutions of Earth have ever known.

Precious Heart, the Company of Heaven is revealing to us an unfolding Divine Plan that will help you and me and the rest of awakening Humanity to clear the way for the activation of the *consciousness codes* within the Millennials and the children.

50

ACTIVATING THE CONSCIOUSNESS CODES OF THE MILLENNIALS AND THE CHILDREN

The Company of Heaven will now share with us the blueprint for the unfolding Divine Plan which will ultimately result in the activation of the *consciousness codes* for the Millennials and the children. These Holy Innocents were not only born karma free, their I AM Presence encoded unique *consciousness codes* within their DNA prior to this embodiment.

The Divine Intent of the *consciousness codes* is to provide the Millennials and the children with easy access to the sacred knowledge they accumulated while they were waiting in the Temples in the electronic belt around the Central Sun of Alpha and Omega prior to beginning their Earthly sojourn. This sacred knowledge resonates with the knowing that "*We are One*" and that "*Love is ALL there is.*" This is the consciousness of the New Earth, and it reflects the *Reverence for ALL Life* that is necessary in order for the Millennials and the children to be able to reach into the *Realms of Cause* where the viable solutions for every single malady on Earth exist.

The Divine Plan for 2018

The Divine Plan that has been revealed to us by the Company of Heaven for 2018, will be a global activity of Light that will unfold week by week under the guidance of our Father-Mother God and the Legions of Light in the Realms of Illumined Truth. Every week the Company of Heaven will share information and reveal a vitally important activity of Light that will be very easy for each and every one of us to participate in. Step by step we will assist ourselves and the rest of Humanity to transcend the dense carbon-based frequencies of the old Earth. As we lift ourselves into higher frequencies of the 5th-Dimensional Crystalline-based Solar Light associated with the New Earth, we will lift every man, woman and child up with us. This is possible because we are One and there is no separation.

Again, I will reiterate that this information and these events are occurring in the Eternal Moment of Now. That means that no matter when you are reading these words, your I AM Presence is assimilating the Light and the benefits from these events in perfect alignment with your Divine Plan.

As these activities of Light are revealed to us step by step, every person's I AM Presence will be in charge of the Divine Alchemy that will take place within his or her physical, etheric, mental and emotional bodies at a cellular level. This shift of vibration will occur within every person on Earth in perfect alignment with his or her Divine Plan and their highest good.

We at *Era of Peace* will freely share the information we are receiving from On High through our Weekly Vlogs, our Monthly Newsletter and our Free Seminars. Information regarding all of these FREE opportunities is available on our website www.eraofpeace.org.

Our Father-Mother God are encouraging all of us to participate in this facet of the Divine Plan according to our Heart's Call. They also want to remind all of us that in addition to the global activities of Light we may be drawn to, each and every one of us has our own Divine Plan that we have been preparing for lifetimes to fulfill during this Cosmic Moment on Earth. We alone can weave our unique and critically important Golden Thread of Life into the Tapestry of Earth's Ascension process that is unfolding now.

So every day, please listen to your inner guidance and focus on your I AM Presence. You will be guided unerringly and you will know intuitively how to add to the Light of the world in every situation that is presented to you. Then you can confidently take positive action knowing that your Lightwork is being amplified a thousand fold through our newly empowered Planetary Grid of Transfiguring Divine Love.

Activating the Consciousness Codes
In the Millennial's and the Children's DNA

In order for the I AM Presence of the Millennials and the children to activate the *consciousness codes* within their DNA, these souls must first transcend the dense carbon-based frequencies of their contaminated 3rd- and 4th-Dimensional Earthly bodies. Only then will they be able to transcend the toxic substances of the old Earth and integrate into the higher frequencies of their 5th-Dimensional Crystalline-based Solar Light Bodies. It is within this higher frequency of Light that their I AM Presence will be able to easily activate their *consciousness codes*. This will enable these precious Ones to begin their missions of cocreating the patterns of perfection for the New Earth, which will greatly benefit Humanity and ALL Life on this planet.

This is exactly what the unfolding Divine Plan for 2018 is designed to do. Week by week the Company of Heaven will guide us through activities of Light that will assist ALL of Humanity to gradually transcend the carbon-based frequencies of our contaminated 3rd- and 4th-Dimensional Earthly bodies, so that we can integrate into our 5th-Dimensional Crystalline-based Solar Light Bodies. This process will daily and hourly build in momentum until we reach the anniversary of Harmonic Convergence in August 2018.

Our Father-Mother God have asked those of us at *Era of Peace* to orchestrate a global activity of Light during that auspicious time that will catapult the Millennials and the children into the highest possible frequencies of their 5th-Dimensional Crystalline-based Solar Light Bodies. Together, we will create a sacred space that will allow the I AM Presence of these precious Ones to activate their *consciousness codes*. This will take place in perfect alignment with each one's Divine Plan and their highest good.

The vehicle that will be used for this global gathering is the *32nd Annual World Congress on Illumination* which will be held within the sacred Portal of Diamond Head in Honolulu, Hawaii, August 11–16, 2018. This is the Portal of Light where the very first World Congress on Illumination was held. During that momentous occasion, the Earth Ascended off of the wheel of karma and reclaimed her rightful place on the Spiral of Evolution. That miraculous event took place during Harmonic Convergence in 1987.

This will be the first time in 32 years we have been called back to this Portal of Light at Diamond Head in Hawaii. The Company of Heaven revealed to us in 1987, that Diamond Head is the Portal through which the Light of God flows into Mother Earth's Crown Chakra. The fact that our Father-Mother God are asking Lightworkers to once again gather within this Portal of Light, indicates the magnitude of the Divine Plan that is destined to be God Victoriously accomplished this year.

Once again through the unified efforts of Lightworkers around the world, on the anniversary of Harmonic Convergence in 2018 miracles will take place. Some of us will be called to be physically present in Honolulu, Hawaii at the *32nd Annual World Congress on Illumination*. Others of us will be drawn to different locations in order to anchor the Light that will enable the I AM Presence of every Millennial and every child to activate their *consciousness codes*.

Every Lightworker will be in his or her right and perfect place. No facet of this Divine Plan is any more important than another. What *is* important, is that you respond to whatever your I AM Presence is guiding you to do. In addition to those who will be inspired to be physically present in Hawaii, there will be others around the world who will join us in consciousness. These Lightworkers will project the Light flowing through their Heart Flames into the Portal of Light where those attending the *32nd Annual World Congress on Illumination* are physically gathered. This will allow our unified efforts to be expanded exponentially. If you have the Heart Call to join us in any way for this holy endeavor, God Bless you for your willingness to be the Open Door for the Light of God during this Cosmic Moment in Earth's Ascension process.

The Company of Heaven has said to Trust and KNOW that if you are being guided to be physically present within the Portal of Light in Hawaii, then your I AM Presence and the Company of Heaven will assist you in clearing the way. This is true whether you may need assistance with time, energy, or money to accomplish this facet of your Divine Mission. All of the Lightworkers who have been prepared to serve in this wondrous way on behalf of Humanity and all Life on this sweet Earth will know who they are through the inner promptings of their heart.

Dear One, next the Beings of Light will help us comprehend why so many of the Millennials and children are suffering if they were born karma free. We will also learn more about how we can help them transcend their painful life experiences.

51

IF THE MILLENNIALS AND THE CHILDREN ARE KARMA FREE WHY ARE SO MANY OF THEM SUFFERING?

The Company of Heaven has been revealing to us who the Millennials and the children are and what their Divine Mission on Earth is at this time. We are learning that in the Inner Realms these souls are known as the Holy Innocents. They include the vast majority of people born on Earth since 1987 after Humanity was freed from our self-inflicted trap on the wheel of karma.

The Holy Innocents have embodied on Earth for the first time. Consequently, they were born karma free. Prior to this embodiment, their I AM Presence encoded special *consciousness codes* within their DNA structures that will be activated in Divine Timing. These *consciousness codes* are designed to help the Holy Innocents easily remember the training they received in the Inner Realms prior to this embodiment. This sacred knowledge will empower them to effectively assist Humanity and the Earth through the final stages of our Ascension process.

When we witness so many of the Millennials and the children all over the world going through extremely challenging life experiences, it is easy to doubt the validity of these revelations. It also makes us question what being karma free really means. The Company of Heaven will help us to comprehend why so many of the Millennials and children are suffering if, in fact, they were born karma free.

When we embody on Earth nothing about our birth circumstances is left to chance. Once we are given permission to embody, or to re-embody, on Earth by our Father-Mother God, our I AM Presence helps us choose the most appropriate conditions for the learning experiences we have volunteered to go through. We choose our parents, our physical body, our race, our nationality, the location on the planet where we will be born, our socioeconomic condition and the family religion we will be exposed to as children.

Prior to our fall from Grace, these choices were always positive and designed to accelerate our spiritual growth and our Divine Mission of learning to become cocreators with our Father-Mother God. After the fall, however, most of these choices had to do with what karmic liabilities we had either deliberately or inadvertently miscreated. Our choices were based on what circumstances we needed to experience in order to help us learn our lessons and transmute our miscreations back into Light as quickly as possible.

In relation to this, there is an interesting fact that the Company of Heaven wants us to contemplate during this confusing and often tumultuous time. Currently, in an attempt to maintain power and control the recalcitrant souls are perpetuating hate, prejudice, suspicion and fear between the various peoples of the world. Their goal is to divide people into aggressive and fear-based opposing factions, so they will not hear the inner voice of their I AM Presence reminding them that they are One with the very people they are opposing and that there is no separation.

The ludicrous thing about this malicious effort is that in most instances those of us who are over the age of 32 have had hundreds of lifetimes on Mother Earth. We have literally chosen to be every gender, race, nationality, religion, socioeconomic class and lifestyle. Our physical body is merely the vehicle we use to navigate around in the physical plane. It is not who we are as a person. We choose these various Earthly experiences because of what we will learn and how we will grow by walking in the shoes of our sisters and brothers. This profound Truth may make you uncomfortable, but our Father-Mother God and your I AM Presence are longing for you to make Peace with this reality.

So the question now is, if the Millennials and the children are embodying on Earth for the first time and they are karma free, why are they experiencing so many painful and negative things? Well, in fulfillment of their Divine Missions, they too have chosen their particular birth circumstances. They are very aware of the challenges Humanity is experiencing due to the accelerated purging of our human miscreations from the old Earth. They know that the asleep and recalcitrant souls are so buried in their past karmic liabilities that they have not been able to raise their heads above the chaos effectively enough to perceive the Light or to hear the still small voice of their I AM Presence.

The Millennials and the children have come to help us through the final stages of Earth's Ascension process. They understand that in order for the remaining masses to awaken quickly, they need exceptional assistance. The Holy Innocents trusted that with the knowledge they accumulated in the Inner Realms while waiting for the opportunity to embody on Earth, and the fact that they were not going to be burdened with karmic liabilities from their past, they would be able to descend into the most painful situations on Earth and return fairly unscathed. The plan was for them to awaken and lift into the Light quickly. They believed they would be able to accomplish this on behalf of unawakened Humanity far more easily than the karma-laden masses would be able to.

A Universal Law that we are all subject to is, *"As I AM lifted up ALL life is lifted up with me."* This is the knowing the Millennials and the children had when they made the choice to descend into the most painful and challenging situations on Earth on behalf of Humanity. Tragically, what the Holy Innocents did not know is the lengths the recalcitrant souls had gone to in order to pollute the Earth with deadly toxic substances that would contaminate the air they would breathe, the water they would drink and the food they would eat.

Due to the unconscionable behavior of the recalcitrant souls, the grossly contaminated physical, etheric, mental and emotional bodies of both Humanity and Mother Earth have wreaked havoc in Earth's Ascension process. The awakening process of the Millennials and the children has been thwarted in many ways. This has delayed these precious ones from actively participating in their Divine Missions.

The encouraging news is that with the initiation of our Father-Mother God's NEW Divine Plan and the empowerment of our Planetary Grid of Transfiguring Divine Love, the recalcitrant souls have been put on notice. The activities of Light that will be cocreated this year through the unified efforts of awakening Humanity and the Company of Heaven will bring the recalcitrant souls' ability to block or interfere with Humanity's awakening to a screeching halt.

To begin this endeavor Archangel Michael and Saint Germain are offering every person on Earth a forcefield of Invincible Protection that will prevent anything that is not of the Light from interfering with the fulfillment of his or her Divine Plan.

If you have the Heart Call to do so, please join with me now and together we will join in consciousness with the I AM Presence of every man, woman and child on Earth. Together, we will establish the gift of this Invincible Protection from the Heavenly Realms around each person's physical, etheric, mental and emotional bodies. This will occur in perfect alignment with each one's Divine Plan and their highest good.

This Gift of Light from the Heavenly Realms will prevent the Holy Innocents from being overwhelmed by the surfacing miscreations of the old Earth, and it will assist them and all of the rest Humanity to transcend the painful experiences of our contaminated carbon-based Earthly bodies. This Forcefield of Protection will also assist Humanity to transcend the contaminated physical, etheric, mental and emotional strata of the old Earth. These are the Elemental Realms of consciousness that are now rebelling against the atrocities the recalcitrant souls have inflicted upon this planet. This rebellion is manifesting as the extreme weather conditions and the horrific natural disasters that are plaguing people around the world.

Please go within to the Divinity of your Heart Flame and focus on your I AM Presence. Breathe in deeply and be here now. And we begin.

Archangel Michael's and Saint Germain's Invincible Forcefield of Protection

I AM my I AM Presence and I AM One with the I AM Presence of all Humanity. What I invoke for myself this sacred and holy day I invoke on behalf of every man, woman and child on Earth. Beloved Archangel Michael and Beloved Saint Germain, we ask you and your Legions of Angels to come forth NOW!

*Archangel Michael, encapsulate each of us, the Millennials, the children and all of Humanity in your invincible Circle of White Lightning, your **"Ring Pass Not of God's First Cause of Perfection."** Prevent anything that is not of the Light from entering this forcefield or interfering with our service to the Light and our Divine Mission of Loving ALL Life free.*

Saint Germain, fill the Circle of White Lightning that is now blazing around every person on Earth with exquisite frequencies of the 5th-Dimensional Violet Flame of God's Infinite Perfection. Instantly transmute into Light every thought, word, feeling or action we have ever expressed, or that we may express in the future, that is less than the Love and Light of our I AM Presence.

Archangel Michael and Saint Germain, we ask that you permanently station an Angel of Protection and an Angel of the Violet Flame within the aura of every person. Direct these Angels to use their power and might to instantly...

CUT US FREE! (repeat 3 times)

from every line of force that would strive in any way to prevent the Immaculate Concept of our Divine Plans from being fulfilled. Free us instantly from any blocks or resistance from our own lower consciousness that might try to impede the God Victorious accomplishment of our heartfelt service to Humanity, Mother Earth and the Light.

Archangel Michael and Saint Germain, we ask that you now seal every person on Earth in the glorious gift of Light you have now established around the physical, etheric, mental and emotional bodies of Humanity and Mother Earth. Increase this Light daily and hourly with every breath we take. We so decree it, and accept it done, through the Power of God, I AM.

And so it is.

Dear One, in the next chapter the Beings of Light will reveal the first steps in transforming the contaminated carbon-based bodies of the Millennials, the children, the rest of Humanity and Mother Earth into 5th-Dimensional Crystalline-based Solar Light Bodies.

52

TRANSFORMING OUR
EARTHLY BODIES

The Company of Heaven is going to lead us step by step through the process of transforming our contaminated 3rd- and 4th-Dimensional carbon-based bodies into 5th-Dimensional Crystalline-based Solar Light Bodies. This Divine Alchemy is occurring within each and every one of us whether we believe it, or whether or not we are aware of it on a conscious level.

This information and this process of Divine Alchemy are being revealed to us now because they are a critical part of the unfolding Divine Plan for 2018. Know, however, that this sharing from On High will never become outdated or obsolete. No matter when you are reading these words you are in the *Eternal Moment of Now.* You are experiencing the full benefit and assistance from the Company of Heaven and every Son and Daughter of God who has woven their magnificent Light into this facet of the Divine Plan.

What we are experiencing on Earth at this time is a perfectly natural part of our evolutionary process. We have successfully moved through the Shift of the Ages. The Earth and all Life evolving upon her are now Ascending up the

Spiral of Evolution into the 5th-Dimensional Crystalline Solar Light frequencies of the New Earth. In order for the Earth and our bodies to withstand these higher frequencies of Solar Light, we must transform them from carbon-based cells to crystalline-based cells.

Our physical, etheric, mental and emotional bodies were always destined to go through the transformation from carbon-based to crystalline-based cells as we Ascend up the Spiral of Evolution into higher and higher frequencies of Light. However, it was never part of the Divine Plan that our Earthly carbon-based bodies be forced to outpicture the horrific mutations of aging, degeneration, disease and every other physical, mental and emotional affliction that Humanity is now experiencing. These gross mutations were inadvertently formed through the self-obsessed and often hateful thoughts, feelings, words and actions of our wayward human egos after we lost awareness of our I AM Presence and fell into the abyss of separation and duality.

It was also never part of the Divine Plan for our fragmented and fear-based egos to pollute Mother Earth and to contaminate, with deadly toxic chemicals, the elemental substances of air, water and food that we need in order for our Earthly Bodies to survive in the physical plane.

Prior to our fall from Grace, the Divine Alchemy of transforming our bodies from carbon-based to crystalline-based cells was a gentle and a very easy process. After the fall and the gross contamination of Mother Earth and our Earthly Bodies, that process became all but impossible. Now, due to miracles that have been God Victoriously accomplished through the unified efforts of awakening Humanity and the Company of Heaven over the past few decades, this process of Divine Alchemy is once again becoming available to Humanity.

This vitally important information is being received through Divine Revelations that are being given to Humanity by the Mighty Elohim and the Directors of the Earth, Air, Fire, Water and Ether Elements. In order for us to implement these revelations, however, we must first reverse the adverse effects of our human egos' miscreations.

One of the most tragic results of our fall from Grace is that we lost the ability to consciously communicate with our I AM Presence and the Company of Heaven. When that occurred, we also lost awareness of the Elemental Kingdom and the Divine Intelligence that directs and maintains the proper functioning of our Earthly Bodies. Remember, we are not our Earthly Bodies. Our physical, etheric, mental and emotional bodies are just the vehicles we use to navigate around in the physical plane, but they are the most amazing and complex instruments on Earth.

Even our scientific community is beginning to realize that our physical body has a degree of intelligence associated with it that is separate from our brain. We eat a carrot and our body digests it and converts it into heart cells, liver cells, brain cells, lung cells, stomach cells, bone cells, blood cells, hormones and myriad other cells with entirely different functions that are necessary for the survival of our body. This happens with every morsel of food we eat without any thought or conscious participation from us at all.

When everything that our body can use from the food we have eaten is distributed to our various cells and organs, the remainder which is considered waste is released from our body through several systems of elimination.

This incredible process does not happen by chance. It is orchestrated through the Divine Intelligence of an Elemental Being known as our Body Elemental. That term may seem brand new to you, but your Body Elemental was assigned to you by our Father-Mother God and the Mighty Elohim when you were first breathed forth from the Core of Creation. This selfless Elemental Being, along with your personal Guardian Angel, has been with you lifetime after lifetime from the moment you were granted permission by our Father-Mother God to begin your lessons of cocreation on the physical plane of Earth.

The Company of Heaven has told us that the first step in the process of reversing the gross miscreations in our Earthly Bodies is for Humanity to consciously remember and willingly cooperate with the intelligent Elemental Beings associated with the elements of earth, air, fire, water and ether. These intelligent Elemental Beings are responsible for manifesting the physical, etheric, mental and emotional strata of Mother Earth, and the physical, etheric, mental and emotional bodies of Humanity. So let me introduce you to the Elemental Kingdom in case you are not familiar with these Beings of Light.

The Mighty Elohim

The highest position held in the Elemental Kingdom is that of the **Mighty Elohim** who are the Builders of Form. The Elohim are responsible for magnetizing from the Heart of God the unformed primal Light substance that will be used by the various Elemental Beings who are responsible for forming the five elements on Earth. In our Solar System there are 12 Masculine Elohim and 12 Feminine Elohim who work together to fulfill the evolving physical needs of the Sons and Daughters of God.

Directors of the Elements and the Elementals

Next are the **Directors of the Elements**. These are powerful Beings of Light who guide and direct the Elemental

Beings who are associated with the five elements and who are responsible for creating Mother Earth and Humanity's Earthly Bodies.

The Directors of the Air Element are known as *Thor and Aries.* Their luminous Presence pulsates above the Earth at the cardinal point to the North. From this position they direct the Elemental Beings associated with the Air. These Beings are known as *Sylphs.* The Air Element is associated with Humanity's Etheric Body. Each person's Body Elemental works closely with the Sylphs in our Etheric Body.

The Directors of the Water Element are known as *Neptune and Lunara.* Their luminous Presence pulsates at the cardinal point to the East of the Earth. From this position they direct the Elemental Beings associated with the Water. These Beings are known as *Undines.* The Water Element is associated with our Emotional Body which is our largest Earthly Body. Our Body Elemental works closely with the Undines in our Emotional Body.

The Directors of the Earth Element are known as *Virgo and Pelleur.* Their luminous Presence pulsates at the cardinal point to the South of the Earth. From this position they direct the Elemental Beings associated with the Earth. These Beings are known as *Nature Spirits.* They include not only the physical substances of Earth but the plants and animals as well. The Earth Element is associated with our Physical Body. Our Body Elemental works closely with the Nature Spirits in our Physical Body.

The Directors of the Fire Element are known as *Helios and Vesta.* Their luminous Presence pulsates at the cardinal point to the West of the Earth. From this position they direct the Elemental Beings associated with the Fire. These Beings are known as *Salamanders.* The Fire Element is associated with our Mental Body. Our Body Elemental works closely with the Salamanders in our Mental Body.

The Directors of the Ether Element are known as *Aeolos and Amaryllis.* Their luminous Presence pulsates in the Divine Momentum within the Sun of Even Pressure in the center of Mother Earth. From this position they direct the Elemental Beings associated with the Ethers. These Beings are known as *Devas and Deva Rajas.* The Ether Element is associated with the more rarified Elemental substances necessary to form our crystalline-based cells. Our Body Elemental is working closely with the Devas and Deva Rajas in the Divine Alchemy of forming our 5th-Dimensional Crystalline-based Solar Light Bodies.

The Company of Heaven is asking us to contemplate this information within the Divinity of our Heart Flames. Awareness of the Divine Intelligence within the Elemental Kingdom may seem foreign to you, but that is okay. In gentle and loving ways your I AM Presence will help your Body Elemental and the Elemental Beings you have learned about today make themselves known to you. It is *only* through their unified efforts with your I AM Presence that the Divine Alchemy necessary for your ultimate Ascension in the Light can be completed.

So don't let this sacred knowledge confuse you. As we move through this process step by step the information being shared by the Company of Heaven will awaken your inner knowing about the Elemental Kingdom. This will clear the way for your conscious cooperation with your I AM Presence and your Body Elemental.

53

OUR RESPONSIBILITY IN TRANSFORMING OUR EARTHLY BODIES

We were told by the ancient prophets and seers that there would come a time in the not too distant future when we would Ascend into "A *New Heaven and a New Earth.*" They revealed that when that happened our Earthly Bodies would be Transfigured into expressions of vibrant health, eternal youth and infinite physical perfection.

Well, we are in the midst of that Cosmic Moment and even though Humanity is receiving more assistance from the Company of Heaven than ever before, our physical transformation from carbon-based to crystalline-based cells will not occur without our deliberate participation. This Divine Alchemy will only occur through our intentional, conscious and cooperative efforts with our I AM Presence, our Body Elemental and the Elemental Kingdom who have selflessly dedicated their lives to helping us.

There are Lightworkers who have been preparing for decades for this moment. Others have recently awakened and are just beginning to realize the opportunity at hand.

There are many others who are still in a deep sleep spiritually and do not have a clue about what is happening to them at this time. For this reason, there is an urgency of the hour.

Because of the urgency of the hour, a special Cosmic Dispensation has been granted by our Father-Mother God. This dispensation is allowing the Mighty Elohim and the Directors of the Elements to assist Humanity in unprecedented ways. These Beings of Light have been given permission to work with the Body Elementals of Humanity to greatly accelerate the Divine Alchemy of transforming our 3rd- and 4th-Dimensional planetary carbon-based cells into 5th-Dimensional Crystalline-based Solar Light Cells. This will allow the I AM Presence of every person including the Millennials, the children, and the asleep and recalcitrant souls to take full dominion of their thoughts, words, actions and feelings much sooner than any of us ever dreamed possible.

The reasons for this Divine Intervention are manifold, but most importantly it is due to the fact that "*As we are lifted up, ALL Life is lifted up with us.*" When we apply the universal Truths associated with physical transformation which are being revealed to Humanity by the Mighty Elohim, we will create an upward rush of Divine Love and Light. This will actually form a pathway for our sisters and brothers in the Family of Humanity to follow as they Ascend up the Spiral of Evolution into the 5th-Dimensional Realms of Infinite Physical Perfection associated with the New Earth.

The Mighty Elohim and the Directors of the Elements have been given permission to amplify a thousand fold every effort we make toward this holy endeavor. This will be accomplished through our newly empowered Planetary Grid of Transfiguring Divine Love. Daily and hourly, these Beings of Light will work with our I AM Presence and our Body Elementals to transform our carbon-based Earthly

Bodies into the infinite physical perfection of our 5th-Dimensional Crystalline-based Solar Light Bodies.

In the beginning, our Body Elemental was able to easily outpicture the vibrant health, eternal youth and infinite perfection encoded in our RNA-DNA messenger codes. This was largely due to the active Elemental Vortices within each of our Earthly Bodies. These vortices energized and sustained the elements within each of our bodies which allowed the Elementals to help us maintain the patterns of physical perfection originally intended by our Father-Mother God. Unfortunately, after the fall everything changed. Our Elemental Vortices became dormant, and Humanity began manifesting the maladies of aging, disease, mental illness and every other human affliction.

Now Humanity is reversing the adverse effects of the fall, and the Directors of the Elements have given our Body Elementals permission to reactivate the Elemental Vortices within our Earthly Bodies. This Heavenly assistance will greatly accelerate our physical transformation.

Humanity's Elemental Vortices

Prior to our embodiment on Earth for the first time, our I AM Presence was assigned a Guardian Angel and a Body Elemental that agreed to serve with us throughout our Earthly sojourns. Once that decision was made, our Body Elemental created five Elemental Vortices designed to energize and rejuvenate our Earthly Bodies on a daily basis.

1. The first vortex to be created was the *Ether Vortex* which pulsates above our head. The Ether Vortex bathes our four Earthly Bodies with rarified Ethers that pulsate with the Divine Potential of limitless physical perfection.

2. The next vortex to be created was the *Air Vortex* which pulsates in the area of our Throat Chakra. The unformed primal Light for our *Etheric Body* is magnetized through this vortex. Our Etheric Body is associated with the *Air Element*. It interpenetrates every cell and organ and extends a little beyond our physical body. Our Etheric Body is comprised of very sensitive chemical ethers that record every thought, word, feeling and action we express. This Earthly Body is considered *"the seat of all memory."* A portion of our Etheric Body serves as our personal Akashic records. This is where all of our etheric records and memories are maintained and this portion of our Etheric Body embodies with us lifetime after lifetime.

3. The next vortex to be established was the *Fire Vortex* which pulsates in the area of our sternum in the middle of our chest. The unformed primal Light for the *Mental Body* is magnetized through this vortex. Our Mental Body is associated with the *Fire Element*. The intent of our Mental Body is to keep our I AM Presence connected with the Divine Mind of God and the Realms of Thought. This vehicle allows us to effectively utilize our creative faculties of thought while we are learning to become cocreators. There is a lot of discussion at this time as to whether the brain and the mind are the same thing or if they are two separate entities. The Company of Heaven has revealed that our mind which is our Mental Body, and our physical brain structure are two separate entities. Our Mental Body functions in alignment with the Divine Mind of God and the Realms of Thought. This vehicle is always whole and complete. Our physical brain is the instrument through which

our Mental Body expresses thoughts in the physical plane. Just like we are not our Physical Body, our brain is not our Mental Body. Our physical brain can be damaged or chemically unbalanced which causes mental illness and prevents us from clearly expressing thoughts, but this does not affect our Mental Body. Even if a person is in a coma or unable to express thoughts in any way, their Mental Body is still processing their experiences and everything is being recorded in their Etheric Body. Nothing in our Earthly experience is ever lost, regardless of outer appearances.

4. The next vortex to be established by our Body Elemental was the *Water Vortex* which pulsates in the area of our Root Chakra at the base of the spine. The unformed primal Light for the *Emotional Body* is magnetized through this vortex. Our Emotional Body is associated with the *Water Element*. This is our largest Earthly Vehicle. Our Emotional Body surrounds our Physical Body and extends for several feet in every direction. Approximately eighty percent of our energy is released through our Emotional Body. The remaining twenty percent is expressed through our thoughts, words and actions.

5. The fifth and final vortex to be established by our Body Elemental was the *Earth Vortex*. This vortex pulsates in the area between our feet. The unformed primal Light for our *Physical Body* is magnetized through this vortex. This vortex grounds our Physical Body and allows us to easily navigate around in the 3rd and 4th Dimensions. Our Physical Body is associated with the *Earth Element*.

The Company of Heaven is asking us to focus on this information so that our I AM Presence and our Body Elemental can prepare our dormant Elemental Vortices to be opened to full breadth. In the next chapter the Elohim and the Directors of the Elements will guide us through an activity of Light that will restore our Elemental Vortices to their full Divine Potential.

54

AWAKENING OUR DORMANT ELEMENTAL VORTICES

This is the 2018 March Equinox which manifests as the perfect balance between night and day. The Company of Heaven has revealed to us that because of our Father-Mother God's recently initiated Divine Plan it is a new day on Planet Earth. Consequently, all of the celestial events we experience throughout the year will provide very powerful opportunities for us to add to the Light of the world.

In our Father-Mother God's new Divine Plan the Lightwork of every single person on Earth is being amplified a thousand fold. This has created a unique opportunity that is giving the Mighty Elohim and the Directors of the Elements permission to utilize the greatly amplified influx of Light from the 2018 March Equinox in ways that were previously unknown to the masses.

Know that no matter when you are reading these words you are being blessed with the full Divine Potential of this Equinox and the activity of Light the Mighty Elohim and the Directors of the Elements will guide us through this sacred and holy day.

The Company of Heaven will utilize the Planetary Grid of Transfiguring Divine Love which they have been assisting awakening Humanity to cocreate for over 50 years. In an unprecedented activity of Light, as we are being held in the full embrace of the March Equinox, the Mighty Elohim will bathe the Earth and all Life evolving upon her with higher frequencies of 5th-Dimensional Crystalline Solar Light than we have ever been able to withstand at a cellular level. It is this unfathomable Light that Humanity's I AM Presences and our Body Elementals will use to awaken and activate the Elemental Vortices within our four Earthly Bodies.

These Elemental Vortices have been dormant since our fall from Grace aeons ago. They are the portals through which our Body Elemental was originally able to restore and rejuvenate our four Earthly Bodies. The Divine Intent of these vortices was to provide our Body Elemental each day with renewed elements that would maintain vibrant health, eternal youth and limitless physical perfection in our Earthly Bodies. Our Father-Mother God directed the Mighty Elohim and the Directors of the Elements to provide this service for the Sons and Daughters of God, so that we would not be distracted from our missions by having to worry about the maintenance of our Earthly Bodies.

Today, through the Gift of God's Amazing Grace, the Mighty Elohim are going to guide us through an activity of Light that will activate Humanity's Elemental Vortices once again. If you have the Heart Call to do so, please join me now in this holy endeavor. Know that our unified efforts are being amplified a thousand fold.

The exercise we are being guided through today by the Mighty Elohim will awaken and activate the Elemental Vortices within our physical, etheric, mental and emotional bodies. These activated vortices will begin raising the vibration within each of our Earthly Bodies which will pave the way for the integration of our I AM Presence. Our activated Elemental Vortices will give our I AM Presence and our Body Elemental the ability to create and sustain the infinite perfection of our 5th-Dimensional Crystalline Solar Light Bodies.

This activity of Light is being stated in the first person so that we will each experience it personally, but know that we are invoking this Light through the I AM Presence of every person on Earth whether he or she is in or out of embodiment. And we begin.

Activating the Elemental Vortices

I AM breathing in and out slowly and deeply. The Holy Breath is an essential part of Life. It is a key factor in unifying the spectrums of Living Light throughout the whole of Creation. As I AM inbreathing and exhaling deeply, I AM attuning myself to the rhythm of the Universe. I AM One with the Heartbeat of my Father-Mother God. I AM One with the Sacred Fire Breath of the Holy Spirit and I AM One with the I AM Presence of every man, woman and child on Earth.

The Mighty Elohim are now guiding my I AM Presence through an activity of Light that will assist the Directors of the Elements and my Body Elemental to awaken and permanently activate my five Elemental Vortices.

As I continue breathing deeply and rhythmically, I begin to clearly see the Elemental Vortices pulsating within my Earthly Bodies. These centers are swirling vortices of Divine Light. They are shining like the Sun. There are five vortices. Each one is specifically designed to nourish, refresh and rejuvenate one of the five elements within my Earthly Bodies.

I first focus my attention on the Ether Vortex which is pulsating above my head. I put the full power of my concentration on this spinning vortex of Light. I breathe the Sacred Fire Breath of the Holy Spirit into the center of the Ether Vortex. It is now expanding and blazing like the Sun. I affirm with deep feeling:

I AM THAT I AM.
I AM THAT I AM.
I AM THAT I AM.

My Body Elemental now awakens and fully activates my Ether Vortex. The Light of God is expanding a thousand fold through this awakened vortex as my Body Elemental bathes my four Earthly Bodies in rarefied Ethers from the 5th- Dimensional Realms of Crystalline Solar Light.

I now focus the full power of my attention on the Air Vortex which is pulsating in the area of my Throat Chakra. I breathe the Sacred Fire Breath of the Holy Spirit into the center of the Air Vortex. It is now expanding and blazing like the Sun. I affirm with deep feeling:

I AM THE BREATH OF THE HOLY SPIRIT.
I AM THE BREATH OF THE HOLY SPIRIT.
I AM THE BREATH OF THE HOLY SPIRIT.

My Body Elemental now awakens and fully activates my Air Vortex. The Light of God is expanding a thousand fold through this awakened vortex as my Body Elemental bathes my Etheric Body in 5th- Dimensional Crystalline Solar Light. Through this Elemental Vortex my Etheric Body is being Transfigured.

I now focus the full power of my attention on the Fire Vortex which is pulsating within the location of my sternum in the center of my chest. I breathe the Sacred Fire Breath of the Holy Spirit into the center of the Fire Vortex. It is now expanding and blazing like the Sun. I affirm with deep feeling:

I AM THE FIRE BREATH OF THE ALMIGHTY.
I AM THE FIRE BREATH OF THE ALMIGHTY.
I AM THE FIRE BREATH OF THE ALMIGHTY.

My Body Elemental now awakens and fully activates my Fire Vortex. The Light of God is expanding a thousand fold through this awakened vortex as my Body Elemental bathes my Mental Body in 5th- Dimensional Crystalline Solar Light. Through this Elemental Vortex my Mental Body is being Transfigured.

I now focus the full power of my attention on the Water Vortex which is pulsating within the location of my Root Chakra at the base of my spine. I breathe the Sacred Fire Breath of the Holy Spirit into the center of the Water Vortex. It is now expanding and blazing like the Sun. I affirm with deep feeling:

I AM THE HARMONY OF MY TRUE BEING.
I AM THE HARMONY OF MY TRUE BEING.
I AM THE HARMONY OF MY TRUE BEING.

My Body Elemental now awakens and fully activates my Water Vortex. The Light of God is expanding a thousand fold through this awakened vortex as my Body Elemental bathes my Emotional Body in 5th-Dimensional Crystalline

Solar Light. Through this Elemental Vortex my Emotional Body is being Transfigured.

I now focus the full power of my attention on the Earth Vortex which is pulsating between my feet. I breathe the Sacred Fire Breath of the Holy Spirit into the center of the Earth Vortex. It is now expanding and blazing like the Sun. I affirm with deep feeling:

I AM THE MASTER OF MY PHYSICAL REALITY.
I AM THE MASTER OF MY PHYSICAL REALITY.
I AM THE MASTER OF MY PHYSICAL REALITY.

My Body Elemental now awakens and fully activates my Earth Vortex. The Light of God is expanding a thousand fold through this awakened vortex as my Body Elemental bathes my Physical Body in 5th-Dimensional Crystalline Solar Light. Through this Elemental Vortex my Physical Body is being Transfigured.

The Mighty Elohim, the Directors of the Elements and my Body Elemental have now fully awakened and permanently activated my five Elemental Vortices. This has created a tremendous pathway of Light through my four Earthly Bodies from head to toe. This dynamic force is quickening the Divine Alchemy taking place within my physical, etheric, mental and emotional bodies as they are transformed from carbon-based Earthly Bodies into 5th-Dimensional Crystalline-based Solar Light Bodies.

Every time I focus on my Elemental Vortices, God's Transfiguring 5th-Dimensional Crystalline Solar Light will expand a thousand fold through my four Earthly Bodies raising my energy, vibration and consciousness to new heights.

I accept and know that this activity of Light has been God Victoriously accomplished.

And so it is.
Beloved I AM. Beloved I AM. Beloved I AM That I AM.

Precious Heart, be gentle with yourself and allow your I AM Presence to assimilate the full magnitude of this activation into your Earthly Bodies at an atomic and subatomic level.

55

THE RESURRECTION FLAME A GIFT FROM ON HIGH

Step by step this year the Company of Heaven is guiding us through celestial opportunities and activities of Light that will help you and me and the Millennials and the children, as well as every other person on Earth, to transcend our contaminated 3rd- and 4th-Dimensional carbon-based Earthly Bodies. This will pave the way for the tangible manifestation of our 5th-Dimensional Crystalline-based Solar Light Bodies. It will also create the sacred space so that the I AM Presences of the Millennials and the children will be able to activate the *consciousness codes* within their DNA. This vitally important facet of the unfolding Divine Plan will also help Mother Earth to transcend the atrocities Humanity has inflicted upon her.

Today, in the Eternal Moment of Now, we are in the midst of Holy Week. This is a time when billions of people around the world pause to acknowledge our Father-Mother God through various spiritual and religious celebrations. On March 30, 2018, we will experience a very powerful Full Moon which this year is greatly enhanced by also being a Blue Moon. This is the first Full Moon following the March

Equinox which ushers in the celebrations of Passover and Easter every year. This year the Passover Full Moon occurs on Good Friday, the day Christian religions acknowledge the crucifixion of Jesus.

Because of our Father-Mother God's newly implemented Divine Plan, Humanity's spiritual focus of attention this week involving billions of people all over the world is creating a greatly empowered collective Cup of Consciousness. This Chalice of Light is forming a *Holy Grail* through which our Father-Mother God and a Mighty Archangel known as the Angel of Resurrection are blessing the Earth with previously unknown frequencies of the Mother of Pearl Resurrection Flame. It is through this *Holy Grail* that our Father-Mother God and the Angel of Resurrection are projecting more intensified frequencies of the Resurrection Flame than Humanity and Mother Earth have ever received. This awesome restorative and rejuvenating frequency of Sacred Fire is being infused into our Planetary Grid of Transfiguring Divine Love for the benefit of all Life on Earth. Today the Company of Heaven wants all of us to have a greater understanding of this incredibly merciful Gift from our Father-Mother God.

The Miracle of the Resurrection Flame

Aeons ago, when the Sons and Daughters of God began experimenting with our Gift of Life and departed from the Love-based qualification of our thoughts and feelings, our Father-Mother God perceived the shadow of our miscreations taking form in the consciousness of our Earthly Bodies. They knew the fruits of those seeds would be aging, disease, disintegration and decay. They further understood that some means of restoration would have to be provided to the children of Earth who would one day desire to return to their original God Estate.

To begin the process of manifesting that restorative power, our Father-Mother God breathed into their Heart Flames from the very Core of Creation the radiance of the Mother of Pearl Resurrection Flame. This Sacred Fire is a multifaceted and multidimensional frequency of Light by which the aged, diseased, distorted and disintegrating carbon-based substance generated by the misuse of Humanity's thoughts and feelings can be purified, restored and rejuvenated back into its original God Perfection.

When all was in readiness, our Father-Mother God summoned a Mighty Solar Archangel from the Great Silence to bring this sacred restoring Flame to Earth. Through the Heart Flame of this Mighty Archangel, who is now known through all Creation as the Angel of Resurrection, the Mother of Pearl Resurrection Flame was anchored on Earth.

From that moment forth, the Angel of Resurrection has accepted the responsibility of bathing the Earth in the Resurrection Flame in a rhythmic momentum. This Sacred Fire flows through the portal formed during the March Equinox every year and bathes the Earth for several weeks. In the Northern Hemisphere the Resurrection Flame is the frequency of Light that awakens the hibernating animals and brings the plants and trees back to life after the dormant winter months. The Resurrection Flame is also the Sacred Fire from the Heart of God that Resurrected Jesus' crucified carbon-based planetary body into his 5th-Dimensional Crystalline-based Solar Light Body. This occurred three days after the crucifixion on what Christians now celebrate as Easter Sunday.

In previous sharings in this book the Company of Heaven has revealed very enlightening information about Jesus' crucifixion and Resurrection, so I will not repeat those revelations here. What the Company of Heaven wants us to know today is how the Resurrection Flame can assist us now with the Divine Alchemy of transforming our own carbon-based planetary bodies into 5th-Dimensional Crystalline-based Solar Light Bodies.

Jesus' Resurrection was a deliberate demonstration of what occurs when our carbon-based 3rd- and 4th-Dimensional bodies are transformed into 5th-Dimensional Crystalline-based Solar Light Bodies. The scriptures state that when Mary Magdalene came to Jesus' tomb, and he appeared to her, he said *"Do not touch me, I am not of this world."* Jesus appeared to Mary in his 5th-Dimensional Crystalline Solar Light Bodies. Even though his carbon-based physical body had been brutalized and crucified, his 5th-Dimensional Crystalline Solar Light Bodies were pulsating with the vibrant health and physical perfection of his I AM Presence.

Forty days after Jesus' Resurrection into his 5th-Dimensional Crystalline Solar Light Bodies, he demonstrated what the next step of our Ascension process is going to be by publically Ascending up the Spiral of Evolution into the 5th-Dimensional Realms of Light. This is the same path that Humanity and Mother Earth are now in the process of completing as we move through the final stages of our Ascension onto the 5th-Dimensional New Earth.

Jesus knew that initially we would not comprehend the full meaning of what he was demonstrating through his Resurrection and Ascension. Nevertheless, he was determined to leave those archetypes so that, in Divine Timing, the Company of Heaven would be able to reveal to Humanity the true meaning of the Divine Alchemy we were destined to experience after the Shift of the Ages.

In the Resurrection and Ascension process we are now going through, we do not need to die in order to be Resurrected from our grossly contaminated carbon-based

Earthly Bodies. Our process is slower than what Jesus experienced because instead of one person Resurrecting their carbon-based bodies and Ascending into the 5th Dimension, this time every person on this planet and Mother Earth herself are going through this Divine Alchemy. That means quite literally that as we Resurrect our carbon-based bodies and Ascend into the 5th Dimension, we are taking Mother Earth and ALL Life evolving upon her with us. This is a tremendous responsibility for every Son and Daughter of God on Earth, but what a glorious opportunity for each and every one of us to be the Instruments of God we have been preparing to be for lifetimes.

Due to the urgent need of the hour, our Father-Mother God have granted the Angel of Resurrection permission to breathe unprecedented frequencies of the Mother of Pearl Resurrection Flame into our Planetary Grid of Transfiguring Divine Love. This monumental amplification of the Resurrection Flame will quicken the vibratory rate of Humanity's and Mother Earth's contaminated carbon-based cells. This will allow our I AM Presence and our Body Elemental to activate the Core of Purity in every atomic and subatomic particle and wave of our Earthly Bodies. Our Body Elemental will then cast the mutated substances contaminating our cells into the Violet Flame where they will be transmuted back into their original perfection. This will clear the way for each cell to be able to receive the full Divine Potential of God's 5th-Dimensional Crystalline Solar Light.

When we invoke and freely partake of the gifts and blessings of the Resurrection Flame, we avail ourselves of its restorative and rejuvenating power. By stating the following decree on a regular basis, each of us will greatly accelerate the Divine Alchemy taking place within our Earthly Bodies.

Please listen to your heart and recite this decree as often as you are inspired to do so. It is a Gift from On High that has been building in momentum for millennia,

I AM the Resurrection and the Life

"I AM the Resurrection and the Life of the Immaculate Concept of Humanity and Mother Earth now made manifest and sustained by Divine Grace."

"I AM the Resurrection and the Life of the Immaculate Concept of Humanity and Mother Earth now made manifest and sustained by Divine Grace."

"I AM the Resurrection and the Life of the Immaculate Concept of Humanity and Mother Earth now made manifest and sustained by Divine Grace."

And so it is.

Dear One, allow the Resurrection Flame to bless you, your Loved Ones, and all Life on Earth in miraculous ways.

56

Ressurecting the Immaculate Concept of Our Divine Missions

We are still in the full embrace of the tremendous influx of the Resurrection Flame that bathed the planet and all her Life during the Passover and Easter celebrations. In order to take full advantage of that resplendent Light our Father-Mother God have given us a message and an invocation that will help us use the Resurrection Flame to empower the Immaculate Concept of our Divine Missions. The first sharing is a quote our Father-Mother God have given to us that will reveal the Truth about YOU and every other Child of God.

Please breathe in deeply and go within to the Divinity of your Heart Flame as you read these words.

The Truth About YOU - A Quote from our Father-Mother God

"You are a precious and Beloved Child of God. Your unique Golden Thread of Life confirms your Divinity and reveals the reality that you are an essential part of Earth's

Ascension in the Light. This knowing will renew your faith in yourself and will remind you that you are a priceless Human Being. Once this realization truly registers in your heart and your conscious mind you will never again say, 'What good could I possibly achieve?' 'What value am I?' 'What difference will one soul make?' *You will recognize those words to be a sacrilege.*

"We are your Father-Mother God. We created you and we have chosen to express some beautiful manifestation of Life through you. You are destined to fulfill a portion of the glorious Divine Plan unfolding on Planet Earth. Now is the time for you to release the unique perfume and music of your Being to bless all Life. The purity of your individual fragrance and keynote is unlike any other ever released by the evolving Sons and Daughters of God. Something sacred is hidden within your Being that has never been known by another. It is an exquisite expression of Life which your I AM Presence alone can externalize. It is time for you to accept this Divine Truth. It is time for you to stand revealed as your mighty I AM Presence grown to full stature. And so it is."

Now Dear One, as we invoke this activity of Light on behalf of ourselves and all Humanity, please allow these words to resonate within the Flame of Truth in your heart.

I AM the Resurrection and the Life of the Immaculate Concept of My Divine Mission

I AM my I AM Presence and I AM One with the I AM Presence of ALL Humanity. What I invoke for myself, I invoke on behalf of every man, woman and child on Earth in perfect alignment with each person's Divine Plan and the highest good for all concerned. This is possible because WE ARE ONE and there is no separation.

I AM the Resurrection and the Life of the Immaculate Concept of my Divine Mission.

I AM the Resurrection and the Life of the Immaculate Concept of my Divine Mission.

I AM the Resurrection and the Life of the Immaculate Concept of my Divine Mission.

I open my heart and mind and I AM receptive to the Divine Directives of my Father-Mother God. In this state of Listening Grace, I AM able to "*hear with new ears and see with new eyes.*"

I AM experiencing a deep inner knowing, I now understand my mission with new clarity. There is an awakening taking place within my Heart Flame. I AM recognizing my responsibility for the conditions existing in my life and on Earth. I remember that through the Universal Law of the Circle, I AM a cocreator of the physical plane.

My thoughts, words, actions and feelings are projected onto the atomic substance of physical matter and they manifest in physical form. As my Life Force flows through me, it picks up the vibrations of my consciousness and then expresses those vibrations in visible form, experiences and circumstances. In other words, what I think about, what I put my feelings and energy into, I bring into form.

Because of the confusion I have experienced in the past, I have given power to physical matter. I have allowed the distorted manifestation of physical matter to become my reality, when, in Truth, it is only an illusion created by my beliefs, thoughts, words, actions and feelings. I now realize with my new level of understanding and clarity, that physical matter is nothing more than a mass of atomic energy controlled by my consciousness. Never does matter control consciousness.

My world reflects my human consciousness. In the past, I have set about trying to change the physical conditions in my world, instead of changing my consciousness. Those conditions are only the reflection of my consciousness. Trying to change physical conditions without changing my consciousness is like trying to change the reflection in a mirror without changing the object causing the reflection. It is a futile effort.

Now, I AM One with my I AM Presence. My consciousness is rising. My Transfiguration is occurring subtly and deeply at an atomic, cellular level. The seed of awareness is growing within me. It is blazing like a Sun and radiating forth Rays of Light. As this occurs, I begin to realize the Truth about me.

I came into this world with a very specific purpose. I came to fulfill a mission. I came to Love Life free and to realize the Truth about me. I came to assist with Humanity's and the Earth's Ascension in the Light.

I AM part of God and the fullness of my Father-Mother God abides in me. In the Mind of God, no one is useless or meaningless. Every single person is valuable and critically important to the balance and order of the Universe. I now know that without me God would be incomplete. Without me the Universe would lose its equilibrium.

All that I AM called to do I will do with happiness and enthusiasm for I now realize that nothing is too insignificant. I AM always embraced in my Father-Mother God's Love, and never again will there be a sense of futility in my life. I AM overflowing with Gratitude for the opportunity to be on Earth at this time. I AM so thankful to be where I AM right now serving all who come my way with Love, Joy, Understanding, Compassion and Forgiveness.

Now, recognizing my true worth, I go forth in deep humility to fulfill my Divine Mission. With my Inner Vision I see the all-encompassing Light of my I AM Presence freely flowing through me. With my physical sight I see the Divine Potential of God's Infinite Abundance and Eternal Peace manifesting everywhere. I AM filled with Divine Love and Infinite Gratitude for I remember who I AM.

I AM a Beloved Child of God and ALL that my Father-Mother God have is mine.

With this awareness now pulsating within my Heart Flame, my Father-Mother God are presenting me with brand new opportunities to be an Instrument of God. On this sacred and holy day, I make the heart commitment to listen for this inner guidance. Then, with the Divine Intervention of my I AM Presence and the assistance of the Company of Heaven, I will accept these opportunities, and I will fulfill my Divine Mission with Love and Abounding Joy.

And so it is.

Dear One, listen for your inner guidance and allow your I AM Presence to Resurrect the Immaculate Concept of your Divine Mission within your Heart Flame and your conscious mind.

57

CLARITY ABOUT OUR PHYSICAL TRANSFORMATION

Our Father-Mother God's newly implemented Divine Plan is creating unprecedented opportunities for our I AM Presence and our Body Elemental to greatly accelerate the Divine Alchemy taking place in our Earthly Bodies. The Company of Heaven is revealing new information and guiding us through activities of Light that have moved us into uncharted waters. They said that what is occurring on Earth at this time is actually a Gift of Divine Grace beyond the comprehension of our finite minds.

Never have such contaminated physical, etheric, mental and emotional bodies which are expressing the gross mutations of aging, degeneration, disease, decay and every other affliction been given the opportunity to be Transfigured into 5th-Dimensional Crystalline Solar Light Bodies through such an accelerated process of Divine Alchemy.

On a daily basis, every person's Lightwork is now being amplified a thousand fold through our newly empowered Planetary Grid of Transfiguring Divine Love. This is allowing Humanity's I AM Presence and our Body Elemental to receive higher frequencies of 5th-Dimensional Crystalline

Solar Light than we have ever been able to withstand at a cellular level.

This Light is disrupting the obsolete patterns of aging and disease that are recorded in our Etheric Body. It is also short circuiting the flawed messenger codes in our DNA that automatically accept these maladies as a normal part of our evolutionary process. In perfect alignment with our individual Divine Plans, our I AM Presence is recalibrating and bringing into balance the right and left hemispheres of our brain. The fragmented pathways that developed within our physical brain structures after our fall from Grace are being reconnected and restored to their original Divine Potential.

These changes are allowing our I AM Presence and our Body Elemental to increase the cellular frequency of our Earthly Bodies the maximum that we can safely withstand in every 24-hour period. This unprecedented increase of vibration into higher frequencies of Light is what is CAUSING the Divine Alchemy within our cells. Our cellular Transfiguration from carbon-based to crystalline-based cells is occurring within each of us at an astonishing pace. That is true even if we may not be able to perceive it in a tangible way just yet.

The reason the Beings of Light are sharing this information with us now is because people are beginning to feel sensations and unusual symptoms in their bodies that are different from anything they have experienced in the past. They are wondering if what they are feeling is related to the Divine Alchemy taking place within them, and they are curious about when they will see physical results in their Earthly Bodies.

The Beings of Light want us to understand that this is a very individual process. The experience for each and every one of us will be different. It is important for us to know this and to be aware of the bigger picture, so that we will not get distracted or discouraged by unrealistic expectations.

At any given moment our life experiences and our Earthly Bodies are reflecting the sum total of everything we have ever experienced through all time frames and dimensions. Every person's life path has been diverse and multifaceted. No two people have the exact same level of contamination or distortion reflecting at a cellular level in their Earthly Bodies. This means that the Divine Alchemy taking place within each and every one of us will manifest in our bodies in different ways and in Divine Timing.

We must remember that we are multidimensional Beings functioning in various dimensions and in various levels of consciousness simultaneously. From the perspective of the physical plane on Earth, we usually evaluate our reality through the concept of linear time and our five physical senses. If we cannot see it, touch it, hear it, taste it or smell it we have difficulty believing that it is real. This is a very limiting and inaccurate way of interpreting the progress of our physical transformation.

When we are willing to just accept at face value the physical appearances of what is happening in the outer world, we make a big mistake. The physical plane of Earth that we think of as being so real is actually *the least real* of all of the dimensions we abide in, and it is the *very last* dimension to reflect the changes we are cocreating with our Father-Mother God and the Company of Heaven.

Every time we invoke the Light of God through our I AM Presence with the intention of cocreating something we would like to manifest in our life, a matrix for what we are invoking is instantaneously formed in the Realms of Cause. This is where everything begins. After our matrix is formed, every time we focus our attention on what we want to create more Light flows into the matrix and it is intensified. Eventually, what we are cocreating reaches its full Divine Potential in the Realms of Cause. At that point, whatever we are cocreating is ready to be magnetized from the Realms of Cause into the world of effects which is the physical plane of Earth.

How long it takes for what we are cocreating to manifest in the physical plane is determined by several variables. It depends on what miscreations we are responsible for from the past that need to be transmuted into the Light before our cocreation can manifest. It also depends on how dedicated we are to magnetizing our cocreation into the world of form through our thoughts, feelings, words and actions.

So how does this information apply in regards to cocreating our 5th-Dimensional Crystalline Solar Light Bodies? Through the sharings from the Company of Heaven we know that *at some level* Divine Alchemy is already taking place within the Earthly Bodies of every person on the planet. That level is being determined by several things. How awake is the person? How contaminated are their Earthly Bodies? Are they consciously participating in this process with their I AM Presence, their Body Elemental and the Company of Heaven?

The Company of Heaven wants us to know that during this critical moment in Earth's Ascension process they have been given permission to assist each and every one of us the maximum that Cosmic Law will allow. All we have to do is align with our I AM Presence and our Body Elemental and ask for the Company of Heaven's Divine Intervention. That is as simple as saying,

"I AM my I AM Presence and I AM One with my Body Elemental. Together, we invoke the maximum assistance from the Company of Heaven that Cosmic Law will allow."

Instead of getting too caught up in outer world appearances, it will be much easier if we just *"keep on keeping on"* with the inner knowing that these changes will manifest in perfect Divine Order the moment we reach a critical mass of the higher frequencies of our Solar Light Bodies.

Through our Weekly Vlogs, our Father-Mother God and the Company of Heaven are giving us incredibly powerful activities of Light. These Gifts from On High are specifically designed to intensify the matrixes for our 5th-Dimensional Crystalline Solar Light Bodies which have already been birthed in the Realms of Cause.

If we consecrate our Life Force to being the Open Door for these activities of Light, and regularly participate in them on behalf of ourselves, our loved ones, Humanity and Mother Earth, we will greatly accelerate the Divine Alchemy taking place at a cellular level. Then, the physical manifestation of our Solar Light Bodies will occur much sooner than we can imagine. So stay focused on the process and you will create miracles.

58

ACTIVATING NEW
STRANDS OF DNA

The Beings of Light in the Realms of Illumined Truth are revealing to us at this time that our Father-Mother God's newly implemented Divine Plan is succeeding in ways beyond what we ever imagined. The fact that every person's Lightwork is being amplified one thousand fold every single day has created new opportunities for our I AM Presence and our Body Elemental to assist us. This greatly amplified influx of Light is enhancing our Body Elemental's ability to reverse some of the most adverse consequences of our fall from Grace.

Prior to the fall, we had twelve strands of DNA that functioned like a very elaborate fiber-optic communication system. These strands of DNA kept us connected with our I AM Presence and the multidimensional aspects of our own Divinity. They also allowed us very clear open heart and mind telepathic communication with our Father-Mother God and the Company of Heaven.

Once we began misqualifying our Life Force by expressing thoughts and feelings that were not based in Love, our DNA dramatically changed. As we fell into denser and denser frequencies of our own misqualified thoughts, feelings, words and actions our twelve strands of DNA began to short circuit and become fragmented. Over time, they deteriorated into a single double helix or the two strands of DNA that our scientists have now discovered.

Our original twelve strands of DNA contained genetic codes and information regarding the multidimensional aspects of who we are as Sons and Daughters of God. What our scientists have discovered within the fragmented strands of our double helix DNA is only a miniscule fraction of the knowledge that will be available to us once again when our twelve strands of DNA are restored to their original capacity and Divine Intent.

When we study what is now known about the genome and genetic codes science is researching in our two strands of DNA, it seems as though there is a lot of information. But amazingly, at one point scientists stated that 98.8% of Humanity's double helix DNA is "*junk DNA*." This simply means that science does not have a clue what the purpose is of that additional DNA. God is incredibly practical and nothing in our Earthly Bodies exists without a purpose. There is no such thing as "*junk DNA*", only DNA that we do not yet understand.

Now, with every person's Lightwork being expanded one thousand fold every day, our I AM Presence is able to integrate into our Earthly Bodies more effectively. This is happening for everyone to some degree, even if the person does not consider what they are doing to be Lightwork. Lightwork is anything we do that adds to the Light of the world. For example, loving someone, giving someone a helping hand, admiring a beautiful sunset, fixing a healthy meal for our family, listening to beautiful music, being compassionate and forgiving, connecting with the Elemental

Kingdom in a loving way, doing our job with the highest level of integrity, honoring our Earthly Bodies and respecting Mother Earth. All of these things add to the Light of the world.

The great amplification of Light we are experiencing through the implementation of our Father-Mother God's new Divine Plan is allowing our I AM Presence to recalibrate and bring into balance the right and left hemispheres of our brain. This is allowing the fragmented pathways within our physical brain structures to be reconnected.

Once these pathways are reconnected, our spiritual brain centers which consist of our pineal gland, our pituitary gland, our hypothalamus gland and the ganglionic centers at the base of our brain will be activated and restored to their full Divine Potential. When these centers within our brain are fully reactivated, our Body Elemental will be able to use the amplified Light flowing through our Grid of Transfiguring Divine Love to restore the fragmented connections within our twelve original strands of DNA.

The Company of Heaven wants us to know that at this time the Earth and Humanity are receiving unprecedented assistance from the Solar Logos in our Solar System. This Divine Intervention has been manifesting for the past several weeks in the form of extremely powerful shifts in Earth's magnetic field. This is being caused by powerful streams of Solar Wind being ejected from the Sun. These streams of Solar Wind are opening portals in Earth's magnetic field that are allowing us to receive higher frequencies of 5th-Dimensional Crystalline Solar Light.

Magnetic shifts of this nature alter our personal energy field and dramatically affect our Mental Body and our physical brain structure. When our magnetic field shifts in this way obsolete crystallized patterns are shattered. Things recorded in our Etheric Body that have been hidden from us are pushed to the surface to be cleared. This allows our I AM Presence and our Body Elemental to remove blocks that have been preventing us from moving forward in the Light.

This Divine Intervention from the Solar Logos in our Solar System is designed to accelerate the reactivation of our spiritual brain centers, so that we can restore the twelve fragmented strands of our DNA. This will be a giant step forward in paving the way for the Lightwork we are being asked to do on behalf of the Millennials and the children during the 32nd Annual World Congress on Illumination which will be held in Honolulu, Hawaii, August 11–16, 2018.

This is a global activity of Light during which the Light of God will flow to activate the *consciousness codes* within the DNA of the Millennials and the children. These are specific DNA codes designed to help these precious Ones remember the training they received prior to embodiment on Earth. This training contains facets of the Divine Plan that will assist Humanity and Mother Earth through the final stages of our Ascension into the 5th-Dimensional frequencies of the New Earth.

With the assistance we are receiving from our Solar Logos and the amplification of Light flowing through our Planetary Grid of Transfiguring Divine Love, the Company of Heaven said the potential of restoring all twelve strands of our fragmented DNA is more possible than ever before. And they are committed, week by week, to helping us accomplish that facet of the Divine Plan.

Scientists used to think of our DNA as being stagnant and fixed in a particular pattern. Now we know that our DNA is a shimmering waveform configuration that is now being modified by God's Light, solar radiation, magnetic fields, sonic impulses, thoughtforms and emotions associated with the newly encoded archetypes and with the Divine Matrix for our 5th-Dimensional Crystalline Solar Light Bodies and the New Earth. These patterns are now pulsating within the mental and emotional strata of Mother Earth awaiting the opportunity to tangibly manifest in the lives of awakening Humanity.

During this Cosmic Moment, our I AM Presence and our Body Elemental are working with the Company of Heaven to restore the genetic codes that were originally imprinted within the RNA and DNA structures in our twelve strands of DNA. These patterns are igniting every cell in our Earthly Bodies as we are lifted into alignment with the 5th-Dimensional frequencies of the New Earth. The 5th-Dimensional Crystalline patterns of our Solar Light Bodies are now flowing through our Heart Flames and being secured within the nucleus of every atomic and sub-atomic particle and wave of our physical, etheric, mental and emotional Earthly Bodies.

In Divine Timing, as our twelve strands of DNA are restored to their original Divine Potential, a reactivation and initiation into multifaceted awareness will occur within every person on Earth. We will then have the ability to step through the doorway into multidimensional realities. Each and every one of us will then be empowered with even more rarified frequencies of our own Divinity. In this Realm, we will recognize and be willing to release and let go of attachments and behavior patterns that do not support our highest good and the Immaculate Concept of our Divine Potential as Sons and Daughters of God.

Dear One, please contemplate this important information. Ask your I AM Presence and your Body Elemental to help you grasp the magnitude of what restoring our twelve strands of DNA will mean for you, the Millennials, the children and every other person on Earth.

59

OUR BODY ELEMENTAL
IS INITIATED INTO THE
5TH DIMENSION

Through the unified efforts of Heaven and Earth this year, a Divine Plan is unfolding that is resulting in opportunities beyond our greatest expectations. Every single day through our Planetary Grid of Transfiguring Divine Love every person's Lightwork is being amplified one thousand fold. When we were originally told that our unified efforts would result in that amazing amplification of Light, we knew it would be wonderful, but I don't think we realized the awesome amount of Lightwork awakening Humanity is doing every day.

Now it is clear what the prophets and seers of ancient times meant when they said Humanity's transformation in these latter days would take place *"in the twinkling of an eye."* The amount of Light that is now bathing the Earth every day is pushing literally hundreds of lifetimes worth of Humanity's human miscreations to the surface to be transmuted back into their original perfection. This critical purging process is allowing every person's I AM Presence and their Body Elemental to raise the frequency of vibration within their Earthly Bodies faster than previously expected.

This year, step by step, the Company of Heaven is guiding us through celestial opportunities and activities of Light that will help you and me and the Millennials and the children, as well as every other person on Earth to transcend our contaminated 3rd- and 4th-Dimensional carbon-based Earthly Bodies. This will pave the way for the tangible manifestation of our 5th-Dimensional Crystalline-based Solar Light Bodies. It will also create the sacred space so that the I AM Presences of the Millennials and the children will be able to activate the *consciousness codes* within their DNA. This vitally important facet of the unfolding Divine Plan will also help Mother Earth to transcend the atrocities Humanity has inflicted upon her.

What the Company of Heaven is revealing to us today is that the success of the activities of Light awakening Humanity has participated in so far this year has cleared the way for our Body Elementals to Ascend into the full embrace of the 5th Dimension. This is a miracle that even our I AM Presence and the Company of Heaven thought would occur much farther down the road.

Since our fall from Grace, these selfless Elemental Beings have loyally stuck with us through every trial and tribulation. They have fulfilled their mission of outpicturing our thoughts and feelings in our Earthly Bodies no matter how distorted or painful that may be. Since the birth of the New Earth in December 2012, they have been functioning in both worlds. They have outpictured the mutated frequencies of the old Earth and our carbon-based bodies while simultaneously helping us cocreate the pristine frequencies of our 5th-Dimensional Crystalline Solar Light Bodies.

Our Father-Mother God have revealed that with the reactivation of Humanity's Elemental Vortices, and the initial impulse of the splicing and restoration of our twelve solar strands of DNA, the collective body of Humanity has reached a critical mass of vibration that will enable our Body Elementals to be permanently initiated into the frequencies of the 5th Dimension. They will still maintain whatever assistance we need with the residue of our carbon-based bodies, but they will never again have to be immersed in the quagmire of the 3rd and 4th Dimensions.

Today the Mighty Elohim and the Directors of the Elements will guide the I AM Presence of every man, woman and child on Earth through an activity of Light that will initiate each person's Body Elemental into the 5th Dimension. We are being asked to be the Open Door for this activity of Light. If you have the Heart Call to participate in this wondrous Gift to Humanity's Body Elementals please join with me and the entire Company of Heaven now.

The Initiation of Humanity's Body Elementals

I AM my I AM Presence and I AM One with the I AM Presence of every man, woman, and child evolving on this planet. I AM One with my Father-Mother God, I AM One with the Solar Logos from Suns beyond Suns beyond Suns, I AM One with the Company of Heaven, and I AM One with the Mighty Elohim, the Directors of the Elemental Kingdom and all of the Beings associated with the Elemental Kingdom and the Angelic Kingdom.

I AM One with every electron of precious Life energy evolving on this planet, and I AM One with every atomic and subatomic particle and wave of energy comprising the physical, etheric, mental, and emotional bodies of Humanity and Mother Earth. I AM also One with all of the spaces in between the atomic and subatomic particles and waves of energy on Earth.

Through the Divine Intervention of this collective Body of Light Beings, I invoke the most intensified frequencies of 5th-Dimensional Crystalline Solar Light from the very Core of Creation that Humanity and the Earth are capable of receiving at this time. I ask that this Crystalline Solar Light accelerates the maximum that Cosmic Law will allow the Divine Alchemy that is transforming the carbon-based bodies of Humanity and Mother Earth into 5th-Dimensional Crystalline Solar Light Bodies.

On this sacred and holy day, I consecrate my physical, etheric, mental, and emotional bodies to be the Open Door for the 5th-Dimensional Crystalline Solar Light that will permanently initiate the Body Elemental of every person on Earth into the 5th-Dimensional Realms of Light.

Now, under the direction of our Father-Mother God, the Mighty Elohim invoke the 5th-Dimensional Directors of the Elements to take their strategic positions in preparation for Humanity's Body Elemental's initiation into the 5th Dimension.

- Thor and Aries, the Directors of the Air Element and the Sylphs of the Air take their positions at the cardinal point to the North.
- Neptune and Lunara, the Directors of the Water Element and the Undines of the Water take their positions at the cardinal point to the East.
- Virgo and Pelleur, the Directors of the Earth Element and the Nature Spirits of the Earth take their positions at the cardinal point to the South.
- Helios and Vesta, the Directors of the Fire Element and the Salamanders of the Fire take their positions at the cardinal point to the West.

- Amaryllis and Aeolos, the Directors of the Ether Element and the Devas and Deva Rajas of the Ethers take their positions within the Sun of Even Pressure in the Center of the Earth.

Now, as One Breath, One Heartbeat, One Voice, and One Energy, Vibration, and Consciousness of pure Divine Love, the Directors of the Elements sound a Cosmic Tone signaling to Humanity's Body Elementals that the time has come to reverse the adverse effects of Humanity's fall from Grace. It is, at long last, time to reclaim the original Divine Plan of outpicturing the perfection that is pulsating within the 5th-Dimensional Crystalline Solar Light Bodies of Humanity's I AM Presence.

Every person's Body Elemental responds with deep gratitude and an exceptional willingness to transform the maladies that they were forced to create in our physical, etheric, mental, and emotional bodies after the fall. With elation and abounding joy, Humanity's Body Elementals accept the opportunity to Transfigure our bodies into the limitless perfection of 5th-Dimensional Crystalline Solar Light Bodies.

The Mighty Elohim are placing new Solar Record Keeper Crystals in Mother Earth's Crystal Grid System. Humanity's pineal glands are being adjusted by our I AM Presence to safely receive more 5th-Dimensional Crystalline Solar Light. The Directors of the Elements now ask the Mighty Elohim to empower Humanity's Body Elementals with the ability to assimilate and integrate these higher frequencies of 5th-Dimensional Crystalline Solar Light.

The Mighty Elohim respond and every person's Body Elemental is initiated into higher frequencies of the 5th Dimension. Once the initiation is complete, the Elohim invest every person's Body Elemental with new skills and abilities that will enable them to accelerate the Divine Alchemy taking place within Humanity's Earthly Bodies. This means our Body Elemental has graduated into a 5th-Dimentional Elemental Being. This will expedite our transformation into our Crystalline Solar Light Bodies.

My I AM Presence and the I AM Presence of every person on Earth now join in harmony with our newly initiated 5th-Dimensional Body Elemental. Together we begin the process of cocreating the final stages of Earth's Ascension into the 5th-Dimensional frequencies of the New Earth.

And so it is.

Dear Heart, focus on your newly empowered 5th-Dimensional Body Elemental. Observe how your I AM Presence and your Body Elemental are working together to accelerate the Divine Alchemy taking place in your Earthly Bodies.

60

THE MYSTICAL MONTH OF MAY

In the Heavenly Realms the month of May is considered a very spiritual and powerful time for Planet Earth. The Company of Heaven refers to May as "*the Mystical Month of May*" because of various activities of Light that take place during this time of year. These activities are orchestrated through the selfless Divine Intervention of both Saint Germain and Mother Mary. This year, because of the initiation of our Father-Mother God's new Divine Plan and our greatly empowered Planetary Grid of Transfiguring Divine Love, we have an extraordinary opportunity to utilize the Gifts being given to us by Saint Germain and Mother Mary.

The first of May is celebrated as Saint Germain's Ascension Day. Every year on the first of May Saint Germain, who is known through all Creation as the Keeper of the Violet Flame, blesses the Earth and all Life evolving upon her with an ever increasing influx of the Violet Flame of God's Infinite Perfection.

Because of the monumental changes taking place within our Earthly Bodies this year, due to the activation of Humanity's Elemental Vortices and the beginning of the process of splicing our 12 strands of DNA, Saint Germain is able to bless us with more intensified frequencies of the

Violet Flame than Humanity has ever been able to safely receive at a cellular level. This influx of Light is the highest frequency of the 5th-Dimensional Crystalline Solar Violet Flame of God's Infinite Perfection that Mother Earth or Humanity has ever known. This unfathomable Light is providing Humanity's newly initiated 5th-Dimensional Body Elemental and our I AM Presence with an unprecedented opportunity.

The Company of Heaven is revealing that with the influx of Light now bathing the Earth every day through our Father-Mother God's newly initiated Divine Plan, we have reached a frequency of vibration that will allow our I AM Presence and our 5th-Dimensional Body Elemental to accelerate the purging of the contaminated substances in our Earthly Bodies, and the Bodies of Mother Earth.

With the cooperation of our I AM Presence and the I AM Presence of every person on Earth, Saint Germain and his Legions of Violet Fire Angels will work to purge the toxic substances that have overwhelmed and contaminated Humanity's and Mother Earth's Bodies since our fall from Grace.

During this "*Mystical Month of May*", Saint Germain will bathe the Earth and all her Life with this new frequency of the Violet Flame for much longer than just one day. This year, Saint Germain and his Legions of Violet Fire Angels will blaze the most intensified frequencies of the Violet Flame that Cosmic Law will allow through every particle and wave of Life on Earth for an extended period of time.

Every single person on this planet and Mother Earth herself will be blessed daily with this intensified frequency of the Violet Flame until the *consciousness codes* of the Millennials and the children are God Victoriously activated. This will take place during the 32th Annual World

Congress on Illumination, August 11–16, 2018. After that global gathering, Saint Germain will evaluate our progress and determine how much longer Humanity and the Earth need to receive this particular assistance.

Beginning today, May 1, 2018, this colossal influx of the 5th-Dimensional Crystalline Solar Violet Flame of God's Infinite Perfection will flow through our Planetary Grid of Transfiguring Divine Love. As this Sacred Fire bathes the Earth day by day, it will be amplified one thousand fold through the Lightwork of every man, woman and child. This will give the I AM Presences and the Body Elementals of the Millennials, the children and the rest of Humanity, the opportunity to purge our Earthly Bodies from the humanly created toxic substances and the gross contaminations that have polluted the air we breathe, the food we eat and the water we drink since our fall from Grace.

This intensified purging will occur for each person in Divine Order and in perfect alignment with their Divine Plan. As usual, this will be a very individual process. The Company of Heaven has assured us, however, that every single person will greatly benefit from this Gift from On High if we will just take a moment everyday to consciously invoke the Violet Flame.

Saint Germain said the Violet Flame Mantra that he gave to Humanity decades ago has been building in momentum. It is now incredibly powerful and will help us to receive and assimilate the full benefit from this Gift of the Violet Flame. Please listen to your heart and repeat this mantra throughout the day as often as you are inspired to do so. It is very easy to memorize.

Begin the mantra by saying, *"I AM my I AM Presence and I AM One with the I AM Presence of all Humanity."* Then repeat the mantra three times.

Violet Flame Mantra

Transmute, transmute by the Violet Fire all causes and cores not of God's desire. I AM a Being of Cause alone; that Cause is Love, the Sacred Tone.

Transmute, transmute by the Violet Fire all causes and cores not of God's desire. I AM a Being of Cause alone; that Cause is Love, the Sacred Tone.

Transmute, transmute by the Violet Fire all causes and cores not of God's desire. I AM a Being of Cause alone; that Cause is Love, the Sacred Tone.

Precious Heart, this frequency of the Violet Flame is powerful beyond what we are able to perceive with our finite minds. Please Trust your I AM Presence. This aspect of your own Divinity knows exactly how powerful this Violet Flame is and how much it will help you to purge the contamination in your Earthly Bodies. So listen to your heart and respond to your intuitive promptings to repeat this Violet Flame Mantra.

Dear One, in the next sharing Mother Mary will tell us what her vitally important contribution to the *Mystical Month of May* will be at this time.

61

MOTHER MARY AND THE
MYSTICAL MONTH OF MAY

The Company of Heaven is sharing information about who Mother Mary actually is and the selfless service she is rendering to each and every person on Earth during this auspicious time. This information may seem new to you, but it is not. Every Child of God evolving on this planet has a very personal and sacred relationship with Mother Mary. This is because of her dedication to holding the Immaculate Concept for each and every one of us to fulfill our Divine Plan. This is true regardless of what your spiritual or lack of spiritual affiliation may be, or how oblivious you are on a conscious level of Mother Mary and her service to Life.

Our Father-Mother God said it is time for this information to be revealed to the masses of Humanity, so every person will have the opportunity to comprehend the magnitude of this moment. Our God Parents issued this Divine Edict because of the urgency of the hour and the importance of the Gift Mother Mary is giving to Humanity during this *Mystical Month of May.*

The Cosmic Being of Light we know as Mother Mary is a Universal exponent of our Mother God and the Divine

Feminine. She has consecrated her Life Force to holding the *Immaculate Concept* for the return of our Mother God and for the restoration and the expansion of the Immortal Victorious Threefold Flame within the heart of every Son and Daughter of God evolving on Earth. This Threefold Flame is the Divinity within every person's heart which was tragically diminished after our fall from Grace.

In the beginning, the Masculine Polarity of our Father God blazed into our left-brain hemisphere activating our rational, logical mind. It then awakened the Power Center of our Throat Chakra and was anchored in the Permanent Seed Atom in our heart as a beautiful Blue Flame of Divine Power. Next, the Feminine Polarity of our Mother God blazed into our right-brain hemisphere activating our creative, intuitive mind. It then awakened the Love Center of our Heart Chakra and was anchored in the Permanent Seed Atom in our heart as a beautiful Pink Flame of Divine Love.

When the Masculine Power of our Father God and the Feminine Love of our Mother God were balanced in the right and left hemispheres of our brain and the Permanent Seed Atom in our heart, the Blue and Pink Flames merged forming the Violet Flame of God's Infinite Perfection. Our Father-Mother God's Violet Flame then activated our spiritual brain centers which consist of our pineal, pituitary and hypothalamus glands and the ganglionic centers at the base of our brain.

Once our brain centers were activated, our Crown Chakra opened to full breadth birthing us into the Enlightened state of Christ Consciousness. This was the original state of awareness we experienced as Sons and Daughters of God. Once our Crown Chakra was opened, the Yellow-gold Flame of Christ Consciousness representing the Wisdom of the Sons and Daughters of God blazed from the Heart of God, through our Crown Chakra, and was anchored in the Permanent Seed Atom in our Heart. This activity of Light completed the formation of the Immortal Victorious Threefold Flame pulsating in every person's heart.

This Sacred Flame is a reflection of the Holy Trinity. The Blue Flame of our Father God's Power, the Pink Flame of our Mother God's Love and the Yellow-gold Flame of the Son and Daughter of God's Wisdom is the Divinity within every person's heart. Our Heart Flame is also the sacred space being referred to in the pronouncement, *"seek ye first the Kingdom of Heaven within and all else will be revealed to you."* It is through the Threefold Flame in our heart that our I AM Presence and the Light of God enter the world of form.

Prior to our fall from Grace, the Light of our Threefold Flame literally enveloped our four Earthly Bodies. At that time, the Light of God flowing through our Heart Flame was a tremendous shaft of Light. Every day through our creative faculties of thought and feeling and our free will choices, we decided how we would use this tremendous influx of Light from our Father-Mother God to add to the Light of the world.

Once we made the fateful decision to use our Father-Mother God's Light in ways that were not based in Love, everything changed. We began experiencing the painful results of our human miscreations. In a futile attempt to stop the pain, we closed our Heart Chakra blocking the portal through which our Mother God entered the physical plane. This forced our Mother God to withdraw her Light which greatly diminished the Pink Flame of Love in our heart. This tragic event caused our right brain to become almost dormant and our spiritual brain centers to atrophy.

Once that occurred, our Mother God was barely able to project enough of her Light through our right brain to sustain consciousness. In our Heart Flame our Father God's Power was no longer balanced with our Mother God's Love. This caused our Crown Chakra to close which, in turn, caused us to lose the Enlightened state of Christ Consciousness. We also lost the ability to communicate with our I AM Presence and the Company of Heaven. These tragic events catapulted us into the abyss of separation and duality.

In a merciful effort to prevent us from being totally over-whelmed by our human miscreations, our Father-Mother God issued a Divine Fiat for our I AM Presence to reduce the amount of Light flowing through our Heart Flame. In response, our I AM Presence withdrew our unbalanced Immortal Victorious Threefold Flame into the Permanent Seed Atom in our heart. Our Threefold Flame which origi-nally enveloped our four Earthly Bodies was reduced to what we now refer to as the "*spark*" of Divinity in our heart. The mighty shaft of Light that originally flowed through our Heart Flame was reduced to what we now refer to as our "*silver cord.*"

When Mother Mary realized the immensity of the situ-ation we had inadvertently created, she knew that the pos-sibility of Humanity fulfilling the Immaculate Concept of our Divine Potential as Sons and Daughters of God was in jeopardy. Mother Mary understood that without our Mother God's Love our right brain could not be restored to its full capacity and our spiritual brain centers would remain atro-phied. She also knew that without the Masculine Polarity of our Father God and the Feminine Polarity of our Mother God being balanced within our Heart Flame, we would not be able to return to Christ Consciousness. Mother Mary was also aware of the profound Truth that returning to Christ Consciousness is the *only* way that we can complete our jour-ney back to the Heart of our Father-Mother God.

With this knowing, Mother Mary appealed to our Father-Mother God for permission to initiate a Divine Plan that would hopefully prevent our Heart Flame from diminishing to the point where it could no longer sustain our existence on Earth. This selfless offering of unparalleled Divine Intervention was welcomed by our Father-Mother God. Mother Mary's Divine Plan received the blessings and the Divine Assistance of both our God Parents and the Company of Heaven.

Mother Mary's Divine Plan

Aeons ago, long before the Piscean Age, as the Sons and Daughters of God were spiraling into the abyss of separation and duality, Mother Mary initiated her Divine Plan. She invoked the Mighty Elohim to create a Heavenly Retreat where she could assist the I AM Presence of every person on Earth to restore their Immortal Victorious Threefold Flame to its original Divine Potential. She knew that this would assure the return of our Mother God and Humanity's return to Christ Consciousness.

In response to Mother Mary's request, the Elohim manifested in the Heavenly Realms an exquisite Crystalline Temple of Light. This Temple is known throughout the Universe as *Mother Mary's Temple of the Immaculate Heart.* The Sacred Fire that blazes on the altar of this Temple is the *Flame of the Immaculate Concept* which is a Crystalline White Flame with a Madonna Blue radiance.

Since that time aeons ago, every year for the entire month of May, Mother Mary magnetizes the I AM Presence of every person on Earth into her Temple of the Immaculate Heart for an activity of Light. This activity is designed to gradually restore the Immaculate Concept and the perfect balance within each person's Threefold Flame. We are multidimensional Beings and this event occurs in our finer body as we sleep at night.

The Company of Heaven said every single person's I AM Presence responds to Mother Mary's Clarion Call each May. This is because they realize how vital this annual activity of Light is in order for our Heart Flames to be balanced, so that the Light of our Mother God can return to Earth.

During the Month of May, Mother Mary and our I AM Presence work together to restore the balance within our Heart Flame. Progress is definitely being made, but because of the gross contamination within Humanity's Earthly Bodies, it has been much slower than Mother Mary anticipated. This year, however, due to the tremendous shifts of energy, vibration and consciousness that are taking place within Humanity's Earthly Bodies, things are different.

Saint Germain is blessing us with an unprecedented influx of the 5th-Dimensional Crystalline Solar Violet Flame of God's Infinite Perfection. This Sacred Fire is purging the contaminated substances within our physical, etheric, mental and emotional bodies in ways we have not previously experienced. This activity of Light is being coordinated with the events taking place in Mother Mary's Temple of the Immaculate Heart.

Mother Mary and Saint Germain are old friends who have worked in tandem for millennia to assist Humanity in the process of returning to Christ Consciousness. He volunteered to embody with Mother Mary during the inception of the Piscean Age in order to assist Jesus and Mary Magdalene to fulfill the Immaculate Concept of their Divine Missions. Saint Germain was Joseph, Mother Mary's husband, in that embodiment. What Mother Mary and Saint Germain did for Jesus and Mary Magdalene in the Piscean Age they are now doing for all Humanity during the inception of the Aquarian Age which we have now entered.

This month, as the contamination in our Earthly Bodies is being purged, Mother Mary is working with each person's I AM Presence and Body Elemental to expand the Permanent Seed Atom in our heart. The Divine Intent of this activity of Light is to transform every person's Permanent Seed Atom into a greatly empowered Chalice of Light that will be able to sustain higher frequencies of the Threefold Flame than we have ever known. This is something Mother Mary has been working toward for a very long time. Now, to the elation of our Father-Mother God this facet of Mother Mary's assistance will be God Victoriously Accomplished this month.

Precious Heart, open your heart and mind and pay attention. Mother Mary is encouraging us to ask our I AM Presence to take us to her Temple of the Immaculate Heart when we meditate and when we go to sleep at night. This will help us to participate on a more conscious level in this process. We can also ask our I AM Presence to help us bring back in the morning the memory of what we experienced in Mother Mary's Temple.

62

A Blessing for Humanity from Mother Mary

The Company of Heaven has been sharing important information with us about the assistance Saint Germain and Mother Mary are giving to Humanity at this time. Now they will share another facet of Mother Mary's service to all of us. This involves what happens once our Father-Mother God have given us permission to embody or re-embody on Earth.

From the time Mother Mary initiated her Divine Plan to help the I AM Presence of every person on Earth restore the balance within our Threefold Flame so that our Mother God could return and we would once again be able to return to Christ Consciousness, she has been rendering another very important service to the incoming children.

On May 1st every year, Mother Mary magnetizes into her Temple of the Immaculate Heart the I AM Presence of every Son and Daughter of God who will be conceived from May 1st that year through April 30th the following year. The first thing Mother Mary does when these precious Ones arrive is to help their I AM Presence select the electrons that will form the Permanent Seed Atom in their heart. These electrons are chosen from the very highest frequencies of electronic Light that these Children of God are capable of sustaining. Mother Mary's Intervention in this way assures that their vitally important Permanent Seed Atom will be able to sustain their Immortal Victorious Threefold Flame in the physical plane of Earth.

Since Mother Mary has been rendering this service to Humanity, our Threefold Flame has not deteriorated any further than the initial stages of our fall from Grace. This is true regardless of how far a person descended into the chaos of separation and duality. The Company of Heaven revealed that without Mother Mary's Divine Intervention and her steadfast determination to hold the Immaculate Concept for the return of our Mother God and Humanity's return to Christ Consciousness, the potential of Earth making it through the Shift of the Ages would have been non-existent.

As the contamination within Humanity's Earthly Bodies is being purged with Saint Germain's Gift of the Violet Flame, Mother Mary is initiating another facet of her Divine Plan. Because of the shifts that have taken place within Humanity's Earthly Bodies during the last few months, Mother Mary is now able to work with our I AM Presence and our 5th-Dimensional Body Elemental to expand the Permanent Seed Atom within our heart.

The Divine Intent of this activity of Light is to transform every person's Permanent Seed Atom into a Chalice of Light that will be able to sustain a balanced and greatly intensified Threefold Flame. This is something for which Mother Mary has been holding the Immaculate Concept for a very, very long time. The Company of Heaven said this is going to benefit all of us in wondrous ways, especially the Millennials and the children.

Transforming the Permanent Seed Atom in Every Person's Heart

Dear One, enter the Divinity of your Heart Flame and listen to these words through the Flame of Illumined Truth pulsating within you as they are revealed to us by Mother Mary.

This year, as we enter the Temple of the Immaculate Heart during the month of May, Beloved Mother Mary will embrace each of us in her Loving arms. As she does, she will awaken within us the remembrance of our sojourn in her Temple prior to this embodiment. She will remind us of the Vow she took to come and assist us at this time during the fulfillment of our missions.

Mother Mary will affirm that we came to Earth during this critical time in Earth's Ascension process with but one desire, to do God's Will. She will help us understand that we volunteered to be powerful Instruments of God during this Cosmic Moment, and that we have been training for aeons of time for this mission. She will also help us remember that we promised to be the full manifestation of Divine Love while serving the Earth and ALL her Life in this embodiment.

With Mother Mary's assistance, we will remember that we chose to bring a portion of the Divine Plan encoded within our Heart Flame through the veil of physical birth. She will also help us to remember the capacity we have to fulfill our Divine Purpose with integrity, dignity, honor and victory.

During the holy month of May, Mother Mary will assist our I AM Presence to expand our Permanent Seed Atom into a Chalice of Light that will hold a greatly intensified and balanced Threefold Flame. When this is complete, our I AM Presence will be able to expand our balanced Immortal Victorious Threefold Flame until it once again envelops our Earthly Bodies.

When the Divinity of our Heart Flame expands to that level, we will become aware of the Presence of God in every cell and atom of our Beings. This will pave the way for the integration of our 5th-Dimensional Crystalline Solar Light Bodies into our physical, etheric, mental and emotional bodies. This is a miraculous process of Divine Alchemy that has been unfolding for a time now. However, during this Mystical Month of May, this process will move forward a quantum leap.

Functioning within the frequencies of our Solar Light Bodies, we will be able to consciously magnify the Divinity within ourselves and all Life until our up-reaching consciousness conducts the patterns of perfection for the New Earth into the world of form.

All of the blessings we are receiving during this *Mystical Month of May* are further preparing the Millennials and the children for the activation of their *consciousness codes* which will take place August 11–16, 2018. Precious Heart, if you are interested in being physically present to serve as an Instrument of God on behalf of the Millennials and the children during the 32nd Annual World Congress on Illumination in Honolulu, Hawaii, August 11–16, 2018, all of the information you need to participate is available on our website www.eraofpeace.org.

Remain centered in your Heart Flame and stay focused on the Gifts Saint Germain and Mother Mary are giving to all of us.

63

Healing Our Contaminated Bodies With the Violet Flame

Saint Germain and his Violet Fire Angels have been working with our I AM Presence and our 5th-Dimentional Body Elemental to help us purge the toxic substances contaminating our Earthly Bodies. During this activity of Light, they are going to take this purging to the next level by guiding us through a powerful Healing that will utilize not only the *5th-Dimensional Crystalline Solar Violet Flame of God's Infinite Perfection*, but also the *Flame of Healing Through the Power of Transmutation.*

This is an exquisite Emerald Green Flame with a Violet Flame radiance that is the most powerful frequency of Healing available to Humanity. If you feel the Heart Call to participate in this Healing Gift from our Father-Mother God, please go within and follow me through this activity of Light with the full power of your attention and your Divine Intentions. And we begin.

Healing Visualization

I AM sitting comfortably in my chair with my spine as straight as possible and my arms and legs uncrossed. This allows me to be an open conduit for the 5th-Dimensional Crystalline Solar Violet Flame of God's Infinite Perfection and the Emerald Green and Violet Flame of Healing Through the Power of Transmutation. I breathe in and out deeply and rhythmically as I completely relax.

I AM my I AM Presence and I AM One with the I AM Presence of every man, woman and child on Earth. What I invoke for myself this sacred and holy day I invoke for all Humanity in perfect alignment with each person's Divine Plan and the highest good for all concerned.

My I AM Presence and my 5th-Dimensional Body Elemental now take command of my Earthly Bodies. Any tension, doubt or fear I have just drops away. This is a very special time just for me, and anything that I need to take care of will be waiting for me when I am through, so for the time being I just let it go.

During this activity of Light, I AM magnetizing into my Heart Flame the most intensified frequencies of the Violet and Emerald Green Flames of Healing that I am capable of receiving from the very Heart of my Father-Mother God. Under the direction of my I AM Presence and my 5th-Dimemsional Body Elemental these Sacred Flames begin to expand into every atomic and subatomic particle and wave of my physical, etheric, mental and emotional bodies. The Emerald Green and Violet Flames penetrate into the core of purity in every cell and organ of my physical body in preparation for the life-transforming Divine Healing and Cleansing that will take place within this vehicle.

With deep concentration, I visualize the Emerald Green and Violet Flames as my I AM Presence and my

5th-Dimensional Body Elemental now direct them to Heal, Cleanse, Rejuvenate, Resurrect and Transfigure the various systems in my Earthly Bodies.

1. My Healing process begins by the Emerald Green and Violet Flames expanding through my physical brain structure, my spinal cord, my nervous system, my Chakra system, and my corresponding meridians and acupuncture points. The Healing Flames instantaneously remove every trace of disease or imbalance of any kind in these systems. My conscious awareness is rising to a higher level. This is increasing my ability to think and to use my creative faculties of thought to cocreate the infinite perfection of the New Earth.

2. Next the Healing Flames flow into my eyes—instantaneously removing every trace of disease or imbalance of any kind. The Healing Flames restore my eyes to perfect sight, allowing me to see and recognize perfection in all Life.

3. The Healing Flames now flow into my ears—instantaneously removing every trace of disease or imbalance of any kind. The Violet and Emerald Green Healing Flames restore my ears to perfect hearing, allowing me to hear the inner voice of my I AM Presence and the Music of the Spheres.

4. The Healing Flames now flow into my nostrils, sinuses, respiratory system, lungs, larynx, vocal chords, trachea, bronchial tubes and every function of my voice and breathing apparatus—instantaneously every trace of disease or imbalance of any kind is removed. The Healing Flames enhance my breathing and enable me to absorb the maximum prana with every Holy Breath I take. I AM now

blessed with the Breath of the Holy Spirit and I AM empowered to speak with *"the tongues of Angels."*

5. Next the Healing Flames flow into my mouth, teeth, gums, tongue, esophagus, stomach, liver, gallbladder, small intestines, ileocecal valve, large intestines, appendix, colon, kidneys, bladder and every aspect of my digestive and elimination systems—instantaneously every trace of disease or imbalance of any kind is removed. The Healing Flames restore all of these aspects of my digestive system to vibrant health, thus allowing me to purify my body and to assimilate my food and drinks perfectly.

6. Now the Healing Flames flow into my spiritual brain centers: my pineal, pituitary, and hypothalamus glands, and the ganglionic centers at the base of my brain. The Violet and Emerald Green Healing Flames now flow into the remainder of my endocrine system: my thyroid, thymus, pancreas, spleen, adrenal glands, gonads and all of the other glands associated with this ductless system. The Healing Flames instantaneously remove every trace of disease or imbalance of any kind as they restore all of these aspects of my Earthly Bodies to perfect balance and function.

7. The Healing Flames now flow through the various facets of my circulatory system. They first flow through my lymph nodes and lymphatic fluid, then into the muscle of my heart and through the chambers, valves, veins, arteries and capillaries. The Emerald Green and Violet Flames now flow through my red and white blood cells and my bone marrow—instantaneously removing every trace of disease or imbalance of any kind in my circulatory system. This

is increasing my ability to feel and to use my creative faculties of feeling in ways that express Divine Love, Oneness and Reverence for all Life.

8. The Healing Flames now flow into my reproductive system: my female or male organs—instantaneously every trace of disease or imbalance of any kind is removed. The Healing Flames restore every aspect of my reproductive system allowing me to hold the sacred space for myself or for anyone else who is destined to bring in the children of the New Earth. The Healing Flames are creating a Chalice of Light in every mother and father, a Holy Grail, through which these precious children will be born. These transfigured reproductive systems will enable the I AM Presence of the incoming children to create perfect vehicles through which they will assist in cocreating the New Earth.

9. Next, the Healing Flames flow into my skeletal and my muscular systems: my bones, muscles, joints, tendons, ligaments, cartilage, fat cells and connective tissue—instantaneously removing every trace of disease or imbalance of any kind. The Violet and Emerald Green Healing Flames restore every aspect of these systems, empowering me with strength, vitality and youth.

10. The Healing Flames now flow through my skin, hair, nails and every remaining facet of my physical body—instantaneously every trace of disease or imbalance of any kind is removed. As the Healing Flames purge every trace of contamination or disease in my Earthly Bodies, I AM transfigured into the Immaculate Concept of my 5th-Dimensional Crystalline Solar Light Bodies of Vibrant Health, Eternal Youth, Radiant Beauty and Infinite Perfection

11. Now, with the Emerald Green and Violet Flames pulsating in, through and around every electron of my Earthly Bodies and the Earthly Bodies of all Humanity, I ask Saint Germain and the Legions of Light associated with these Sacred Flames to blaze them in, through and around the entire Elemental Kingdom and the physical, etheric, mental and emotional strata of Mother Earth.

I know and accept that this Healing activity of the Violet and Emerald Green Flames has been God Victoriously accomplished in the Realms of Cause. The Divine Matrix has been formed and will be amplified one thousand fold by my I AM Presence and the Company of Heaven every time I participate in this activity of Light. For this, I AM Eternally Grateful. And so it is.

Dear One, please focus on this powerful Healing Gift from Saint Germain and our Father-Mother God and take full advantage of this life-transforming opportunity.

64

JOURNEY INTO MOTHER MARY'S TEMPLE OF THE IMMACULATE HEART

Our Father-Mother God want to secure the epic Gifts and Healings we have received through the Divine Intervention of Saint Germain and Mother Mary. This will be accomplished through the following activity of Light as we journey in consciousness into Mother Mary's Temple of the Immaculate Heart.

A Journey in Consciousness

This activity of Light is stated in the 1st person, so that we will each experience it personally, but KNOW that we are serving as surrogates on behalf of every man, woman, and child on Earth.

I AM my I AM Presence and I AM One with the I AM
Presence of ALL Humanity.
As I AM lifted up all Life is being lifted up with me.

Archangel Michael has enveloped me in an invincible forcefield of Light, which prevents anything from interfering or distracting me from this sacred activity of Light.

I breathe in deeply, and as I do I enter the Divinity of my Heart Flame. There I kneel before the altar of Love and surrender my lower human consciousness to the perfection of my I AM Presence. My physical, etheric, mental and emotional bodies are being brought into alignment, and the energy, vibration and consciousness of my Earthly Bodies is accelerating to higher frequencies than I have ever experienced.

Suddenly, I realize that I AM Ascending through a mighty shaft of Light into the Realms of Illumined Truth. In the twinkling of an eye, I find myself tangibly present in the Pure Land of Boundless Splendor and Infinite Light. For a sublime moment I absorb the wonder of this magical place.

Gradually, I become aware that Beloved Mother Mary is beside me. We are standing in front of her magnificent Crystalline Temple of the Immaculate Heart.

She beckons me, and together we ascend the steps of the Temple and pass through the massive Golden Doors. Mother Mary takes my hand and escorts me through the alabaster hallway into a resplendent Sanctuary of Light in the center of the Temple.

Pulsating in the center of this Sanctuary is a huge crystalline lotus blossom. Blazing as the stamen of the lotus blossom is a magnificent Crystalline White Flame with a Madonna Blue radiance. This is the Flame of the Immaculate Concept. The Flame of the Immaculate Concept pulsates with the Divine Blueprint, the full Divine Potential, of every facet of Life contained within the Causal Body of God. Mother Mary is the Keeper of the Flame of the Immaculate Concept, and it is through this Sacred Fire that she sustains the Immortal Victorious Threefold Flame within the heart of every Child of God.

As I look around this central chamber, Mother Mary points out that there are four smaller chambers at the cardinal points of this massive room. Each of these chambers has a smaller crystalline lotus blossom with the Flame of the Immaculate Concept blazing in the center.

Mother Mary motions for me to enter the Flame of the Immaculate Concept in the large crystalline lotus blossom in the central Sanctuary, and I gratefully respond.

I stand within the scintillating essence of this Crystalline White and Madonna Blue Flame, and I begin to experience the vibratory rate of my physical, etheric, mental, and emotional bodies being accelerated.

My consciousness is being lifted up, and I perceive more clearly than ever before the Divine Blueprint—the Immaculate Concept—for my Earthly Bodies. This blueprint is the template for my 5th-Dimensional Crystalline Solar Light Bodies.

Pouring forth now from the very Heart of my Father-Mother God is a tremendous Shaft of Light that is pulsating with higher frequencies of the Flame of Transfiguring Divine Love than I have ever been able to receive. Emanating from this unfathomable frequency of Love are the Divine Qualities of Healing, Restoration, Resurrection, Transformation and Transfiguration.

This shaft of Light descends into the Flame of the Immaculate Concept in the lotus blossom in the central Sanctuary, and it begins blazing in, through, and around my four Earthly Bodies. This shaft of Light now expands into the lotus blossoms in the four smaller chambers at the cardinal points of this Sanctuary.

Mother Mary reveals to me that each of these chambers is dedicated to the Transfiguration of one of my four Earthly Bodies.

The chamber to the East is dedicated to the Transfiguration of my Emotional Body.

The chamber to the West is dedicated to the Transfiguration of my Mental Body.

The chamber to the North is dedicated to the Transfiguration of my Etheric Body.

The chamber to the South is dedicated to the Transfiguration of my Physical Body.

1. Now Mother Mary directs me to consciously project my Emotional Body and all of my feelings and emotions into the Flame of the Immaculate Concept in the crystalline lotus blossom in the chamber at the cardinal point to the East.

The Flame of Transfiguring Divine Love and the Divine Qualities of Healing, Restoration, Resurrection, Transformation and Transfiguration blaze in, through and around my Emotional Body, transmuting every trace of imbalance or imperfection.

My I AM Presence now projects the Divine Blueprint for my Emotional Light Body through this vehicle, and it begins pulsating as a Light Pattern, Transfiguring this body instantly into the Immaculate Concept of my 5th-Dimensional Crystalline Emotional Solar Light Body.

2. Mother Mary now directs me to consciously project my Mental Body and all of my thoughts into the Flame of the Immaculate Concept in the crystalline lotus blossom in the chamber at the cardinal point to the West.

The Flame of Transfiguring Divine Love and the Divine Qualities of Healing, Restoration, Resurrection, Transformation and Transfiguration blaze in, through and around my Mental Body, transmuting every trace of imbalance or imperfection.

My I AM Presence now projects the Divine Blueprint for my Mental Light Body through this vehicle, and it begins pulsating as a Light Pattern, Transfiguring this body instantly into the Immaculate Concept of my 5th-Dimensional Crystalline Mental Solar Light Body.

3. Mother Mary now directs me to consciously project my Etheric Body and all of my memories and records of the past into the Flame of the Immaculate Concept in the crystalline lotus blossom in the chamber at the cardinal point to the North.

The Flame of Transfiguring Divine Love and the Divine Qualities of Healing, Restoration, Resurrection, Transformation and Transfiguration blaze in, through and around my Etheric Body transmuting every trace of imbalance or imperfection.

My I AM Presence now projects the Divine Blueprint for my Etheric Light Body through this vehicle, and it begins pulsating as a Light Pattern, Transfiguring this body instantly into the Immaculate Concept of my 5th-Dimensional Crystalline Etheric Solar Light Body.

4. Mother Mary now directs me to consciously project my Physical Body and every cell, atom, gland, muscle, organ and function of this vehicle into the Flame of the Immaculate Concept in the crystalline lotus blossom in the chamber at the cardinal point to the South.

The Flame of Transfiguring Divine Love and the Divine Qualities of Healing, Restoration, Resurrection, Transformation and Transfiguration blaze in, through and around my Physical Body, transmuting every trace of imbalance or imperfection.

My I AM Presence now projects the Divine Blueprint for my Physical Light Body through this vehicle, and it begins pulsating as a Light Pattern, Transfiguring this body instantly into the Immaculate Concept of my 5th-Dimensional Crystalline Physical Solar Light Body.

Now, one by one, I magnetize my 5th-Dimensional Crystalline Solar Light Bodies back into the Flame of the Immaculate Concept in the lotus blossom in the central Sanctuary where they are brought into perfect alignment: first my Physical Crystalline Solar Light Body, now my Etheric Crystalline Solar Light Body, now my Mental Crystalline Solar Body and finally my Emotional Crystalline Solar Light Body. Through my I AM Presence, Mother Mary seals the frequency of these perfected vehicles within the Flame of the Immaculate Concept.

With the completion of this activity of Light, I gently return my consciousness to the physical plane. Within the physical plane my I AM Presence seals this activity of Light in the core of purity within every electron of my Earthly Bodies, and the Earthly Bodies of ALL Humanity.

I now breathe in deeply and return my attention to the room. I become aware of my physical body. I exhale and gently open my eyes. For a moment I just relax and allow these Divine Energies to be assimilated into my physical, etheric, mental and emotional bodies.

Dear One, please contemplate the Gifts Mother Mary and Saint Germain have given to you and open your heart in preparation for the next phase of our journey into the Light.

65

INTEGRATING OUR
RECALIBRATED HEART FLAME

Our Father-Mother God and the Company of Heaven are expressing with a greater frequency of elation than I have ever felt from them, the fact that Mother Mary's Divine Intervention during the Month of May succeeded God Victoriously. Within the heart of every single person's I AM Presence the Permanent Seed Atom has been Transfigured into a greatly empowered Chalice of Light and recalibrated to withstand brand new 5th-Dimensional Solar frequencies of the Immortal Victorious Threefold Flame.

This means that no matter how asleep or how recalcitrant a person is now, or how far he or she may be from awakening, their I AM Presence is standing in readiness and will integrate these new frequencies of the Permanent Seed Atom and the Threefold Flame into their physical heart the moment they are capable of receiving them. Of course, in addition to the people who are still asleep there are millions of awakened and awakening people all over the world who are ready to receive this incredible blessing right here and right now.

In order for us to grasp the magnitude of what this expansion of our Permanent Seed Atom and our Threefold Flame really means, it will help to remember that our Immortal Victorious Threefold Flame is how our Father God, our Mother God and our full Divine Potential as Sons and Daughters of God are anchored within us. Our Threefold Flame is the sacred space being referred to when we were told from On High, "*Seek ye first the Kingdom of Heaven within and all else will be revealed to you.*"

Our Threefold Flame is a reflection of our Father-Mother God, the Cosmic I AM, ALL That Is. This means quite literally that everything pulsating within the Divine Matrix of our Father-Mother God's Causal Body is within this Sacred Flame. This is why each and every one of us can affirm the profound Truth, "*All that my Father-Mother God have is mine.*"

It is within the Divinity of our Threefold Flame that we experience the Oneness of ALL Life. It is within this Sacred Fire that we are interconnected, interdependent and inter-related to every particle and wave of Life throughout the whole of Creation. When we remember this fact, it is easy to realize the Truth within the statement "*As I AM lifted up ALL Life is lifted up with me.*"

Today the Company of Heaven is going to lead us through an activity of Light that will assist the I AM Presence of every person on Earth to begin the process of integrating our newly empowered Permanent Seed Atom and our newly balanced and recalibrated 5th-Dimensional Solar Threefold Flame into our physical Heart Flame. This will occur in perfect alignment with every person's Divine Plan and our highest good. So let's begin.

Integrating Our Transfigured Permanent Seed Atom and Our Newly Balanced and Recalibrated 5th-Dimensional Threefold Flame

As One Voice, One Breath, One Heartbeat and One Consciousness of Pure Divine Love, we center ourselves by breathing in and out deeply and rhythmically through our Heart Flame.

I AM my I AM Presence and I AM One with the I AM Presence of ALL Humanity. What I invoke for myself I invoke on behalf of every man, woman and child on Earth in perfect alignment with each person's Divine Plan and their highest good.

I AM aware of my Presence in the world of form and I know I AM One with all Life. I now gently remove my attention from the outer world, and I reverently enter the Divinity of my Heart Flame.

I know that the Holy Breath is the vehicle for the assimilation and the expansion of my Immortal Victorious Threefold Flame in the physical plane of Earth. My balanced and recalibrated 5th-Dimensional Solar Threefold Flame has a dual pulsation. The first pulsation is the Inbreath—assimilation and absorption. The second pulsation is the Outbreath—expansion and radiation. On the Inbreath, my Threefold Flame extends up in vibration piercing into the very Heart and Mind of God the Source of never-ending perfection. On the Outbreath, my Threefold Flame radiates the blessings from the Heart and Mind of God into the physical plane, eventually projecting these Gifts throughout the planet and into the Universe. On every Inbreath my Heart Flame Ascends into new heights of Divinity, and on each Outbreath my Heart Flame becomes a stronger pulsation of God's blessings into the world of form.

Because of this dual activity, my Heart Flame is both the portal to the Kingdom of Heaven within me, as well as the Source of all Divine Blessings for Humanity and the planet. My Threefold Flame is both the inward portal to my 5th-Dimensional I AM Presence, and the Open Door for the Gifts of my Father-Mother God radiating outward into my daily life.

As I Breathe the Holy Breath in and out through my Heart Flame, my inner journey to God and my outer service to Life are brought into perfect balance. It is within the balance of my Threefold Flame that I AM able to return to Christ Consciousness, and it is within this balance that I reconnect with my I AM Presence, the master within me, the Keeper of my Heart Flame.

It is now, within this same balance, that my I AM Presence will integrate my Transfigured Permanent Seed Atom and my recalibrated 5th-Dimensional Solar Threefold Flame into my physical Heart Flame. This is being accomplished in perfect alignment with my Divine Plan and my highest good.

On the Holy Breath my I AM Presence now integrates into the Permanent Seed Atom in my heart the *appropriate frequency* of my newly Transfigured Permanent Seed Atom. This is instantaneously accomplished in perfect Divine Order.

Now on the Holy Breath my I AM Presence integrates into the Threefold Flame in my heart the *appropriate frequency* of my newly balanced and recalibrated 5th-Dimensional Solar Threefold Flame. This is also instantaneously accomplished in perfect Divine Order.

From this moment forth, as I progress step by step through the final stages of my Ascension process, my I AM Presence will increase the frequency of my transfigured

Permanent Seed Atom and my balanced 5th-Dimensional Solar Threefold Flame. This will occur as I AM lifted up in energy, vibration and consciousness, thus accelerating the Divine Alchemy within my Earthly Bodies, the Earthly Bodies of ALL Humanity and the physical, etheric, mental and emotional strata in the Bodies of Mother Earth.

My I AM Presence is now encoding this knowing within my heart and mind, so that I will be consciously and intuitively aware of this profound Truth with every breath I take.

And so it is. Beloved I AM That I AM.

Dear One, as you go about your day focus on your Inbreath and your Outbreath and be cognizant of what you have experienced through this activity of Light.

66

PURIFYING HUMANITY AND MOTHER EARTH

The Light of God flowing through our Planetary Grid of Transfiguring Divine Love is amplifying the Lightwork of every person on Earth one thousand fold every day. This is giving Saint Germain and his Legions of Violet Fire Angels the ability to Gift us with an unparalleled opportunity to cleanse our contaminated Earthly Bodies and the various polluted systems associated with the Earth.

As we are learning, it is the toxic substances and the gross contaminations polluting the air we breathe, the food we eat and the water we drink that are causing the maladies in our Earthly Bodies and blocking the activation of the *consciousness codes* in the DNA of the Millennials and the children. The Company of Heaven will lead us through an activity of Light that will greatly empower the purification taking place within the Earthly Bodies of Humanity and Mother Earth. If you have the Heart Call to do so, please join with me and the thousands of Lightworkers around the world who are participating with us in this activity of Light.

And we begin.

The Violet Flame of God's Infinite Perfection Invocation

I AM my I AM Presence and I AM One with the I AM Presence of ALL Humanity. As One Voice, One Breath, One Heartbeat, and One Energy, Vibration, and Consciousness of Pure Divine Love we invoke the most intensified frequencies of the 5th-Dimensional Crystalline Solar Violet Flame of God's Infinite Perfection that Cosmic Law will allow.

We invoke Saint Germain and his Legions of Violet Fire Archangels who are associated with this unfathomable frequency of the Violet Flame.

Beloved Ones come forth NOW!

We ask that you blaze this Violet Flame with the power and might of a thousand Suns in, through and around all contamination within Humanity's and Mother Earth's physical, etheric, mental and emotional bodies. Expand this Violet Flame through all inharmonious actions, all lower human consciousness and all obstructions of the Light that any person, place, condition or thing has ever placed on the pathway of Life's perfection.

Transmute this negative energy cause, core, effect, record and memory back into its original perfection and seal it in an invincible forcefield of God's Transfiguring Divine Love.

Legions of Light, we ask that you now expand this activity of Light and project this Violet Flame of God's Infinite Perfection with the power and might of a thousand Suns into the human miscreations that are surfacing all over the Earth to be healed and transmuted back into Light.

a) Blaze the Violet Flame with the power and might of a thousand Suns through the thoughts, words, actions and feelings of every man, woman and child evolving on Earth until every person individually acknowledges and accepts the Divinity within ALL Life, and every expression made by Humanity is a healing benediction to every part of Life on this planet.

b) Blaze this Violet Flame through all incoming babies, the children and the Millennials until the *consciousness codes* within ALL youth are activated, and these precious Ones are raised up in energy, vibration and consciousness to hear and carry out the directives of their I AM Presence.

c) Blaze this Violet Flame through all parents, guardians, leaders, teachers, instructors and professors in every line of endeavor. Now expand this Violet Flame through all youth centers, schools, colleges and universities. Create a sacred space for the Millennials and the children to express the Divine Wisdom, God Illumination and Enlightenment pulsating within the *consciousness codes* of their DNA.

d) Blaze this Violet Flame through all religious and spiritual teachings until Divine Love, Truth, Tolerance, Oneness, Understanding and Universal Sisterhood and Brotherhood become a manifest reality.

e) Blaze this Violet Flame through all doctors, nurses, healers, hospitals, insurance companies, pharmaceutical conglomerates and every institution associated with Healing of any kind until Divine Mercy, Compassion, Caring, Healing and Integrity are tangible realities for every person.

f) Blaze this Violet Flame through all banking and financial institutions, all economic systems, all money and the people associated with monetary interactions of any kind until every person on Earth is openly demonstrating true Integrity, Honesty,

Generosity, Fairness, Abundance and the God Supply of all Good Things.

g) Blaze this Violet Flame through all places of incarceration and all employed there. Now intensify this Violet Flame through every correctional institution, every law enforcement officer, every judge, jury and court of law until Divine Justice is manifest and eternally sustained for every person.

h) Blaze this Violet Flame through ALL of the governments of the world and every person, place, condition and thing associated with the governments of the world at national, state and local levels. Intensify this Violet Flame until every government is focusing on the highest good for ALL concerned, and cocreating an environment of Divine Love, Oneness and Reverence for ALL Life for every person in every single instance.

i) Blaze this Violet Flame through all space activities throughout the world until every nation unites in cooperative service, so that God's Will may be manifest with our sisters and brothers throughout the Universe.

j) Blaze this Violet Flame through the physical, etheric, mental and emotional bodies of Humanity until all aging, all disease, all human miscreations and their cause and core are purified, dissolved and transmuted into Vibrant Health, Eternal Youth and Infinite Physical Perfection.

k) Blaze this Violet Flame through the food and water industries and through all of the food and water used for human consumption until every particle of food and every molecule of water are filled with Light. Empower this Elemental substance to raise the vibratory action of Humanity's physical, etheric, mental and emotional bodies until every person's 5th-Dimensional Crystalline Solar Light Bodies become a manifest and Eternally sustained reality.

l) Beloved Ones, now blaze this Violet Flame in, through and around every remaining electron of precious Life energy on this planet until we have completed our Ascension into the full embrace of the Immaculate Concept of the New Earth.

We accept and know that the unparalleled frequency of the Violet Flame of God's Infinite Perfection which Saint Germain and his Legions of Violet Fire Archangels have blessed us with this sacred and holy day is God Victoriously accomplishing this facet of the Divine Plan even as we Call.

We also accept and KNOW that every time we participate in this activity of Light our efforts will be amplified one thousand fold through our Planetary Grid of Transfiguring Divine Love.

And so it is! Beloved I AM, Beloved I AM, Beloved I AM.

Dear One, this exceptionally powerful Gift of the Violet Flame which Saint Germain and his Violet Fire Archangels are blessing us with at this time will be available until the Divine Mission we are all being called to assist with this year is God Victoriously accomplished. The goal of this Violet Flame activity is for awakening Humanity to help the I AM Presences of the Millennials and the children to prepare their physical, etheric, mental and emotional bodies for the events that will take place on their behalf during the *32nd Annual World Congress on Illumination, August 11–16, 2018.*

During that event, Lightworkers from around the world will gather within the Portal of Light at Diamond Head in Honolulu, Hawaii. We will unify our newly recalibrated Heart Flames and form a mighty transformer through which the Light of God will flow to activate the *consciousness codes* that the I AM Presences of the Millennials and the children encoded within their DNA prior to this embodiment.

These *consciousness codes* contain sacred knowledge that these precious Ones were given in the inner realms prior to this embodiment. The specific purpose of these codes is to accelerate the awakening of the Millennials, who are 17 to 32 years old, and the children being born now and those through the age of sixteen. Once these incoming souls are awakened, they will remember who they are and why they are here. This will empower them in ways that will enable them to assist the Earth and all Life evolving upon her through the final stages of our Ascension process into the 5th-Dimensional New Earth.

The Millennials and the children, who are known in the Heavenly Realms as the Holy Innocents, began embodying on Earth for the first time after this planet Ascended off of the wheel of karma and reclaimed our rightful place on the Ascending Spiral of Evolution. This occurred during Harmonic Convergence in August of 1987. Now the activation of their *consciousness codes* is a critical step in the process of accomplishing the final stages of Earth's Ascension process.

Dear One, listen to your heart and repeat the Violet Flame activity of Light that has been shared with us as often as you feel inspired to do so.

67

A QUANTUM SHIFT DURING THE JUNE SOLSTICE

If you have been participating in the activities of Light the Company of Heaven has been guiding us through so far this year during our Weekly Vlogs and our Monthly Free Seminars, you are aware of the amazing assistance Humanity is receiving from the Beings of Light at this time.

This Divine Intervention is the result of our Father-Mother God's newly initiated Divine Plan which is utilizing the Planetary Grid of Transfiguring Divine Love that Lightworkers have been cocreating for over 50 years. Through this Grid of Love which is now enveloping the entire planet, the Lightwork of every person on Earth is being amplified one thousand fold every single day.

This increase of Light has shifted the energy, vibration and consciousness of Humanity and accelerated the Divine Alchemy taking place within our Earthly Bodies and the Bodies of Mother Earth in astonishing ways. The Company of Heaven said that these events have paved the way for a quantum shift up the Spiral of Evolution that will involve the Earth and all Life evolving upon her. According to these

Beings of Light, not even they anticipated that a shift of this magnitude would be able to occur this soon.

This shift into higher frequencies of the 5th-Dimension will take place during the influx of Light that will flow through our Planetary Grid of Transfiguring Divine Love on the *June 21st Solstice*. Our Grid of Love is a multifaceted and multidimensional Forcefield of Light that envelopes the entire Planet Earth. It consists of various sacred geometric patterns and it extends from the densest frequencies of Humanity's miscreations into the highest frequencies of Light in the 5th-Dimensional New Earth. The Company of Heaven refers to our Grid as the *BRIDGE TO FREEDOM*, and it is the vehicle through which our Father-Mother God are expanding the Lightwork of every person on Earth one thousand fold every single day.

In order for every man, woman and child, and Mother Earth herself, to receive the maximum benefit from the influx of Light on the *June 21st Solstice*, our Father-Mother God are asking us to take some time today to recalibrate our Planetary Grid of Transfiguring Divine Love to a higher frequency. By participating in this activity of Light, our Planetary Grid will be raised into the highest frequencies of Transfiguring Divine Love we have ever been able to receive.

A wonderful artist named Endre Balogh has cocreated an exquisite image of our Planetary Grid of Transfiguring Divine Love. I will show you this powerful image as we focus on the invocation that was given to us by our Father-Mother God.

If you have the Heart Call to be the Open Door for this activity of Light on behalf of Mother Earth and all Life evolving upon her, please follow me through this visualization. Together, with the Company of Heaven and the I AM

Presence of every man, woman and child on Earth, we will empower our Planetary Grid to receive greater frequencies of Transfiguring Divine Love than we have ever experienced. And we begin.

Empowering Our Planetary Grid of Transfiguring Divine Love

Breathe in deeply and go within to the Divinity of your Heart Flame as you participate in this activity of Light with the full power of your attention and your Divine Intentions.

I AM my I AM Presence and I AM One with the I AM Presence of ALL Humanity. As One Voice, One Breath, One Heartbeat and One Energy, Vibration and Consciousness of Pure Divine Love we invoke our Father-Mother God and the Legions of Light throughout Infinity.

Beloved Ones, come forth NOW!

We are One with ALL of these magnificent Forces of Light. Through our sincere Heart Call, they have joyously come to help Humanity's I AM Presence empower our Planetary Grid of Transfiguring Divine Love one thousand fold.

Beloved Legions of Light, we ask that you gather up every electron of precious Life energy being expended by Humanity during this sacred and holy time. Purify this energy with the power and might of a thousand Suns using the New 5th-Dimensional Solar Frequencies of the Violet Flame of God's Infinite Perfection. Weave this purified energy into the collective Cup of Humanity's Consciousness, so that every electron of precious Life energy released by the Sons and Daughters of God on Earth at this time will be used to exponentially expand the Light of God through the Planetary Grid of Transfiguring Divine Love which is now enveloping the entire Planet Earth.

Beloved Father-Mother God, we ask that you now Breathe the highest possible frequencies of Divine Love, Oneness and Reverence for All Life into every person's newly recalibrated Heart Flame.

In Oneness with the I AM Presence of every person on Earth and the entire Company of Heaven, we now affirm within the Divinity of our 5th-Dimensional Solar Heart Flame:

"I AM the Cup, the Holy Grail, through which the Light of God now flows to bless every particle and wave of Life evolving on this precious planet.

"I AM my I AM Presence, and I now invoke my Father-Mother God to Breathe their Infinite Light into our Planetary Grid of Transfiguring Divine Love. As this NEW and exquisite frequency of Light blazes through our Grid of Love it bathes the Earth and expands every person's Lightwork one thousand fold."

This unfathomable influx of our Father-Mother God's Infinite Light lifts every atomic and subatomic particle and wave of Life on Earth into a Higher Order of Being.

As this wondrous Light is anchored within the Divinity of every person's 5th-Dimensional Solar Heart Flame, it expands into the 5th-Dimensional Solar Heart Flame of every other person on Earth unifying Heart Flame with Heart Flame. Through this amazing activity of Light, the I AM Presence of every person becomes a power point of Divine Love and Oneness unified in consciousness with the I AM Presence of every other person.

Through this unified effort involving Heaven and Earth, we are greatly empowering our Planetary Grid of Transfiguring Divine Love. This Forcefield of Light is extending from the very depths of Humanity's pain and suffering into the highest frequencies of the 5th-Dimensional Realms of God's Infinite Light that Humanity has ever experienced. This Grid of Transfiguring Divine Love is the **Bridge to Freedom** over which this blessed planet and ALL her Life are now Ascending into the 5th-Dimensional Realms of Perfection on the New Earth.

Through this activity of Light, we are reclaiming our Divine Birthright as Sons and Daughters of God. We are truly becoming Love in action. We are collectively changing the core vibration of the primal Light substance that has gone into creating the present negative conditions that are surfacing all over the planet to be healed and transmuted into Light. The I AM Presence within every person is the Open Door for these NEW and resplendent patterns of Transfiguring Divine Love.

We are now the CAUSE of Divine Love being permanently re-established on Earth. Together we are setting in place the basic spiritual forces of Divine Love over which the Earth and ALL her Life are at last Ascending out of our long exile in darkness into the 5th-Dimensional Realms of Light where the New Earth abides. The Love of God is now thriving on Earth through each of us, and through the I AM Presence of every person on this planet.

Through this activity of Light, Humanity is being raised into a profound awakening of supreme Love Consciousness. We are, here and now, the Masters of Love we were always destined to be. We are Beings of Love, accepting responsibility for Loving this sweet Earth and ALL her Life FREE. We are One with this blessed planet, and the planet is One with us.

Our Father-Mother God and the Company of Heaven are now intensifying their Light through every person's

Heart Flame. This influx of Light is lifting ALL Humanity into a higher octave of Divine Service in preparation for the shift up the Spiral of Evolution that will occur during the *June 21st Solstice*. Every person on Earth is being permanently invested with a Cosmic Forcefield of Transfiguring Divine Love. This forcefield is initiating each of us into a higher order of service to both Humanity and Mother Earth, as our Lightwork is intensified one thousand fold through our newly empowered Planetary Grid of Transfiguring Divine Love.

Beloved Father-Mother God, we accept that this activity of Light has been
God Victoriously Accomplished. And so it is!

Beloved I AM, Beloved I AM, Beloved I AM That I AM.

Dear One, thank you for your willingness to be the Open Door for this powerful expansion of Light within our Planetary Grid of Transfiguring Divine Love.

To bring the image of this Grid of Light tangibly into your personal space we have produced a beautiful poster of the picture Endre cocreated for us. If you are interested in having this poster to bless you in your home or office it is available on our website www.eraofpeace.org.

68

THE 12 ASPECTS OF DEITY
ASSOCIATED WITH THE
NEW EARTH

The Company of Heaven has confirmed that during the June Solstice the Earth and all Life evolving upon her God Victoriously Ascended up the Spiral of Evolution into higher frequencies of the 5th Dimension than we have ever experienced. They said that the I AM Presences of Humanity en masse are now able to receive the full Divine Momentum of the Twelve Solar Aspects of Deity. This is the Light of God that Humanity will use to cocreate the patterns of perfection for the New Earth.

During the next few chapters the Company of Heaven will guide us through activities of Light that will reveal to us just how to utilize this Gift of Light from our Father-Mother God in ways that will help us to transform our Earthly Bodies and our Life experiences into what we want them to be.

The Beings of Light will begin this process by familiarizing us with the NEW frequencies and the Divine Qualities of the Twelve Solar Aspects of Deity. Please join with me now and allow your I AM Presence to bathe your Earthly

Bodies with these NEW frequencies of Light. This is the Light of God that we will use to cocreate the New Earth and move through the final stages of our Ascension in the Light. And we begin.

New Solar Frequencies of the Twelve Solar Aspects of Deity

I AM my I AM Presence and I AM One with I AM Presence of every person on Earth. On this sacred and holy day, as One unified consciousness, we collectively prepare to receive the Divine Blessings of our Father-Mother God's Twelve Solar Aspects of Deity in frequencies beyond anything we have previously experienced. Please center yourself within your Heart Flame and follow me through this visualization.

I accept and know that the Twelve Solar Aspects of Deity from the very Heart of my Father-Mother God will flow through the newly recalibrated and balanced Solar Threefold Flame that is now pulsating within the I AM Presence and the physical Heart Flame of every man, woman and child. As this exquisite Light flows through every Heart Flame and bathes the physical, etheric, mental and emotional bodies of every person, the 5th-Dimensional Body Elemental within each of us will assimilate this Light into the Core of Purity in every atomic and subatomic particle and wave of our Earthly Bodies.

The collective Forcefield of Light that reflects all Twelve of the Solar Aspects of Deity from the Heart of our Father-Mother God is known through all Creation as *The Circle of the Sacred Twelve.*

On the Holy Breath, our Father-Mother God now Breathe the highest frequencies of the Circle of the Sacred Twelve that Humanity is capable of assimilating into every person's Heart Flame.

We now experience the Twelve Solar Aspects of Deity, one by one, as they bathe our Earthly Bodies.

The Twelve 5th-Dimensional Crystalline Solar Aspects of Deity

1. The 1st Solar Aspect of Deity is Sapphire Blue.

The Divine Qualities associated with the 1st Solar Aspect of Deity are God's Will, Illumined Faith, Power, Protection and God's First Cause of Perfection. This is the Ray of Light that reflects the Masculine Polarity of our Father God. Feel the frequency of this Sapphire Blue Light as it bathes your Earthly Bodies.

2. The 2nd Solar Aspect of Deity is Sunshine Yellow.

The Divine Qualities associated with the 2nd Solar Aspect of Deity are Enlightenment, Wisdom, Illumination and Constancy. This is the Ray of Light that reflects the Christ Consciousness of the Sons and Daughters of God. Feel the frequency of this Sunshine Yellow Light as it bathes your Earthly Bodies.

3. The 3rd Solar Aspect of Deity is Crystalline Pink.

The Divine Qualities associated with the 3rd Solar Aspect of Deity are Transfiguring Divine Love, Oneness, Reverence for ALL Life, Adoration and Tolerance. This is the Ray of Light that reflects the Feminine Polarity of our Mother God, the Holy Spirit. Feel the frequency of this Crystalline Pink Light as it bathes your Earthly Bodies.

4. The 4th Solar Aspect of Deity is White.

The Divine Qualities associated with the 4th Solar Aspect of Deity are Purity, Hope, Restoration, Resurrection,

Ascension and the Immaculate Concept. Feel the frequency of this White Light as it bathes your Earthly Bodies.

5. The 5th Solar Aspect of Deity is Emerald Green.

The Divine Qualities associated with the 5th Solar Aspect of Deity are Illumined Truth, Healing, Consecration, Concentration and Inner Vision. Feel the frequency of this Emerald Green Light as it bathes your Earthly Bodies.

6. The 6th Solar Aspect of Deity is Ruby-Gold.

The Divine Qualities associated with the 6th Solar Aspect of Deity are Divine Grace, Healing, Devotional Worship, Peace and the Manifestation of the Christ. Feel the frequency of this Ruby-Gold Light as it bathes your Earthly Bodies.

7. The 7th Solar Aspect of Deity is Violet.

The Divine Qualities associated with the 7th Solar Aspect of Deity are Mercy, Compassion, Forgiveness, Transmutation, Liberty, Justice, Freedom, Victory and God's Infinite Perfection. This is the Ray of Light that reflects the perfect balance of the Masculine and Feminine Polarities of our Father-Mother God. The Violet Flame of God's Infinite Perfection will be the predominant frequency of Light bathing the Earth during the Aquarian Age which we have now entered. Feel the frequency of this Violet Light as it bathes your Earthly Bodies.

8. The 8th Solar Aspect of Deity is Aquamarine.

The Divine Qualities associated with the 8th Solar Aspect of Deity are Clarity, Divine Perception, Discernment and Understanding. Feel the frequency of this Aquamarine Light as it bathes your Earthly Bodies.

9. The 9th Solar Aspect of Deity is Magenta.

The Divine Qualities associated with the 9th Solar Aspect of Deity are Harmony, Balance, Assurance and God Confidence. Feel the frequency of this Magenta Light as it bathes your Earthly Bodies.

10. The 10th Solar Aspect of Deity is Gold.

The Divine Qualities associated with the 10th Solar Aspect of Deity are Eternal Peace, Prosperity, Abundance and the God Supply of ALL Good Things. Feel the frequency of this Golden Light as it bathes your Earthly Bodies.

11. The 11th Solar Aspect of Deity is Peach.

The Divine Qualities associated with the 11th Solar Aspect of Deity are Divine Purpose, Enthusiasm and Joy. Feel the frequency of this Peach Light as it bathes your Earthly Bodies.

12. The 12th Solar Aspect of Deity is Opal.

The Divine Qualities associated with the 12th Solar Aspect of Deity are Transformation and Transfiguration. Feel the frequency of this Opal Light as it bathes your Earthly Bodies.

Beloved Father-Mother God, I thank you for the clarity and the assistance you are giving to Humanity during this momentous time. We accept and know that through every person's I AM Presence these NEW frequencies of the Twelve Solar Aspects of Deity have been secured in the Core of Purity in every atomic and subatomic particle and wave of Life on Earth.

We also accept and know that the influx of this resplendent Light will daily and hourly accelerate Earth's Ascension up the Spiral of Evolution into the full embrace of the New Earth. And so it is.

Beloved I AM, Beloved I AM, Beloved I AM.

Precious Heart, the Beings of Light have said that the assistance you are rendering to Humanity and the Earth, through your willingness to be the Open Door for the activities of Light being given to us by our Father-Mother God and the Company of Heaven during this auspicious time on Planet Earth is truly beyond the comprehension of your finite mind. For this, they are Eternally Grateful to YOU.

69

ANSWERS ABOUT HUMANITY'S PHYSICAL TRANSFORMATION

Our Father-Mother God's newly initiated Divine Plan is resulting in an expansion of Light on this planet beyond anything the Earth has ever experienced. This is assisting us through our Ascension process in wondrous ways. The difficult thing is that as the Light of God increases on Earth, everything that conflicts with that Light is pushed to the surface at a greatly accelerated pace in order to be healed and transmuted back into its original perfection. All we have to do to confirm that Truth is watch the nightly news.

Since outer appearances make it seem as though we are descending into an abyss of chaos and fear, the Company of Heaven wants to remind us of something very important. The Earth and ALL her Life have already made it through the Shift of the Ages victoriously and there is *no* turning back. The matrix for the 5th-Dimensional New Earth was birthed in the Realms of Cause, in all of her resplendent glory, during the December Solstice in 2012. Now that the New Earth's matrix has been formed in the Realms of Cause, *nothing* can prevent that perfection from eventually manifesting in the world of effects which is the physical plane. The only variable is how long that will take and that is up to you and me and the rest of awakening Humanity.

When we focus just on what we see happening in the outer world it is easy to lose perspective of the bigger picture. In the face of all of the adversity we are witnessing, it is imperative that we remember that we are multidimensional Beings functioning simultaneously in various dimensions and frequencies of Light. What we are able to see with our physical sight is *only* the contaminated physical plane of the old Earth. This is the densest and the *least real* of all of the dimensions we abide in. It is also the *very last* dimension to reflect the changes and the patterns of perfection from the New Earth we are magnetizing from the Realms of Cause through our Heart Flames.

When we acknowledge this Truth, we know that what we are perceiving with our physical sight is a miniscule fraction of what is actually taking place on this planet. So instead of allowing outer appearances to overwhelm and discourage us, we need to align with our I AM Presence and take the necessary steps to be the Instrument of God we have been preparing for lifetimes to be.

What the Beings of Light want us to understand now is that if we will participate deliberately and consciously in our Ascension process by volunteering to be the Open Door for the Twelve 5th-Dimensional Crystalline Solar Aspects of Deity that form the New Earth, we will assist Humanity and Mother Earth to move through this painful purging process much more quickly. In the last chapter, the Company of Heaven led us through an activity of Light that allowed us to experience these new frequencies of Light. Now they will share some background that will give us greater clarity and help us know how to be the Open Door for this exquisite Light from our Father-Mother God.

We Have Twelve 5th-Dimensional Crystalline Solar Chakras

The following information is something every person's I AM Presence is very aware of, but it is now time for all of us to realize this on a conscious level. I know that when we talk about transforming our carbon-based cells into crystalline-based cells through a process of Divine Alchemy, that concept is often foreign and confusing to people, but this is an imperative part of our Ascension process. The more we know about how and why this process is happening, the easier it will be for us to participate consciously in our physical transformation.

Our Father-Mother God initially created their Children within the highest dimensions of Light. In these frequencies there is no such thing as time or space. Only the Eternal Moment of Now is relevant. Eventually, our Father-Mother God wanted their Children to learn how to become cocreators with them. In order for that to happen in a timely manner, the Sons and Daughters of God needed to experience what we were cocreating through our thoughts, words, feelings and actions in a time and space continuum. This meant that the Sons and Daughters of God needed to step their frequency of vibration down into the 3rd and 4th Dimensions which are the only dimensions where time and space exist. In our case, we descended into the 3rd-Dimensional Earth.

In order to accomplish this, our I AM Presence remained in the timeless, spaceless 5th-Dimensional Realms of Light and projected a stepped down reflection of itself into the 4th Dimension. This 4th-Dimensional Aspect of our Divinity is known as our *Solar Christ Presence*. Next our 4th-Dimensional Solar Christ Presence projected a stepped down reflection of itself into the 3rd Dimension. This 3rd-Dimensional Aspect of our Divinity is known as our *Planetary Christ Presence*.

Our I AM Presence has a 5th-Dimensional Permanent Seed Atom and a 5th-Dimensional Immortal Victorious Threefold Heart Flame. Our I AM Presence also has a 5th-Dimensional Solar Spine with Twelve Solar Chakras. Each Chakra is a sphere of Light that pulsates with all Twelve Solar Aspects of Deity simultaneously. The Divine Light radiating through each of the Twelve Chakras in our I AM Presence is known as *The Circle of the Sacred Twelve*.

In the 4th Dimension we began to experience the initial frequencies of a time and space continuum. This changed the way we were experiencing the Twelve Solar Aspects of Deity. Our Solar Christ Presence has a 4th-Dimensional Permanent Seed Atom and a 4th-Dimensional Immortal Victorious Threefold Heart Flame. It also has a 4th-Dimensional Solar Spine with Twelve Solar Chakras. But since the 4th Dimension is so much denser than the 5th Dimension, in our Solar Christ Presence the Twelve Solar Aspects of Deity reflect very differently through the Twelve Chakras. Instead of all Twelve Aspects of Deity radiating through all Twelve Chakras simultaneously, in our 4th-Dimensional Solar Christ Presence only one of the Twelve Solar Aspects of Deity radiates through each Chakra.

Our Planetary Christ Presence was the first expression of our Divinity to enter into the full restrictions of a time and space continuum. That stepped down frequency required that our Planetary Christ Presence be transformed from a crystalline-based Solar Being into a carbon-based Planetary Being. This dramatically changed the way the Twelve Solar Aspects of Deity entered the world of form through our physical spinal column and our 3rd-Dimensional Chakra system.

As the Twelve Solar Aspects of Deity passed through the prism from the 4th Dimension into the 3rd Dimension, that Solar Light was stepped down into the pigment octave of color and Light. This is exactly what happens when a ray of Sunlight passes through a crystal and we see the sevenfold spectrum of the Rainbow on the other side. The Rainbow reflects the pigment octave of color and Light.

Our Planetary Christ Presence has a 3rd-Dimensional Permanent Seed Atom and a 3rd-Dimensional Immortal Victorious Threefold Heart Flame. It also has a 3rd-Dimensional Planetary Spine with only Seven Chakras. Each Chakra pulsates with one of the colors of the Rainbow. In our Planetary Christ Presence our Root Chakra at the base of the spine is red, our Sacral Chakra is orange, our Solar Plexus Chakra is yellow, the Heart Chakra is green, the Throat Chakra is blue, the Third Eye Chakra is indigo and the Crown Chakra is violet.

The process of stepping down our frequency of vibration from the higher Realms of Light into the time and space continuum of a 3rd-Dimensional reality is called involution. The original plan was that after our Planetary Christ Presence completed learning to be a cocreator with our Father-Mother God we would reverse this process and begin our evolutionary journey back to the Heart of God by Ascending step by step up the Spiral of Evolution.

Our fall from Grace and our self-inflicted entrapment on the wheel of karma caused this process to be delayed for aeons of time. As the Company of Heaven has revealed to us, there was a great chance that we might never have been able to reclaim our rightful place on the Spiral of Evolution in time for the Shift of the Ages if we had not received superhuman Divine Intervention. In the next few chapters the Company of Heaven is going to share with us some of the miracles that took place over the past few decades, thus assuring that every man, woman and child on Earth would make it successfully through the Shift of the Ages. These events brought us to this very moment and prepared the way for the miracles we are being called to cocreate NOW with the Company of Heaven.

When we are consciously aware of how our physical transformation has been unfolding over the past few decades, through the unified efforts of Heaven and Earth, the Divine Alchemy taking place in Humanity's and Mother Earth's physical, etheric, mental and emotional bodies will make perfect sense. This sacred knowledge will also encourage us and inspire us in powerful ways to be *the Open Door that no one can shut.*

70

PREPARATION FOR THIS COSMIC MOMENT

The Company of Heaven is sharing with us vitally important information that will give us greater clarity so that we can grasp the magnitude of this moment on Planet Earth and comprehend the greatest need of the hour.

In previous chapters we have been told that the Earth is in the midst of a unique experiment that has never been attempted in any system of worlds. Never has a planet that has fallen to the depths of separation and duality that the Earth is experiencing been given the opportunity to Ascend through two dimensional shifts in such a short period of time. This experiment can only be accomplished through the unified efforts of Heaven and Earth. The success of this unprecedented experiment is dependent upon the Sons and Daughters of God embodied on Earth working in cooperation with our Father-Mother God and the Company of Heaven.

This experiment was initiated with what the Beings of Light refer to as *Earth's 500-year Period of Grace*. Since that time in the 15th Century incredible things have transpired that have moved this planet and all her Life forward in the

Light. I have documented what the Company of Heaven has shared with us over the years about these events. This information is transcribed in my various books which are available on our website www.eraofpeace.org. However, today we are going to focus on some of the miraculous events that have taken place in recent decades. These events prepared us for what we are all being called to do now in Earth's Ascension process.

During Harmonic Convergence which took place in August 1987, Lightworkers around the world and the Company of Heaven anchored the Light of God on Earth in ways that allowed the Mighty Elohim to lift the Earth off of the wheel of karma that Humanity had inadvertently miscreated. The Elohim then placed the Earth back on the Spiral of Evolution where we were always supposed to be. The success of that event cleared the way for the next vitally important facet of the experiment that was unfolding on Earth.

When Mother Earth reclaimed her rightful place on the Spiral of Evolution, the Light of God still flowing through her meridians from Harmonic Convergence reactivated her Crystal Grid System. This system, which is actually Mother Earth's acupuncture system, had been almost dormant since our fall from Grace. For aeons of time, Mother Earth had been able to receive barely enough Light from our Father-Mother God to maintain her survival.

The Company of Heaven told us that Harmonic Convergence was initiating a 25-year period during which awakening Humanity had the opportunity to avert the potential catastrophic predictions for the end times that were fast approaching. They said that during the first five years awakening Humanity would be guided through myriad activities of Light that would prepare the Earth and all her Life for our initial ascent into the 4th Dimension.

Our Father-Mother God and the Company of Heaven encoded the sacred knowledge revealing these activities of Light onto the unformed primal Light substance in the mental and emotional strata of Mother Earth. That allowed this information to be tangibly available to every single person who was willing to lift up in consciousness. During that 5-year period, hundreds of thousands of Lightworkers around the world responded to their inner guidance and orchestrated various activities of Light that added to the Light of the world. Many of these Lightworkers were oblivious to what anyone else on the planet was doing. They just intuitively knew that they were being called to a higher service on behalf of Humanity and Mother Earth.

As the five years following Harmonic Convergence were drawing to a close, awakening Humanity became aware of a celestial alignment and a global event that the Company of Heaven referred to as *"Moving through the Doorway of 11:11."* Eleven is the master number that reflects the transformation from the physical into the Divine. 11:11 is a sacred geometric code that our I AM Presence encoded within our DNA prior to this embodiment. The Divine Intent of this code is to alert our I AM Presence that the time has arrived to begin the Divine Alchemy of transforming our Earthly Bodies from carbon-based planetary Beings into crystalline-based Solar Light Beings.

The event referred to as *"Moving through the Doorway of 11:11"* involved a six month activity of Light that culminated in Earth's Ascension up the Spiral of Evolution into the initial impulses of the 4th-Dimension. Like Harmonic Convergence, hundreds of thousands of Lightworkers participated in this event in their own way. The collective frequency from every activity of Light ushered Mother Earth and ALL her Life into the 4th-Dimension God Victoriously.

This event began with a very powerful Solar Eclipse on July 11, 1991. This was the first eleven of the 11:11 Doorway. The influx of Light Humanity and Mother Earth received that day built in momentum and frequency until the celestial alignment that occurred on January 11, 1992. That was the second eleven of the 11:11 Doorway. The influx of Light Humanity and Mother Earth received that day catapulted us up the Spiral of Evolution into the initial frequencies of the 4rh Dimension.

This is the event that initiated the Divine Alchemy that began the process of transforming our Earthly Bodies from carbon-based cells into crystalline-based cells. When we Ascended into the initial frequencies of the 4th-Dimension on January 11, 1992, our I AM Presence breathed our 3rd-Dimensional *Planetary Christ Presence* and our 3rd-Dimensional Spine and Sevenfold Chakra System into the full embrace of our 4th-Dimensional *Solar Christ Presence* and our 4th-Dimensional Solar Spine and Twelvefold Solar Chakra System. When that occurred our Planetary Christ Presence merged with our Solar Christ Presence and they became One. From that moment on, we were no longer a 3rd-Dimensional Planetary Being. We were a 4th-Dimensional Solar Being who was beginning the Divine Alchemy of becoming a 5th-Dimensional Crystalline Solar Light Being. This Divine Alchemy was also beginning within the physical, etheric, mental and emotional strata of Mother Earth.

For *eleven years* following the events of "*Moving through the Doorway of 11:11,*" awakening Humanity participated in myriad activities of Light involving the unified efforts of Heaven and Earth. Day by day our I AM Presence and our Body Elemental assisted us in assimilating 4th-Dimensional frequencies of the Twelve Solar Aspects of Deity through our

4th-Dimensional Solar Spine and our Twelve 4th-Dimensional Solar Chakras.

Then, in 2003, the Company of Heaven revealed to us that we were ready for the next phase of our Ascension process. Awakening Humanity, in unison with the Beings of Light in the Realms of Illumined Truth, cocreated a global activity of Light designed to move Mother Earth and all Life evolving upon her into the initial impulse of the 5th-Dimension.

Ascending Into the 5th Dimension

On the anniversary of Harmonic Convergence in August of 2003, Humanity en masse reached a frequency of vibration that allowed us to Ascend up the Spiral of Evolution into the initial impulse of the 5th Dimension.

During a global activity of Light in August of 2003, our 5th-Dimensional *I AM Presence* breathed our 4th-Dimensional *Solar Christ Presence* and our 4th-Dimensional Solar Spine and Twelve Solar Chakras into the initial embrace of our I AM Presence's 5th-Dimensional Solar Spine and Twelve 5th-Dimensional Solar Chakras. When that occurred our *Solar Christ Presence* and our 4th-Dimensional Solar Spine and Twelve Solar Chakras merged and became One with our 5th-Dimensional *I AM Presence* and our I AM Presence's 5th-Dimensional Solar Spine and Twelve Solar Chakras.

With the God Victorious success of that facet of our Ascension process, our I AM Presence began the Divine Alchemy of integrating into to our Earthly Bodies at a cellular level for the very first time. Now our 5th-Dimensional I AM Presence no longer has to step down its frequency of vibration into our 4th-Dimensional Solar Christ Presence and then into our 3rd-Dimensional Planetary Christ Presence in order to interact with our Earthly Bodies.

Our Planetary Christ Presence and our Solar Christ Presence have Ascended in energy, vibration and consciousness. They have permanently merged and become One with our I AM Presence. That means that all we need to do now is focus on our 5th-Dimensional I AM Presence, our 5th-Dimensional Solar Spine and our Twelve 5th-Dimensional Solar Chakras.

Our Father-Mother God have assured us that the events that took place in August of 2003 were victoriously accomplished through the I AM Presence of every man, woman and child on Earth. They revealed that this miraculous facet of our Ascension process paved the way for the return of our Mother God.

Dear One, meditate on this information that the Company of Heaven has shared with us. Ask your I AM Presence to assist you in tangibly experiencing your 5th-Dimensional Solar Spine and your Twelve 5th-Dimensional Solar Chakras.

71

THE NEXT PHASE OF OUR PHYSICAL TRANSFORMATION

In the last chapter the Beings of Light told us about the Divine Intervention and the activities of Light that paved the way for the return of our Mother God. Our God Parents said that the return of our Mother God is the ultimate reason why *every* man, woman and child on Earth was mercifully allowed to make it through the Shift of the Ages. In this chapter, the Company of Heaven will share information about the return of our Mother God and additional acts of Divine Intervention that have propelled us forward in the Light. These events brought us to the phase of our physical transformation that is unfolding right now.

The catalyst for our fall from Grace was Humanity's fateful decision to close our Heart Chakra. We erroneously believed that this would prevent us from feeling the pain of the human miscreations we inadvertently created when we began expressing our thoughts and feelings in ways that were not based in Love.

When we closed our Heart Chakra, our Mother God was forced to reduce the Divine Love she perpetually breathed into our right-brain hemisphere and our Heart Flame to a fraction of its original intensity. This caused our right brain to become almost dormant and our spiritual brain centers to atrophy. In turn, our Crown Chakra closed and we lost Christ Consciousness. This prevented us from being able to communicate on a conscious level with our I AM Presence and the Company of Heaven.

Since that tragic event aeons ago, everything our Father-Mother God and the Company of Heaven have done to help the Sons and Daughters of God on Earth, has been designed to inspire us to open our Heart Chakra and to return to the Path of Divine Love, so that our Mother God could reclaim her rightful place in every person's Heart Flame. Every single Being of Light in the Realms of Illumined Truth knows that the return of our Mother God 's Divine Love is the *only* way the Children of Earth will ever be able to return to Christ Consciousness.

In August of 2003, after our 4th-Dimensional Solar Christ Presence merged and became One with our 5th-Dimensional I AM Presence and our 5th-Dimensional Solar Spine and Twelve 5th-Dimensional Solar Chakras, Lightworkers around the world became aware of another activity of Light. The Divine Intent of that activity was for Humanity to create an Open Door through which our Mother God would help us begin the process of opening our 5th-Dimensional Heart Chakras.

That activity of Light was a complex and multifaceted global event called *Harmonic Concordance*. It occurred during a very powerful Eclipse Series that began with a Lunar Eclipse on November 8, 2003 and culminated with a Solar Eclipse on November 23, 2003. These Eclipses coincided with a rare celestial alignment that opened a portal of Divine Consciousness that extended from the Heart of our

Father-Mother God into the Sun of Even Pressure in the Heart of Mother Earth.

During that event, Lightworkers around the world responded to our Mother God's Clarion Call and cocreated a collective Cup of Consciousness that empowered the I AM Presence of every person on Earth to begin the process of gently opening our 5th-Dimensional Solar Heart Chakra. This miraculous event initiated the return of our Mother God within the Heart Flame of every man, woman and child on Earth.

Since that Cosmic Moment, our Mother God has been working in unison with the I AM Presence of every person to intensify the Divine Love that is now flowing to some degree through each person's right brain and Heart Flame. This is a very individual process that is unfolding for every person in perfect alignment with his or her Divine Plan.

After several years of assimilating our Mother God's Divine Love into our Heart Flames, in December of 2010 we were told by the Company of Heaven that Humanity had reached a critical mass that would allow Lightworkers to cocreate a New Planetary CAUSE of Divine Love. People around the world responded and in unison with our Father-Mother God and the Company of Heaven. Awakening Humanity fulfilled that miraculous facet of the Divine Plan.

Once again, that global event was God Victoriously accomplished within the full embrace of a very rare Eclipse Series. During the December 21st Solstice in 2010, we experienced a rare Full Moon Lunar Eclipse. Astrologers at the time reported that a Lunar Eclipse had only occurred during the December Solstice one other time in the past 2,000 years.

On that day, Lightworkers around the world formed a collective Cup of Consciousness that allowed our

Father-Mother God to encode a New Planetary CAUSE of Divine Love within the 5th-Dimensional frequencies of every person's Heart Chakra. That influx of Light bathed the Earth through the Heart Flame of every man, woman and child. The matrix for our New Planetary CAUSE of Divine Love built in momentum until the powerful Solar Eclipse that occurred on January 4, 2011. That Eclipse permanently sealed the patterns of perfection for our Planetary CAUSE of Divine Love in the Core of Purity in every atomic and subatomic particle and wave of Life on Mother Earth.

After that event, our Planetary CAUSE of Divine Love bathed the planet and gradually prepared Mother Earth and all Life evolving upon her at a cellular level for the approaching Shift of the Ages.

During the Solstice on December 21st and 22nd in 2012, we reached that Cosmic Moment that the Company of Heaven had been helping Humanity prepare for during our *500-year Period of Grace and the 25 years following Harmonic Convergence.* On those sacred and holy days, Mother Earth aligned with the Galactic Core of the Milky Way and was instantaneously Inbreathed by our Father-Mother God up the Spiral of Evolution into the next phase of our evolutionary process. That Inbreath simultaneously occurred for every particle and wave of Life throughout the whole of Creation.

The Shift of the Ages birthed the New Earth in all of her resplendent glory in the Realms of Cause. This means that the Divine Matrix for the 5th-Dimensional Crystalline Solar New Earth and all of the patterns of perfection associated with her are ready and waiting to be magnetized into the world of form. This can only be accomplished if you and I and the rest of awakening Humanity invoke the exquisite patterns for the New Earth through our newly recalibrated

Solar Heart Flame and our 5th-Dimensional Crystalline Solar Spine and Twelve Solar Chakras. Our I AM Presence and the Company of Heaven are standing in readiness awaiting the opportunity to help each and every one of us fulfill this essential facet of our Ascension process.

Dear One, if you have been participating in the activities of Light the Company of Heaven has been guiding us through during our Weekly Vlogs since our Father-Mother God initiated their new Divine Plan in January 2018, you realize the amazing assistance we are being provided at this time. The Divine Intent of this Heavenly Assistance is to help every one of us transcend the contamination and chaos surfacing on the old Earth to be healed and transmuted into Light. Nothing will help us to do that more effectively than learning how to consciously invoke the patterns of perfection for the New Earth through our Heart Flame and our 5th-Dimensional Solar Spine and Twelve Solar Chakras.

72

ACTIVATING OUR
5ᵀᴴ-DIMENSIONAL SOLAR SPINE
AND TWELVE SOLAR CHAKRAS

The activities of Light the Company of Heaven have guided us through since the initiation of our Father-Mother God's new Divine Plan have moved Mother Earth and all Life evolving upon her a quantum leap further up the Spiral of Evolution into the 5th-Dimensional frequencies of the New Earth.

These events have allowed our I AM Presence and our 5ᵗʰ-Dimensional Body Elemental to greatly accelerate the Divine Alchemy taking place within our Earthly Bodies. This alchemy is transforming our carbon-based planetary cells into crystalline-based Solar Light Cells. As a result of this Divine Intervention, our physical, etheric, mental and emotional bodies are now able to withstand higher frequencies of the Twelve 5ᵗʰ-Dimensional Solar Aspects of Deity than we have ever been able to assimilate at a cellular level.

To understand just how important this is, we need to remember that the atrocities we have inflicted on our Earthly Bodies and Mother Earth since our fall from Grace cannot be sustained in the full embrace of 5ᵗʰ-Dimensional Crystalline Solar Light. In other words, once we complete our Ascension into the 5ᵗʰ-Dimensional frequencies of the New Earth, we will permanently transcend the negative energy and the toxic substances that have polluted the Earth and contaminated our Earthly Bodies causing aging, disease, decay, degeneration and every other physical malady.

This negative energy and these toxic substances from the old Earth are also what have prevented the I AM Presences of the Millennials and the children from being able to activate the *consciousness codes* within their DNA. These codes contain sacred knowledge that will help the Millennials and the children to awaken and to connect with the life-transforming information they have brought with them into embodiment.

When the *consciousness codes* of these Holy Innocents are activated, they will begin to remember who they are and why they are on Earth during this auspicious time. These precious Ones will then remember the viable solutions they learned in the Inner Realms that will help them transmute every malady existing on Earth back into Light. Their activated codes will let them know that they already have within them all of the knowledge, wisdom, skill and courage they need to be God Victorious in assisting this sweet Earth and ALL her Life through the final stages of our Ascension into the 5ᵗʰ-Dimensional New Earth.

In this chapter the Company of Heaven will guide us through the next phase of the transformational process they have been leading us through this year. This activity of Light is the next step in preparing our Earthly Bodies to receive the incredible influx of Light that will activate the *consciousness codes* of the Millennials and the children during the anniversary of Harmonic Convergence in 2018.

In order to prepare for this activity of Light, the Mighty Elohim who are the Builders of Form have placed above the Earth and also upon the head of every single person, a Twelve-pointed Crown. This forcefield of Light is called the Crown of the Elohim. This is the vehicle through which our Father-Mother God will breathe the highest 5th-Dimensional Crystalline Solar frequencies of the Twelve Solar Aspects of Deity that the Earth and Humanity are capable of receiving at this time.

As we begin this activity of Light, the Company of Heaven want us to know that the Light of God that is flowing through the Crown of the Elohim upon our head flows through our 5th-Dimensional Solar Spine and our Twelve 5th-Dimensional Solar Chakras in a unique way.

In our 5th-Dimensional Crystalline Solar Spine each Chakra is a sphere of Light that pulsates with all Twelve Solar Aspects of Deity simultaneously. These twelve spheres of Light are aligned along our spinal column from our Crown Chakra at the top of our head to our Root Chakra at the base of our spine. The Twelve Solar Aspects of Deity that simultaneously radiate through each of our Twelve 5th-Dimensional Solar Chakras are known as *The Circle of the Sacred Twelve*.

In our 5th-Dimensional Crystalline Solar Spine, all Twelve Chakras reflect all Twelve Solar Aspects of Deity all of the time. However, if we want to amplify one of the Solar Aspects of Deity for a particular reason or in a particular situation, all we have to do is simply ask our I AM Presence to increase that specific Aspect of Deity. Instantaneously, the Light and Divine Qualities from that Solar Aspect of Deity begin pulsating at an intensified level through all Twelve Chakras.

For instance, if we want to increase the 5th Solar Aspect of Healing through our own physical bodies or project it to a person or a location on Earth, we simply ask our I AM Presence to amplify the 5th Solar Aspect of Healing. Instantly the Emerald Green Healing Light associated with the 5th Aspect of Deity begins blazing through all Twelve Solar Chakras until each one becomes a resplendent Emerald Green Sun of Healing. If we want to increase the 3rd Solar Aspect of Divine Love, we simply ask our I AM Presence to amplify the 3rd Solar Aspect of Deity. Instantly the Crystalline Pink frequencies of Divine Love blaze through all Twelve Solar Chakras until each one becomes a resplendent Pink Sun of Divine Love.

Our I AM Presence always monitors the situation and when the appropriate amount of Healing or Divine Love has been projected through our Twelve Solar Chakras, the Circle of the Sacred Twelve is balanced once again in every Chakra. We can amplify one or more of the Aspects of Deity through our 5th-Dimensional Solar Chakras anytime we want to, and we can do it as often as we like according to the need of the hour and our service to the Light.

The Company of Heaven said that at this time Humanity is experiencing major changes at a cellular level through our 5th-Dimensional Crystalline Solar Spines and Twelve Solar Chakras. This increase in vibration is actually altering and rebuilding our nervous systems. These pathways of Light are being strengthened to accommodate the greatly intensified 5th-Dimensional Crystalline Solar Light now pouring into the planet. Our nervous systems are being recalibrated to withstand higher levels of Divine Wisdom and Sacred Knowledge.

Our spiritual brain centers are also being altered in profound ways through this new infusion of Crystalline Solar Light. As Christ Consciousness filters into our outer mind, our I AM Presence is releasing new visions of possibility in which Oneness, Divine Love and Reverence for ALL Life are becoming tangible realities for every Human Being.

Now, if you have the Heart Call to do so, the Company of Heaven will lead us through an activity of Light. One by one, our Father-Mother God will breathe the Twelve Solar Aspects of greatly intensified 5th-Dimensional Crystalline Solar Light through the Crown of the Elohim above the Earth and the Crown of the Elohim now pulsating on every person's head. These Twelve Solar Aspects of Deity will flow through the Twelve Points on the Crown of the Elohim in a clockwise position beginning with the First Aspect of Deity at the one o'clock position and ending with the Twelfth Aspect of Deity at the twelve o'clock position. And we begin.

Amplifying the Twelve 5th-Dimensional Crystalline Solar Aspects of Deity

I AM my I AM Presence and I AM One with the I AM Presence of every man, woman and child on Earth. As One unified Heart Flame, we now invoke the Mighty Solar Elohim to project their luminous Presence into the atmosphere of Earth.

Blessed Ones, accelerate the expansion of the Circle of the Sacred Twelve and the Divine Qualities associated with each of the Twelve Solar Aspects of Deity through the Crown of the Elohim above the Earth and upon every person's head. Anchor this Divine Light through every person's 5th-Dimensional Crystalline Solar Spine and Twelve Solar Chakras.

1. I invoke the 1st Solar Aspect of Deity which is Sapphire Blue.

The Divine Qualities associated with the 1st Solar Aspect of Deity are God's Will, Illumined Faith, Power, Protection and God's First Cause of Perfection. This is the Ray of Light that reflects the Masculine Polarity of our Father God. All 12 of my Chakras are now blazing Sapphire Blue Suns of Light.

2. Now I invoke the 2nd Solar Aspect of Deity which is Sunshine Yellow.

The Divine Qualities associated with the 2nd Solar Aspect of Deity are Enlightenment, Wisdom, Illumination and Constancy. This is the Ray of Light that reflects the Christ Consciousness of the Sons and Daughters of God. All 12 of my Chakras are now blazing Sunshine Yellow Suns of Light.

3. I now invoke the 3rd Solar Aspect of Deity which is Crystalline Pink.

The Divine Qualities associated with the 3rd Solar Aspect of Deity are Transfiguring Divine Love, Oneness, Reverence for ALL Life, Adoration and Tolerance. This is the Ray of Light that reflects the Feminine Polarity of our Mother God, the Holy Spirit. All 12 of my Chakras are now blazing Crystalline Pink Suns of Light.

4. I invoke the 4th Solar Aspect of Deity which is White.

The Divine Qualities associated with the 4th Solar Aspect of Deity are Purity, Hope, Restoration, Resurrection, Ascension and the Immaculate Concept. All 12 of my Chakras are now blazing White Suns of Light.

5. Now I invoke the 5th Solar Aspect of Deity which is Emerald Green.

The Divine Qualities associated with the 5th Solar Aspect of Deity are Illumined Truth, Healing, Consecration,

Concentration and Inner Vision. All 12 of my Chakras are now blazing Emerald Green Suns of Light.

6. I now invoke the 6th Solar Aspect of Deity which is Ruby-Gold.

The Divine Qualities associated with the 6th Solar Aspect of Deity are Divine Grace, Healing, Devotional Worship, Peace and the Manifestation of the Christ. All 12 of my Chakras are now blazing Ruby-Gold Suns of Light.

7. I invoke the 7th Solar Aspect of Deity which is Violet.

The Divine Qualities associated with the 7th Solar Aspect of Deity are Mercy, Compassion, Forgiveness, Transmutation, Liberty, Justice, Freedom, Victory and God's Infinite Perfection. This is the Ray of Light that reflects the perfect balance of the Masculine and Feminine Polarities of our Father-Mother God. The Violet Flame of God's Infinite Perfection will be the predominant frequency of Light bathing the Earth during the Aquarian Age which we have now entered. All 12 of my Chakras are now blazing Violet Suns of Light.

8. Now I invoke the 8th Solar Aspect of Deity which is Aquamarine.

The Divine Qualities associated with the 8th Solar Aspect of Deity are Clarity, Divine Perception, Discernment and Understanding. All 12 of my Chakras are now blazing Aquamarine Suns of Light.

9. I now invoke the 9th Solar Aspect of Deity which is Magenta.

The Divine Qualities associated with the 9th Solar Aspect of Deity are Harmony, Balance, Assurance and God

Confidence. All 12 of my Chakras are now blazing Magenta Suns of Light.

10. I invoke the 10th Solar Aspect of Deity which is Gold.

The Divine Qualities associated with the 10th Solar Aspect of Deity are Eternal Peace, Prosperity, Abundance and the God Supply of ALL Good Things. All 12 of my Chakras are now blazing Golden Suns of Light.

11. Now I invoke the 11th Solar Aspect of Deity which is Peach.

The Divine Qualities associated with the 11th Solar Aspect of Deity are Divine Purpose, Enthusiasm and Joy. All 12 of my Chakras are now blazing Peach Suns of Light.

12. And finally I invoke the 12th Solar Aspect of Deity which is Opal.

The Divine Qualities associated with the 12th Solar Aspect of Deity are Transformation and Transfiguration. All 12 of my Chakras are now blazing Opal Suns of Light.

Now that this NEW frequency of 5th-Dimensional Crystalline Solar Light is secured through every person's Solar Spine and our Twelve Solar Chakras our I AM Presence returns each Chakra to the balanced frequency of the *Circle of the Sacred Twelve.*

We accept and know that this resplendent Light will be amplified one thousand fold every single day through our Planetary Grid of Transfiguring Divine Love.

Beloved Father-Mother God and Beloved Elohim, we thank you for the assistance you are giving to Humanity during this momentous time.

And so it is. Beloved I AM That I AM.

Precious Heart, focus on this incredible Gift of Light that has been given to us by our Father-Mother God. In the next chapter we will be blessed with another activity of Light that will take us through the next phase of the Divine Alchemy we are all experiencing.

73

ACTIVATING OUR
5TH-DIMENSIONAL CRYSTALLINE
SOLAR LIGHT BODIES

In the last few chapters, the Company of Heaven has clearly revealed to us what the *Twelve Solar Aspects of Deity* are and how important this 5th-Dimensional Crystalline Light is in the Divine Alchemy of transforming our Earthly Bodies and the Bodies of Mother Earth from carbon-based cells into Crystalline-based Solar Light Cells. This sacred knowledge makes it much easier for us to comprehend what an incredible Gift the following activity of Light is for Humanity and Mother Earth.

Our Father-Mother God have given us this powerful activity of Light which will help our I AM Presence and our Body Elemental accelerate the Divine Alchemy taking place in our Earthly Bodies. All we have to do to receive the full benefit of this Gift is to allow our I AM Presence and our 5th-Dimensional Body Elemental to download these patterns into the Core of Purity in every electron of our physical, etheric, mental and emotional bodies. If you have the Heart Call to be the Open Door for this Gift from our

God Parents on behalf of yourself and all Humanity, please follow me through this guided visualization with the full power of your attention and your Divine Intentions. And we begin.

I AM Cocreating My 5th-Dimensional Crystalline Solar Light Bodies

I AM my I AM Presence and I AM One with the I AM Presence of every man, woman and child evolving on this planet. I AM One with my Father-Mother God, I AM One with the Solar Logos from Suns beyond Suns beyond Suns, I AM One with the entire Company of Heaven, and I AM One with all of the Beings of Light associated with the Elemental Kingdom and the Angelic Kingdom.

I AM One with every electron of precious Life energy evolving on this planet, and I AM One with every atomic and subatomic particle and wave of energy comprising the physical, etheric, mental, and emotional bodies of Humanity and Mother Earth. I AM also One with all of the spaces in between the atomic and subatomic particles and waves of energy on Earth.

Through the Divine Intervention of this collective Body of Light Beings, I invoke from the Core of Creation the most intensified frequencies of the 5th-Dimensional Crystalline Twelve Solar Aspects of Deity that Humanity and Mother Earth are capable of receiving at this time.

Now, under the direction of our Father-Mother God, the 5th-Dimensional Directors of the Elements take their strategic positions in preparation for this powerful activity of Light.

Thor and Aries, the Directors of the Air Element and the Sylphs of the Air take their positions at the cardinal point to the North.

Neptune and Lunara, the Directors of the Water Element and the Undines of the Water take their positions at the cardinal point to the East.

Virgo and Pelleur, the Directors of the Earth Element and Nature Spirits of the Earth take their positions at the cardinal point to the South.

Helios and Vesta, the Directors of the Fire Element and the Salamanders of the Fire take their positions at the cardinal point to the West.

Amaryllis and Aeolos, the Directors of the Ether Element and the Devas and Deva Rajas of the Ethers take their positions within the Sun of Even Pressure in the Center of the Earth.

Now, all is in readiness. I breathe in deeply and go within to the Divinity of my Heart Flame.

I first perceive my glorious **5th-Dimensional Crystalline Etheric Light Body**. This vehicle is associated with the Air Element. This is the vehicle that is encoded with my full Divine Potential and my Divine Plan. My Etheric Body is the seat of all memory. When trapped on the wheel of karma which was created after the fall, Humanity had little chance of experiencing vibrant health, eternal youth or radiant beauty in our physical bodies. Now, however, my I AM Presence and my 5th-Dimensional Body Elemental take command. The wheel of karma no longer exists. The Ascending Spiral of Evolution and the Law of the Circle now reveal the Immaculate Concept of my Divine Plan and the perfection of my Crystalline Etheric Light Body.

Within my Etheric Body, my I AM Presence now declares to all obsolete karmic patterns, "*Stand aside for the I AM Presence and the perfection of my Crystalline Etheric Light Body.*" The karmic patterns are instantaneously transmuted into Light by the new Solar Frequencies of the Violet Flame.

My Mother God, the Holy Spirit, now Baptizes my Crystalline Etheric Light Body with Sacred Fire. This blessing seals the 5th-Dimensional frequencies of the Air Element within this vehicle and a scintillating forcefield of infinite perfection is formed.

My **5th-Dimensional Crystalline Emotional Light Body** now comes into view. This vehicle is associated with the Water Element. It is the body through which the Love Nature of my Father-Mother God is expressed in the world of form. This is my most powerful vehicle. Eighty percent of my Life Force is released through my Emotional Body.

My I AM Presence and my 5th-Dimensional Body Elemental step forth to take command of this vehicle. As they do, the full Divine Momentum of my Father-Mother God's Love begins to flow through my Heart Flame. The Love of God expands through my Crystalline Emotional Light Body and forms a Cosmic Forcefield of Divine Love that encompasses the entire Planet Earth.

This forcefield of my Father-Mother God's Transfiguring Divine Love intensifies the Love flowing through every person's Heart Flame, and expands each person's 5th-Dimensional Solar Heart Flame to new breadths. Divine Love reigns supreme through all Creation, and this activity of Light ensures that the patterns of perfection for the New Earth are becoming a tangible reality.

Within this all-encompassing Forcefield of Divine Love, the last vestige of my human ego surrenders to my I AM Presence. Within the embrace of my I AM Presence my ego lets go of its resistance to my Divine Plan and its desire to block my Divine Potential as a Beloved Son or Daughter of God.

My ego dissolves into the Loving embrace of my I AM Presence where it is permanently transformed by the Love of my Father-Mother God. My ego is scientifically, psychologically, physiologically and spiritually transformed. My I AM Presence now inbreathes and absorbs the transformed residue of my human ego into the fullness of my true God Reality and all aspects of my own Divinity.

My Mother God now Baptizes my most powerful Crystalline Emotional Light Body with Sacred Fire. Through this blessing, my feeling nature becomes One with the Feeling Nature of God. My emotional world is now filled with God's Infinite Love and all of the various aspects of God's wondrous Love.

Now my **5th-Dimensional Crystalline Physical Light Body** comes to the fore. My Physical Body is associated with the Earth Element. The limitless physical perfection of my I AM Presence is reflected in my magnificent Crystalline Physical Light Body. My I AM Presence and my 5th-Dimensional Body Elemental take command of this vehicle.

My Crystalline Physical Light Body is composed of Crystalline Cells that are absorbing the Twelve Solar Aspects of Deity from the Infinite Universe and assimilating this Crystalline Light into the atoms and molecules that form each cell of my Physical Body. I AM my I AM Presence inbreathing, absorbing, expanding and projecting the fullness of this Crystalline Light into my flesh vehicle. Every cell of my body is becoming a Crystalline Cell. This amazing influx of Light is generating unexplored levels of limitless physical perfection, vibrant health, eternal youth, radiant beauty and God's Infinite Bliss.

My Physical Body will never again accept karma dictating the reality of its physical functioning or its appearance. The old purpose of the flesh vehicle being the repository for karmic lessons that were never learned has been transmuted forever.

My Mother God now Baptizes my Crystalline Physical Light Body with Sacred Fire. Through this blessing the infinite physical perfection of my I AM Presence is sealed in the cellular structures of my Physical Body.

My 5th-Dimensional Crystalline Mental Light Body now reveals itself to me. This vehicle is associated with the Fire Element. My Crystalline Mental Light Body is One with the Divine Mind of God. My I AM Presence and my 5th-Dimensional Body Elemental take command of this vehicle causing it to blaze like a great Sun of Light forming a halo around my head. As the halo of Light expands through my Mental Body, it encompasses all of my Crystalline Light Bodies and I AM a radiant Sun of Infinite Light.

The Fire Breath of my Father-Mother God activates my Divine Mind, and I clearly receive Divine Thoughts, Ideas, Concepts, Imagination and all aspects of Divine Mind beyond Imagination. All of these reflections of Divine Intelligence and Divine Mind are anchoring and reflecting into my outer consciousness.

Slowly but surely, I become aware of this process. It begins with a soft effulgent Light filling my Mental Body. It leads me past the imagination of hopes and dreams of a future Divinity into the ever present moment of Divine Enlightenment, Illumination, Christ Consciousness and Cosmic Wisdom which all Ascended and Cosmic Beings enjoy right now.

All of the layers of human thought, conscious, subconscious and unconscious mind, that were derived from my human ego now slowly dissolve into this Crystalline Light, thus setting up an entirely new Divine Process for assimilating information.

I now perceive everything as energy, vibration and consciousness whether it is something in my daily life or coming to me from dimensions beyond: I watch for this in my meditations and in my awakened life.

My Mother God now Baptizes my Crystalline Mental Light Body with Sacred Fire. Through this blessing the Divine Mind of God is sealed within my conscious mind and perpetually reflects through my Mental Body.

I AM my I AM Presence and as a multidimensional Being I AM now abiding on the New Earth in my Etheric, Emotional, Physical and Mental 5th-Dimensional Crystalline Light Bodies. I accept this profound Truth, and I agree to stay focused on my Earthly Bodies while deeply enjoying the Divine Alchemy that is continually unfolding within them.

And so it is. Beloved I AM, Beloved I AM, Beloved I AM.

Dear One, be gentle with your Earthly Bodies and allow your I AM Presence and your 5th-Dimensional Body Elemental time to integrate this activity of Light at a cellular level.

74

FINAL CRITICAL STEPS
OF PREPARATION

When the Company of Heaven shared the following information we were being held in the embrace of a rare Eclipse Series that was assisting Humanity and Mother Earth through the final steps of preparation prior to the activation of the *consciousness codes* within the DNA of the Millennials and the children.

This three-part Eclipse Series began with a New Moon Solar Eclipse on July 12, 2018. The influx of Light from that Solar Eclipse built in momentum and was greatly enhanced by the Full Moon Lunar Eclipse that took place July 26th and 27th. That Full Moon was called the Blood Moon, and it was the longest total Lunar Eclipse we will experience this century.

That Lunar Eclipse built in momentum and was followed by a very powerful third Eclipse which was another New Moon Solar Eclipse. That Solar Eclipse occurred on August 11th, the day of the Opening Ceremonies for the 32nd Annual World Congress on Illumination. Three Eclipses in a row are rare, but it was not surprising that we experienced that series of Eclipses during the final stages of preparation our Father-Mother God and the Company of Heaven had been guiding us through since the beginning of 2018.

During the Eclipse Series, our Father-Mother God reminded us of the greatest need of the hour. In the silence of every person's newly recalibrated Heart Flame, our Father-Mother God were sounding a Cosmic Tone with the Divine Intent of awakening within each of us the KNOWING that we are ONE and that there is no separation. Through the wondrous activities of Light that the Company of Heaven had been guiding us through, step by step, Humanity was awakening and beginning to lift above the chaos. People around the world were volunteering to be the Open Door for the Light of God. That was pushing everything that conflicted with the Light to the surface to be healed and transmuted back into its original perfection. This accelerated purging was designed to help Humanity complete our Ascension into the full embrace of the New Earth much more quickly.

The chaos and negativity we were witnessing in the outer world were the result of surfacing residue from the miscreations our fragmented and fear-based human egos manifested when we lost awareness of our I AM Presence and the fact that we are Beloved Sons and Daughters of God. As these patterns of separation and duality were being pushed to the surface, in some instances, they triggered Humanity's obsolete etheric records of hatred, prejudice, abuse of power, greed, corruption and selfishness, as well as the dog-eat-dog, looking out for number one and us against them illusions which are all based in ignorance and fear. Our Father-Mother God encouraged awakening Humanity to transcend the illusions of separation and duality we were witnessing. They inspired us to redouble our efforts and to embrace these fearful Sons and Daughters of God with Divine Love.

Outer-world appearances and painful life experiences have caused many people to become cynical about Love and the concept of the Oneness of ALL Life. They think this kind of unconditional Love is unrealistic and superficial. So during that critical stage of our preparation, our Father-Mother God reminded us of an important Truth that they shared with Humanity once our Mother God was finally able to return to Earth.

Please go within to the Divinity of your heart and contemplate these words from On High within the Flame of Illumined Truth.

"So much has been written about Love that it has almost become a platitude, but the Transfiguring Divine Love of our Mother God is the mightiest force in the Universe. It is the vibration from which we were born out of the Heart of God and it is the vibration through which we must now evolve and Ascend back into the Heart of God. The Love of our Mother God has no bonds, nor barriers, nor conditions. Within the infinite power of our Mother God's Love there is no pain or sorrow, no lack or limitation. Her Love contains within its essence the full potential to rise above all human conditions, all self-inflicted suffering, and all manner of chaos, confusion, hopelessness and despair.

"Our Mother God's Love heals the illusion of separation. It rejuvenates, revitalizes and makes whole all that it embraces. It is the single greatest source of Forgiveness, and it reverberates with the full gathered momentum of our Eternal Freedom in the Light. Our Mother's Love is the foundation of ALL Creation. It is the indivisible, unchanging ecstasy that allows us to know Love in all things. When we experience the Love of our Mother God, we understand that we are all One. We KNOW that every particle and

wave of Life is interconnected, interdependent and inter-related. Whether we are a magnificent Sun, a person or a blade of grass, we are united in the Body of our Father-Mother God by the all encompassing cohesive Light of our Mother God's Transfiguring Divine Love.

"As our Mother God reclaims this Earth and once again anoints Humanity with her Infinite Love, we are beginning to experience a deep Reverence for ALL Life. Our Mother's Love is now pulsating within the core of our Beings, it is NOT outside of us. We no longer need to seek the Divine Feminine from afar. We need to merely accept that our Mother God has returned, and that she is now abiding within every person's Heart Flame. Her Love is pulsating within the silent rhythm of every heartbeat, every breath. It is the universal language now speaking to all Humanity through our Gift of Life. As we take the time to listen in the silence of our Heart, we hear the tones and whisperings of our Mother's Love inspired by the wonders of Nature and the Music of the Spheres.

"Our Mother God is now reestablishing her Covenant of Divine Love with the Children of Earth which will enhance our ability to once and for all accept the Gift of Eternal Peace and God's Infinite Abundance. Through this Covenant, the supply of all good things will forever and ever flood into the hands and use of the Sons and Daughters of God. The glory of God's Eternal Peace and Infinite Abundance will be a manifest reality not only in this moment, but far beyond the Earth and time into Eternity."

I AM LOVING ALL LIFE FREE

Our Father-Mother God are now asking us to participate in an activity of Light that will assist every person on Earth, even the most recalcitrant and asleep Sons and Daughters of God, to hear the Cosmic Tone that is reverberating within every person's newly recalibrated Heart Flame. Our selfless participation in this activity of Light will help to awaken within every person on Earth the knowing that "*We are One.*"

Please listen to your heart and participate in this activity of Light as often as you are inspired to do so. And we begin.

I AM my I AM Presence and I AM One with the I AM Presence of every person on Earth. As One Unified Heart, we invoke our Father-Mother God and the entire Company of Heaven to help us raise every person on Earth from a consciousness of separation and duality into a consciousness of Oneness and Reverence for ALL Life. This is being accomplished by every person's I AM Presence in perfect alignment with his or her Divine Plan and the highest good for all concerned.

Beloved Father-Mother God, we ask that you now expand your Divine Love which is pulsating within the Divinity of every person's newly recalibrated Heart Flame. Allow your Love to flow through each person's 5th-Dimensional Heart Chakra until it envelops the entire Planet Earth, greatly intensifying our Planetary Grid of Transfiguring Divine Love. As this unfathomable influx of Light bathes the Earth, every facet of Life is lifted into a Higher Order of Being.

Each person's I AM Presence now creates a sacred space in which they are able to open their 5th-Dimensional Crown Chakra of Enlightenment to full breadth. This allows each person to Ascend ever higher into the awakened state of Christ Consciousness.

As this occurs, multidimensional and multifaceted 5th-Dimensional Crystalline Solar Light expands from the Heart of our Father-Mother God into every cell of Humanity's Earthly Bodies allowing the I AM Presence of every person to take full dominion of their physical, etheric, mental and emotional bodies.

Now, all is in readiness. Through their I AM Presence, every person on Earth is participating at both inner and outer levels in this activity of Light which is raising the consciousness of the masses of Humanity and assisting every person to shift from the illusion of separation and duality into the Reality of Oneness and Reverence for ALL Life.

I now reach up into the Infinity of my own Divine Consciousness. As I AM lifted up, all of Humanity is lifted up with me. In this frequency of Divine Consciousness, I see that Humanity's free will is becoming One with God's Will. The I AM Presence of each person affirms, *"I AM ready to Love ALL Life FREE!"*

Instantaneously, I see the Truth of every person on Earth. I see ALL of my Sisters and Brothers in the Family of Humanity, even the most recalcitrant souls, as precious Sons and Daughters of God, no matter how far their behavior patterns or their life experiences may be from reflecting that Truth. I perceive all of the painful human miscreations associated with my Sisters and Brothers as innocent primordial energy entering my awareness now to be transmuted back into Light and Loved FREE.

I happily greet all of these Children of God and all of their misqualified energy the same way my Father-Mother God would greet them. I greet them with Love from within the embrace of Eternal Peace, Detachment, God Confidence, and Supreme Authority.

Within an Invincible Forcefield of God's Infinite Love, I take my Sisters and Brothers into the Kingdom of Heaven within my Heart Flame, and I hold them in my arms of Light as I would an injured child. They cannot overwhelm me or control me in any way, nor do I need to fear them or shun them. I simply hold them and Love them until they surrender to the Love of God, desiring on their own to enter the Kingdom of Heaven within the Divinity of their own Heart Flame.

Now, rather than feeling rejected and thus perpetuating their negative behavior patterns, my Sisters and Brothers feel accepted and Loved as the innate Sons and Daughters of God they are. They voluntarily release themselves into the Light, and they begin to KNOW that they are ONE with ALL Life.

I rejoice that every person and their unascended energies are at long last finding their way Home and I release myself into the Peace of knowing:

"My I AM Presence is handling ALL imperfection perfectly."

As these precious Ones surrender to the Light, they remember that they are Beloved Sons and Daughters of God. With this sacred knowledge, they once again find their proper place in the Family of Humanity. In perfect Divine Order, they are set FREE to live and cocreate the patterns of Love, Oneness and Reverence for ALL Life on the New Earth. And so it is.

God Bless you, Dear One. I AM Eternally Grateful for you and your willingness to add to the Light of the world.

75

BE HERE NOW!

This is the sharing that was transmitted around the world via our Weekly Vlog during the 32nd Annual World Congress on Illumination. I am going to repeat it in its entirety so you can experience the full moment of this Gift from On High.

As you watch Vlog 75, I AM in Honolulu, Hawaii with Lightworkers from all over the world who responded to their Heart's Call and volunteered to travel to the Portal of Light at Diamond Head to serve as surrogates on behalf of Humanity during the 32nd WCI. We have unified our newly recalibrated 5th-Dimensional Heart Flames and formed a Chalice of Light that is now cradling the entire Planet Earth. Together, we are serving as a mighty transformer through which the Light of God is flowing to accomplish the Divine Plan of activating the *consciousness codes* within the DNA of the Millennials and the children. We are sending all of you our Eternal Gratitude for your willingness to join with us in consciousness today for this vitally important facet of our collective Divine Missions.

Today, our Father-Mother God and the Company of Heaven are going to assist the I AM Presence of every man, woman and child on Earth through the next phase of our physical preparation. Our I AM Presence will work in unison with the Company of Heaven and, step-by-step, we will Ascend to the next level of the incredible physical transformation process we have been experiencing this year.

Know that this activity of Light is occurring in the Eternal Moment of NOW. That means that no matter when you are watching this Vlog or reading this chapter, you are receiving the full gathered momentum of this Gift from our God Parents and the Company of Heaven. So, in deep humility and gratitude, go within to the Divinity of your Heart Flame and BE HERE NOW!

Together, from the deepest recesses of our hearts we affirm,

"The Light of God is ALWAYS Victorious and WE are that Light."

On this sacred and holy day, our Father-Mother God are Consecrating every person's Heart Flame to be the Open Door for this activity of Light which will help the Sons and Daughters of God on Earth to Ascend to the highest possible level of our physical transformation process. This will prepare each and every person on Earth at a cellular level to participate in the life-transforming events that will take place on Wednesday and Thursday, August 15th and 16th, 2018.

During those events, the Light of God will flow through the transformer that has been formed by the Lightworker's unified Heart Flames within the Portal of Light at Diamond Head. This unparalleled frequency of Light from the Heart of our Father-Mother God will permanently activate the pre-encoded *consciousness codes* within the DNA of the Millennials and the children.

To ensure the God Victorious accomplishment of this Divine Plan, Archangel Michael and Saint Germain have agreed to station one of their powerful 5ᵗʰ-Dimensional Archangels within the aura of every person on Earth. Archangel Michael's Angels of Protection will sustain an invincible Forcefield of Protection around every person. Saint Germain's Violet Flame Archangels will daily and hourly transmute into Light everything within this Forcefield of Protection that is surfacing to be healed and restored back into its original perfection. And we begin.

I AM my I AM Presence and I AM One with my Father-Mother God, I AM One with the entire Company of Heaven, I AM One with my Family and Friends who are joining with me from the Heavenly Realms, I AM One with the I AM Presences of the Millennials, the children and every other person on Earth. I AM also One with the Elemental Kingdom, the Angelic Kingdom and Mother Earth.

Archangel Michael and Saint Germain, we ask that you and your Legions of 5ᵗʰ-Dimensional Archangels come forth NOW! Beloved Ones, send your Archangels north, south, east and west. Direct an Angel of Protection and an Angel of the Violet Flame to descend into the aura of every man, woman and child on Earth.

Archangel Michael, encapsulate the Millennials, the children and the rest of Humanity in your invincible Circle of White Lightning, your *"Ring Pass Not of God's First Cause of Perfection."* Prevent anything that is not of the Light from entering this forcefield or interfering with our service to the Light and our Divine Mission of Loving ALL Life FREE.

Saint Germain, place below the feet of every person a 5ᵗʰ-Dimensional Violet Flame Lotus Blossom. Fill the Circle of White Lightning that is now blazing around every person on Earth with exquisite frequencies of the 5ᵗʰ-Dimensional Violet Flame of God's Infinite Perfection. Instantly transmute into Light every thought, word, feeling or action we have ever expressed, or that we may express in the future, that is less than the Love and Light of our I AM Presence as we decree:

"Transmute, transmute by the Violet Fire all causes and cores not of God's desire. I AM a Being of Cause alone; that Cause is Love, the Sacred Tone."

As a Gift to awakening Humanity, Archangel Michael and Saint Germain are now directing their Archangels to remain within the aura of every person on this planet until Humanity and Mother Earth have completed our Ascension onto the New Earth.

Now, our Father-Mother God invoke the 5th-Dimensional Directors of the Five Elements and the newly initiated 5th-Dimensional Body Elemental within the Earthly Bodies of every Son and Daughter of God evolving on this planet. The Directors of the Five Elements will now breathe the highest possible frequencies of the Ether, Air, Fire, Water and Earth Elements through Humanity's newly activated Elemental Vortices. This 5th-Dimensional Elemental Substance will renew, rejuvenate and lift Humanity's physical, etheric, mental and emotional bodies into the highest frequencies of 5th-Dimensional Crystalline Elemental Light that Cosmic Law will allow.

We begin by focusing our attention on the Ether Vortex which pulsates above our head. We breathe the Sacred Fire Breath of the Holy Spirit into the center of the Ether Vortex and affirm with deep feeling:

I AM THAT I AM.
I AM THAT I AM.
I AM THAT I AM.

We now focus the full power of our attention on the Air Vortex which is pulsating in the area of our Throat Chakra. We breathe the Sacred Fire Breath of the Holy Spirit into the center of the Air Vortex and affirm with deep feeling:

I AM THE BREATH OF THE HOLY SPIRIT.
I AM THE BREATH OF THE HOLY SPIRIT.
I AM THE BREATH OF THE HOLY SPIRIT.

We now focus the full power of our attention on the Fire Vortex which is pulsating within the location of our sternum in the center of our chest. We breathe the Sacred Fire Breath of the Holy Spirit into the center of the Fire Vortex and affirm with deep feeling:

I AM THE FIRE BREATH OF THE ALMIGHTY.
I AM THE FIRE BREATH OF THE ALMIGHTY.
I AM THE FIRE BREATH OF THE ALMIGHTY.

We now focus the full power of our attention on the Water Vortex which is pulsating within the location of our Root Chakra at the base of our spine. We breathe the Sacred Fire Breath of the Holy Spirit into the center of the Water Vortex and affirm with deep feeling:

I AM THE HARMONY OF MY TRUE BEING.
I AM THE HARMONY OF MY TRUE BEING.
I AM THE HARMONY OF MY TRUE BEING.

We now focus the full power of our attention on the Earth Vortex which is pulsating between our feet. We breathe the Sacred Fire Breath of the Holy Spirit into the center of the Earth Vortex and affirm with deep feeling:

I AM THE MASTER OF MY PHYSICAL REALITY.
I AM THE MASTER OF MY PHYSICAL REALITY.
I AM THE MASTER OF MY PHYSICAL REALITY.

Our Five Elemental Vortices are now receiving the highest frequencies of 5th-Dimensional Crystalline Elemental Light that we are capable of withstanding at a cellular level.

We now move to the next step in our physical preparation. In May, Mother Mary assisted the I AM Presence of every person on Earth to Transfigure the Permanent Seed Atom within our heart that holds our Immortal Victorious Threefold Flame. Every person's Permanent Seed Atom is now a 5th-Dimensional Crystalline brazier of Light that is capable of sustaining NEW 5th-Dimensional frequencies of our recalibrated and balanced Threefold Flame which consists of the Blue Flame of our Father God's Power, the Pink Flame of our Mother God's Love and the Yellow-gold Flame of the Sons and Daughters of God's Wisdom and Christ Consciousness. Today our Father-Mother God are taking this expansion of our Heart Flames to brand new levels.

The Holy Breath is the vehicle for the assimilation and the expansion of our Immortal Victorious Threefold Flame. As we Breathe the Holy Breath in and out through our Heart Flame, our inner journey to God and our outer service to Life are brought into perfect balance. It is within this balance that we are able to return to Christ Consciousness, and it is within this balance that we permanently reconnect with our I AM Presence which is the Keeper of our Heart Flame.

It is now within this balance that our Father-Mother God take this activity of Light to the next level. On the Holy Breath, our Father-Mother God are now integrating into the Permanent Seed Atom in our hearts higher frequencies of our balanced and recalibrated 5th-Dimensional

Solar Threefold Flames than we have ever experienced. As our I AM Presence assimilates this Gift from On High, the Threefold Flame within every person's heart expands and expands until it envelops our physical, etheric, mental and emotional bodies.

Now all is in readiness, and our Father-Mother God will breathe through the Twelve-pointed Crown of the Elohim above the Earth, and the Twelve-pointed Crown of the Elohim pulsating on every person's brow, the most intensified frequencies of the 5th-Dimensional Crystalline Twelve Solar Aspects of Deity that Humanity is capable of receiving.

These Twelve Solar Aspects of Deity will flow one by one through the Twelve Points on the Crown of the Elohim in a clockwise position, beginning with the First Aspect of Deity at the one o'clock position and ending with the Twelfth Aspect of Deity at the twelve o'clock position. And we begin.

Our Father-Mother God and the Mighty Elohim now intensify the expansion of the Circle of the Sacred Twelve and the Divine Qualities associated with each of the Twelve Solar Aspects of Deity through the Crown of the Elohim above the Earth and upon every person's brow. As these brand NEW 5th-Dimensional Crystalline Solar frequencies of Light are received, one by one, they flow through every person's 5th-Dimensional Crystalline Solar Spine and are secured within every person's Twelve 5th-Dimensional Solar Chakras.

1. We begin by receiving brand new frequencies of the 1st Solar Aspect of Deity which is Sapphire Blue.

The Divine Qualities associated with the 1st Solar Aspect of Deity are God's Will, Illumined Faith, Power, Protection and God's First Cause of Perfection. This is the Ray of Light that reflects the Masculine Polarity of our Father God.

As this exquisite Light flows through our 5th-Dimensional Spinal Column, all 12 of our Chakras become blazing Sapphire Blue Suns of Light.

2. **We now receive brand new frequencies of the 2nd Solar Aspect of Deity which is Sunshine Yellow.**

The Divine Qualities associated with the 2nd Solar Aspect of Deity are Enlightenment, Wisdom, Illumination and Constancy. This is the Ray of Light that reflects the enlightened state of Christ Consciousness within every Son and Daughter of God. This new frequency of Light now flows through all 12 of our Chakras transforming them into blazing Sunshine Yellow Suns of Light.

3. **We now receive brand new frequencies of the 3rd Solar Aspect of Deity which is Crystalline Pink.**

The Divine Qualities associated with the 3rd Solar Aspect of Deity are Transfiguring Divine Love, Oneness, Reverence for ALL Life, Adoration and Tolerance. This is the Ray of Light that reflects the Feminine Polarity of our Mother God, the Holy Spirit. This new frequency of Light now flows through all 12 of our Chakras transforming them into blazing Crystalline Pink Suns of Light.

4. **We now receive brand new frequencies of the 4th Solar Aspect of Deity which is White.**

The Divine Qualities associated with the 4th Solar Aspect of Deity are Purity, Hope, Restoration, Resurrection, Ascension and the Immaculate Concept. This new frequency of Light now flows through all 12 of our Chakras transforming them into blazing White Suns of Light.

5. We now receive brand new frequencies of the 5th Solar Aspect of Deity which is Emerald Green.

The Divine Qualities associated with the 5th Solar Aspect of Deity are Illumined Truth, Healing, Consecration, Concentration and Inner Vision. This new frequency of Light now flows through all 12 of our Chakras transforming them into blazing Emerald Green Suns of Light.

6. We now receive brand new frequencies of the 6th Solar Aspect of Deity which is Ruby-Gold.

The Divine Qualities associated with the 6th Solar Aspect of Deity are Divine Grace, Healing, Devotional Worship, Peace and the Manifestation of the Christ. This new frequency of Light now flows through all 12 of our Chakras transforming them into blazing Ruby-Gold Suns of Light.

7. We now receive brand new frequencies of the 7th Solar Aspect of Deity which is Violet.

The Divine Qualities associated with the 7th Solar Aspect of Deity are Mercy, Compassion, Forgiveness, Transmutation, Liberty, Justice, Freedom, Victory and God's Infinite Perfection. This is the Ray of Light that reflects the perfect balance of the Masculine and Feminine Polarities of our Father-Mother God. The Violet Flame of God's Infinite Perfection will be the predominant frequency of Light bathing the Earth during the Aquarian Age which we have now entered. This new frequency of Light now flows through all 12 of our Chakras transforming them into blazing Violet Suns of Light.

8. We now receive brand new frequencies of the 8th Solar Aspect of Deity which is Aquamarine.

The Divine Qualities associated with the 8th Solar Aspect of Deity are Clarity, Divine Perception, Discernment and Understanding. This new frequency of Light now flows through all 12 of our Chakras transforming them into blazing Aquamarine Suns of Light.

9. We now receive brand new frequencies of the 9th Solar Aspect of Deity which is Magenta.

The Divine Qualities associated with the 9th Solar Aspect of Deity are Harmony, Balance, Assurance and God Confidence. This new frequency of Light now flows through all 12 of our Chakras transforming them into blazing Magenta Suns of Light.

10. We now receive brand new frequencies of the 10th Solar Aspect of Deity which is Gold.

The Divine Qualities associated with the 10th Solar Aspect of Deity are Eternal Peace, Prosperity, Abundance and the God Supply of ALL Good Things. This new frequency of Light now flows through all 12 of our Chakras transforming them into blazing Golden Suns of Light.

11. We now receive brand new frequencies of the 11th Solar Aspect of Deity which is Peach.

The Divine Qualities associated with the 11th Solar Aspect of Deity are Divine Purpose, Enthusiasm and Joy. This new frequency of Light now flows through all 12 of our Chakras transforming them into blazing Peach Suns of Light.

12. And now we receive brand new frequencies of the 12th Solar Aspect of Deity which is Opal.

The Divine Qualities associated with the 12th Solar Aspect of Deity are Transformation and Transfiguration. This new frequency of Light now flows through all 12 of our Chakras transforming them into blazing Opal Suns of Light.

Now that these brand NEW frequencies of the Twelve 5th-Dimensional Crystalline Solar Aspects of Deity are secured through every person's Solar Spine and our Twelve Solar Chakras, our I AM Presence returns each Chakra to the balanced frequency of the *Circle of the Sacred Twelve.* Within the *Circle of the Sacred Twelve* all Twelve Aspects of Deity reverberate through all Twelve 5th-Dimemsional Solar Chakras simultaneously.

Precious Heart, for the next several days be gentle with yourself. Stay focused in your Heart Flame. Breathe deeply and drink lots of water. Know that Love is ALL there is. And TRUST that your I AM Presence has guided you through this preparation in perfect alignment with your Divine Plan. You have been preparing for lifetimes to be *"The Open Door that no one can shut"* for the Light of God during this Cosmic Moment on Planet Earth.

76

INFINITE GRATITUDE FROM OUR FATHER-MOTHER GOD AND THE COMPANY OF HEAVEN

Our Father-Mother God and the Company of Heaven are flooding the Millennials, the children, awakening Humanity and the I AM Presence of every other Son and Daughter of God on Earth with Infinite Gratitude and Love. This blessing from On High reflects our God Parent's deep appreciation for our willingness to serve as Instruments of God during the critical phase of Earth's Divine Plan that we have just accomplished God Victoriously.

Through the unified efforts of Heaven and Earth, the I AM Presence of every Millennial and every child was able to permanently activate the *consciousness codes* within their DNA. The sacred knowledge within the *consciousness codes* of these precious Ones is now permanently available to them. Our Father-Mother God have assured us that now, in Divine Timing, viable solutions for every malady existing on the old Earth will begin surfacing into the conscious minds of the Holy Innocents through their intuitive inner knowing.

The Holy Innocents were born karma free. The Divine Intent of their *consciousness codes* is to provide these enlightened souls with easy access to the Divine Wisdom they accumulated while they were learning and growing in the Temples in the electronic belt around our Central Sun of Alpha and Omega. They learned this sacred knowledge during the aeons of time they spent in the Temples of the Sun while waiting for the Cosmic Moment when Humanity and the Earth would, at long last, Ascend off of the wheel of karma. That Cosmic Moment arrived during Harmonic Convergence in August of 1987.

Our Father-Mother God have revealed that while waiting in the Inner Realms, the Millennials and the children were trained in unique and powerful ways that will help the rest of us to transcend the pain and suffering of our human miscreations. Their *consciousness codes* resonate with the profound Truth that *"We are One"* and that *"Love is ALL there is."* This knowing is the enlightened consciousness of the New Earth and it reflects *"Reverence for ALL Life."*

Whether or not they are consciously aware of it at this time, the Millennials and the children have come to help all of us to transmute into Light the atrocities Humanity has inflicted on Mother Earth and all Life evolving upon her. As the purging is completed, the Millennials and the children will help the rest of Humanity to easily cocreate the patterns of perfection for the New Earth. The Company of Heaven said that this will occur in wondrous ways that we have not yet imagined.

As we bask in the embrace of Gratitude and Love from our Father-Mother God, the Company of Heaven is encouraging us to take full advantage of the assistance Saint Germain and his Violet Flame Archangels are giving to us. Now that the *consciousness codes* of the Millennials and the children have been activated, everything you and I and the rest of awakening Humanity do to assist in transmuting the surfacing negativity into Light will greatly accelerate the effectiveness of this activation within their DNA.

If you have the Heart Call to do so, please join with the Lightworkers all over the world who are joining with us in the timeless, spaceless Eternal Moment of Now. And we begin.

Invoking the Violet Flame

Through the Beloved Presence of God, I AM, now blazing in my heart and in the hearts of ALL Humanity, I invoke the Legions of Light throughout Infinity who are associated with the 5th-Dimensional Crystalline frequencies of the Violet Flame of God's Infinite Perfection.

Beloved Ones, on behalf of myself and ALL Humanity I ask that you bathe the Earth and all her Life in the most intensified frequencies of this Violet Flame that we are capable of withstanding at a cellular level.

Blaze this Sacred Fire in, through and around every atomic and subatomic particle and wave of Life on Earth that is vibrating at a frequency less than the patterns of perfection for the New Earth.

Beloved I AM Presence, look into my life and the lives of ALL Humanity. See what human miscreations remain that we need to transmute into Light.

Blaze the Violet Flame through every thought, feeling, word or action we have ever expressed to any person, place, condition or thing that may have wronged them at any time, in any way, for any reason whatsoever.

Beloved I AM Presence, reach your great loving hands of Light into all of the positively qualified energy we have released throughout our Earthly sojourns. Draw forth a thousand times as much perfection as we have ever done wrong.

Fashion from this substance of perfection a Gift of Love, whatever is necessary, in order to balance every debt we have created which still remains unpaid to any part of Life.

Beloved Father-Mother God, we ask you to Forgive every person, place, condition or thing that may have wronged us at any time, in any way, for any reason whatsoever. Balance with your Divine Love all debts owed to us by Life everywhere.

We accept that our prayers are being God Victoriously accomplished even as we Call And so it is.

God Bless you, Dear One. Mother Earth and the I AM Presence of every person on this planet are Eternally Grateful for you and your willingness to add to the Light of the world.

77

Empowering the Patterns of Perfection for the New Earth

Several years ago, in response to a request from our Father-Mother God, awakening Lightworkers began downloading the patterns of perfection for the New Earth from the Realms of Cause and anchoring these patterns into the Divinity of our Heart Flames. Everything begins in the Realms of Cause. In order for something from the Realms of Cause to then manifest in the physical world of form which is the world of effects, it must be drawn through the Divinity within the Heart Flame of the Sons and Daughters of God abiding in the physical plane.

The Beings of Light said that beginning the process of downloading the patterns of perfection for the New Earth was a necessary first step for eventually manifesting those patterns in the physical plane. Lightworkers accepted this mission and have been diligently downloading these patterns ever since. Periodically over the years, as more of Humanity awakened, these patterns for the New Earth were raised into higher and higher frequencies of 5th-Dimensional Crystalline Solar Light.

Now that the masses of Humanity are experiencing an incredible acceleration of the Divine Alchemy taking place within our bodies, and the *consciousness codes* within the DNA of the Millennials and the children have been activated, our Father-Mother God have given the I AM Presence of every person permission to take the patterns of perfection that have been building in momentum within our Heart Flames to brand new levels.

This Cosmic Dispensation will trigger within the Millennials and the children the sacred knowledge within their *consciousness codes* that will help them to bring these multidimensional and multifaceted patterns for the New Earth into physical manifestation much more quickly.

If you have the Heart Call to participate in this activity of Light, please join with me and Lightworkers all over the world who have been selflessly downloading these patterns for years. Through our I AM Presences, we will offer the collective Cup of our unified Heart Flames as the Open Door through which these greatly enhanced patterns of perfection for the New Earth will now be downloaded.

Take a deep breath, go within to the Divinity of your Heart Flame, and BE here now.

Downloading the Patterns of Perfection

I AM my I AM Presence and I AM One with my Father-Mother God, I AM One with the entire Company of Heaven and I AM One with the I AM Presence of every man, woman, and child on Earth.

As One Breath, One Heartbeat, One Voice and One Energy, Vibration and Consciousness of pure Divine Love we offer the Cup of our unified Heart Flames as the Open

Door for this activity of Light which we are invoking on behalf of the Lightworkers, the Millennials, the children and every other person on this planet.

Beloved Father-Mother God and the Legions of Light throughout Infinity download NOW from the Realms of Cause the highest and most exquisite frequencies of the patterns of perfection for the New Earth that Cosmic Law will allow.

As we invoke these patterns one by one, we ask that they be downloaded instantaneously into Humanity's newly balanced and recalibrated 5th-Dimensional Solar Immortal Victorious Threefold Flames. We know and accept that this will occur through each person's I AM Presence in perfect alignment with their Divine Plan and the highest good for all concerned. And we begin.

1. Beloved Father-Mother God download now the 5th-Dimensional Crystalline patterns of perfection from the Realms of Cause that are associated with the flow of Eternal Peace and God's Infinite Abundance, Opulence, Financial Freedom and the God-Supply of ALL good things.

2. Download now the 5th-Dimensional Crystalline patterns of perfection from the Realms of Cause that are associated with Eternal Youth, Vibrant Health, Radiant Beauty and the Perfect Form and Function of our Earthly Bodies.

3. Download now the 5th-Dimensional Crystalline patterns of perfection from the Realms of Cause that are associated with perfect health habits including Eating and Drinking Habits, Exercise, Work, Relaxation and Recreation Habits, and Spiritual Devotion, Meditation and Contemplation Habits.

4. Download now the 5th-Dimensional Crystalline patterns of perfection from the Realms of Cause that are associated with Divine Family Life, Loving Relationships, Adoration, Divine Love, Divine Sexuality, True Understanding, Clear and Effective Communication, Open Heart Sharing, Oneness and the Unification of the Family of Humanity.

5. Beloved Ones download now the 5th-Dimensional Crystalline patterns of perfection from the Realms of Cause that are associated with Harmony, Balance, Oneness and Reverence for ALL Life.

6. Download now the 5th-Dimensional Crystalline patterns of perfection from the Realms of Cause that are associated with Empowerment, Success, Fulfillment, Divine Purpose, a Rewarding Career, Self Esteem, Spiritual Development, Enlightenment, Divine Consciousness and Divine Perception.

7. Download now the 5th-Dimensional Crystalline patterns of perfection from the Realms of Cause that will initiate conscious open heart and mind telepathic communication through our I AM Presence with our Father-Mother God, the Company of Heaven, and the Angelic and Elemental Kingdoms.

8. Beloved Ones download now the 5th-Dimensional Crystalline patterns of perfection from the Realms of Cause that will inspire Creativity through Music, Singing, Sound, Toning, Dance, Movement, Art and Education.

9. Download now the 5th-Dimensional Crystalline patterns of perfection from the Realms of Cause that are associated with Laughter, Joy, Playfulness, Fun, Self-expression, Elation, Enthusiasm, Bliss, Ecstasy, Wonder and Awe.

10. And download now the 5th-Dimensional Crystalline patterns of perfection from the Realms of Cause that are associated with the tangible manifestation of Heaven on Earth and our NEW Planetary CAUSE of Divine Love.

We now accept and know that these NEW 5th-Dimensional Crystalline patterns of perfection have been successfully downloaded through our newly balanced and recalibrated 5th-Dimensional Solar Heart Flames. This activity of Light has been God Victoriously accomplished for the highest benefit of ALL Life evolving on this precious planet.

As we focus on these patterns day by day, our Father-Mother God will amplify them one thousand fold through our Planetary Grid of Transfiguring Divine Love.

Now in deep Humility, Divine Love and
Gratitude we decree, It is done. And so it is.

Beloved I AM. Beloved I AM. Beloved I AM That I AM.

78

Victory is Ours!

After the *32nd Annual World Congress on Illumination* I wrote our Monthly Newsletter describing step by step the miracles that took place during that sacred conclave. Our Newsletter is free and if you would like to receive it you may subscribe through our website www.eraofpeace.org.

I know there is a school of thought that professes *"there is no such thing as a miracle."* They say that whatever appears to be a miracle is just the synchronicity of energy, vibration and consciousness merging with the Natural Laws of Quantum Physics in ways that tangibly manifest change in the physical world of form. This belief, incidentally, is absolutely true. However, in my perception, the fact that you and I through our free will choices and our creative faculties of thought and feeling have the ability to use our Life Force to cocreate profound changes with the Company of Heaven in wondrous ways is a miracle in itself. So as we continue to move through this life-transforming Cosmic Moment in our Ascension process, I will continue to use the term miracle.

Now that the I AM Presence of each and every one of us has had the opportunity to assimilate and integrate the events that took place during the week of August 11 – 16, 2018, our Father-Mother God and the Company of Heaven are asking us to empower those miraculous activities of Light by focusing on them step by step. We will begin that process in this chapter continue for through the final chapters of this book. As we focus our attention on each of the miracles that were God Victoriously accomplished through the unified efforts of Heaven and Earth, these events will be amplified and empowered through the mental and emotional strata of this planet. This will allow the masses of Humanity to become much more aware of what has occurred on a conscious level. I will begin by sharing the events that took place on August 11, 2018.

When I began transcribing the wonders that took place during the *32nd WCI* I was overwhelmed, humbled and elated in ways I have not previously experienced. The Company of Heaven confirmed that hundreds of thousands of people around the world consciously joined with those of us gathered within the Portal of Light at Diamond Head in Honolulu, Hawaii from their various points of Light all over the planet. I was also clearly shown by our Father-Mother God that the I AM Presence of every single person on Earth assisted through the multidimensional aspects of their superconscious mind to cocreate the miracles that took place that week whether the person was consciously aware of it or not. Please read these words from within the Flame of Illumined Truth pulsating in the Divinity of your heart. Know that YOU were an essential part of this facet of our Father-Mother God's unfolding Divine Plan and that you God Victoriously succeeded in fulfilling a mission you have been preparing to accomplish for lifetimes.

The Hawaiian Islands are mountain peaks on the huge continent of Lemuria that used to exist in the Pacific Ocean. That is where the initial impulse of our fall from Grace took place aeons ago. When it was clear that we were spiraling into an abyss of our own making, our Father-Mother God determined that the continent of Lemuria must be submerged beneath the healing waters of the Pacific Ocean. When that catastrophic event occurred, Lemuria broke apart and a portion of it was pushed into the Southern Hemisphere. The islands of the South Pacific, Australia and New Zealand are all part of Lemuria.

In 2018 we were called back to Honolulu and the Portal of Light at Diamond Head for the 32nd WCI because our Father-Mother God and the Company of Heaven perceived that the awakening taking place within the hearts and minds of the masses of Humanity had reached the potential of reversing the adverse effects of our fall from Grace back to the initial impulse of the fall on Lemuria. They knew that if the Sons and Daughters of God embodied on Earth could accomplish that miracle, it would assure that the Millennials and the children would be able to transcend the toxic substances and the gross contaminations within their Earthly Bodies that had been preventing their I AM Presence from activating their *consciousness codes.*

There were both Celestial and Earthly events that assisted in paving the way for this monumental endeavor. For several weeks prior to the World Congress, the Earth and all her Life were bathed in powerful planetary alignments and a triple Eclipse Series that was brought to fruition during the Opening Ceremonies of the World Congress which took place on August 11, 2018. That weekend was also the peak of the annual Perseid Meteor Shower. As comets and meteors pass the Earth, they shake the ethers and break down the obsolete crystallized patterns and archetypes of Humanity's miscreations. This allows the Mighty Elohim, who are the Builders of form, to create a fluid field of unmanifest Divine Potential upon which new patterns associated with the unfolding Divine Plan can be encoded by Humanity and the Company of Heaven.

In addition to the assistance we received from the Cosmos in order to help Humanity and Mother Earth prepare for the upcoming events, there were several powerful outer-world activities that occurred as well. For several weeks prior to the conference the Elohim and the Directors of the Elements assisted in relieving the pressure building up in the body of Mother Earth through the accelerated Divine Alchemy she was experiencing in her Ascension process. This release of pressure was necessary in order for Mother Earth to be able to safely receive the unprecedented frequency of Light that would be needed to activate the *consciousness codes* within the DNA of the Holy Innocents. That release of pressure was accomplished during the eruption of the *Kaleo Volcano, on the Big Island of Hawaii.*

On July 22nd which is celebrated in the outer world as Mary Magdalene's Ascension Day, we entered the Sun Cycle of Leo. Leo represents the power and might within the Heart of a Lion. For millennia August 8th has been celebrated around the world as the Opening of the Lion's Gate. On August 8th every year a Portal of Light above the Pyramid and the statue of the Sphinx in Giza, Egypt is opened to full breadth. During that time, the Light of God flows through the Lion's Gate and empowers the I AM Presence of every person to strengthen the Immortal Victorious Threefold Flame in their heart.

This year as the Portal of the Lion's Gate was opened our Father-Mother God assisted the I AM Presence of every person to empower the Cosmic Tone reverberating within our newly recalibrated and balanced Heart Flames. The Divine Intent of that Cosmic Tone was to awaken within each of us the KNOWING that we are ONE and that there is no separation.

On that same day, *Hurricane Hector passed by the Hawaiian Islands clearing the atmosphere of the last vestiges of the surfacing dross prior to the activities of Light that would take place during the World Congress on Illumination.*

On August 11ᵗʰ the World Congress began with the Opening Ceremonies. That event was free and opened to the public allowing many Lightworkers from Honolulu and the surrounding areas to weave their magnificent Light into the Chalice of our unified Heart Flames.

During that event, our Father-Mother God infused our Planetary Grid of Transfiguring Divine Love with the highest frequencies of Light that Mother Earth and Humanity were capable of withstanding at an atomic and subatomic cellular level. This unfathomable frequency of Transfiguring Divine Love flooded the Earth amplifying the Divine Intentions of the Lightwork of every person on Earth one thousand fold in preparation for the miracles that were destined to be accomplished throughout the entire week.

During the Opening Ceremonies the attendees at the World Congress on Illumination were told the following:

"The most important presenter at this event is YOU. Your presence is the key to the fulfillment of this facet of the Divine Plan. Here is a brief biography of you which has been given to us by our Father-Mother God.

'You are a magnificent, multifaceted and multidimensional reflection of your Father-Mother God. You are a radiant Sun expressing ALL of the various frequencies of Divinity

pulsating in the Causal Body of God. You have volunteered to be an Instrument of God, and you are participating in the greatest leap in consciousness ever experienced in any system of worlds. Together we are cocreating a new octave of Godhood. Your service to the Light is expanding the Body of God without measure, and you are lifting every particle of Life ever breathed forth from the core of Creation into the dawn of a new Cosmic Day'."

The attendees were also told the following:

"The Divine Plan you have come to fulfill requires only one thing from you. That is your One-pointed Consciousness focused in buoyant Joy, Divine Love and Reverence for ALL Life.

"As you progress through these Holy Days, remember that above all things, your responsibility is to release the most loving, joyous, playful, uplifting, and harmonious energy you can possibly express. No matter what challenges or tests may be presented to you, know that nothing is worth moving you away from the Harmony of your True Being. It is time for you to BE the Peace Commanding Presence you have been preparing to be for aeons. And it is time for you to BE the most powerful force of Divine Love you are capable of being. This is your moment! And YOU are ready!"

The following was also shared with the attendees:

"Your I AM Presence prompted you to be physically present at this wondrous event because of the specific preparation you have experienced over myriad lifetimes. You have worked diligently for thousands of years to learn what you must do to victoriously accomplish this facet of the Divine Plan. This sacred knowledge is blazing in the deepest recesses of your heart, and it will easily be recalled when you need it.

"At this conclave you will join in consciousness with awakened Light Beings you have worked with for millennia, both in Celestial Realms and on Earth. When you are introduced to a new friend, know that you are merely renewing old friendships and reuniting with the loved ones you have known throughout time.

"As we sojourn through these Holy Days together, the activities of Light will be revealed to us step by step under the guidance of our Father-Mother God and the Company of Heaven. Each day as the activities are God Victoriously accomplished, the next phase of the Divine Plan will be set into motion. The activities of one day will be contingent on how well we succeeded in fulfilling our mission of Light the preceding day. This is a monumental moment in the evolution of this blessed Planet Earth. So BE HERE NOW!"

Dear One, please contemplate this information knowing that we are One and there is no separation.

79

CLEANSING THE PSYCHIC ASTRAL REALM

In this chapter I will share with you the next phase of the miraculous Divine Plan that was accomplished during the *32nd Annual World Congress on Illumination*. Every day we had enlightened presenters, wonderful singers, musicians, music, meditations and visualizations that blessed the attendees and enhanced the ability of every one of us to stay focused on the Light and our Divine Mission. Day by day, our Father-Mother God and the Company of Heaven guided us through activities of Light that enabled us to accomplish the facet of the Divine Plan intended for that day. Those activities of Light were multidimensional and were God Victoriously accomplished through the unified efforts of our Father-Mother God, the Company of Heaven and the embodied Lightworkers who participated at both inner and outer levels.

On August 12, 2018 our Father-Mother God said that the greatly intensified purging process Humanity had been going through since the beginning of the year had pushed tons of our human miscreations, negative thoughtforms and behavior patterns to the surface to be transmuted back into Light. They said this powerful purging process caused an unintended accumulation of negativity in the Psychic Astral Realm surrounding the Earth. Our God Parents revealed that this dense and very dark energy was interfering with the influx of Light from our Planetary Grid of Transfiguring Divine Love.

The Psychic Astral Realm is the sea of negativity surrounding the Earth that people who have gone through a near-death experience describe when they talk about passing through a *"dark tunnel"* on their journey into the Light. Our Father-Mother God said that cleansing the Psychic Astral Realm was a critical step in assuring the success of our Divine Mission.

We were all asked to be the Open Door for an activity of Light the Company of Heaven would lead us through. That activity was designed to transmute the dense negativity in the Psychic Astral Realm, so that the Light of God necessary for the activation of the consciousness codes within the DNA of the Millennials and the children would not be blocked from Earth. I will describe that awesome activity of Light step by step, so you can experience the magnitude of that Divine Intervention.

First, the Mighty Elohim who are the Builders of Form descended into the atmosphere of Earth and took their strategic positions equal distances around the equator of the planet. The Elohim were followed by Archangel Michael and his Legions of Power and Protection. Archangel Michael directed these tremendous Beings of Light to traverse the Earth and to project their powerful Swords of Blue Flame into all of the vulnerable areas and the wounds in the body of Mother Earth. Archangel Michael's Legions projected their Swords of Blue Flame into all of the tectonic plates, cracks, faults, fissures and weak areas in the body of Mother Earth. They also reinforced the areas where mining, drilling for oil, fracking and nuclear testing had taken place.

Next, under the direction of Saint Germain, Legions of 5th-Dimensional Violet Flame Archangels of Infinite Transmutation took their positions throughout the Psychic Astral Realm and within the atmosphere of every country, province, state, city, town and hamlet on Planet Earth.

Once this was accomplished, the Directors of the Elements took their positions at the four Cardinal Points. Thor and Aries and the Sylphs of the Air were stationed at the Cardinal Point to the North, Neptune and Lunara and the Undines of the Water were stationed at the Cardinal Point to the East, Pelleur and Virgo and the Nature Spirits of the Earth were stationed at the Cardinal Point to the South, Helios and Vesta and the Salamanders of the Fire were stationed at the Cardinal Point to the West and Aeolus and Amaryllis and the Devas and Deva Rajas of the Ether were stationed within the Sun of Even Pressure in the center of the Earth.

As all of these Beings of Light stood in readiness, our Father-Mother God bathed Mother Earth and all Life evolving upon her with a Healing unguent of their Divine Love and Comfort in preparation for the unprecedented cleansing process that was about to take place.

To begin the cleansing process, Saint Germain sounded a Cosmic Tone signaling his Violet Flame Archangels to begin blazing the most intensified frequencies of the Violet Flame of Infinite Transmutation that Cosmic Law would allow in, through and around the Psychic Astral Plane. Instantaneously, this unfathomable frequency of the Violet Flame shattered every remaining thoughtform, pattern, archetype and matrix that Humanity had either deliberately or inadvertently miscreated since our fall from Grace aeons ago.

When that facet of the cleansing process was complete, Saint Germain directed the Violet Flame Archangels standing within the atmosphere of every country, province, state, city, town and hamlet on Earth to blaze this powerful 5th-Dimensional Violet Flame of Infinite Transmutation in, through and around every current thought, feeling, word, action, memory and belief that the Sons and Daughters of God were expressing that were not based in Love.

After that unparalleled cleansing process was victoriously accomplished, the electronic Light substance and the atomic and subatomic particles and waves of energy that were forced to out picture those gross mutations by a fallen Humanity were taken into the Heart of our Father-Mother God and bathed with their Healing unguent of Comfort and Love.

As this previously distorted and grossly mutated intelligent electronic Light substance was Loved free and transmuted back into its original perfection, the electrons and the atomic and subatomic particles and waves of energy associated with this intelligent Light substance began to awaken to their Divine Potential.

As this happened, these precious particles of our Father-Mother God's Life Force began to remember their purpose and reason for being. They remembered that their original commitment was to assist the Sons and Daughters of God to out picture the patterns of perfection from the Causal Body of God in the physical world of form.

As the Directors of the Elements witnessed this awakening, they began magnetizing from the very Heart of God the most gentle frequencies of 5th-Dimensional Crystalline Solar Light that this previously distorted electronic Light substance was capable of receiving. Instantaneously, these precious Life Forms received, along with Humanity and all of the rest of Life evolving on Mother Earth, the next level of our Father-Mother God's Healing Blessings.

That wondrous Gift from On High was a Baptism by Sacred Fire from our Mother God, the Holy Spirit. As the Company of Heaven watched in breathless awe, our Mother God breathed her Holy Breath through the Portal of Light at Diamond Head and Baptized the Earth and all her Life with the Sacred Fire of her Transfiguring Divine Love.

Once that Gift of Sacred Fire was received by every particle and wave of Life on Earth, the Mighty Elohim Inbreathed Mother Earth and all her Life up the Spiral of Evolution into higher frequencies of the 5th-Dimensional Crystalline Solar New Earth than we had ever experienced.

Once that occurred, our Father-Mother God and the Company of Heaven bathed the I AM Presence of every man, woman and child on Earth with their Infinite Gratitude.

80

REMEMBERING THE ONENESS
OF ALL LIFE

This is the next phase of the activities of Light that cleared the way for the activation of the *consciousness codes* within the Millennials and the children during the 32nd WCI. On August 13th the Company of Heaven told us that through the cleansing activities of Light that were victoriously accomplished the previous day, the very dark and distorted energy in the Psychic Astral Realm was successfully transmuted into a veil of gossamer Light. They said this gossamer veil was now allowing greatly enhanced frequencies of Light to bathe the Earth through our Planetary Grid of Transfiguring Divine Love which paved the way for a new opportunity.

We were told by the Beings of Light that important shifts of energy, vibration and consciousness had taken place within the hearts and minds of the masses of Humanity since our Father-Mother God's new Divine Plan was initiated in January of 2018. They said these shifts allowed more Light than ever before to flow through every person's newly balanced and recalibrated Heart Flame during the opening of the Lion's Gate on August 8th.

That influx of Light allowed the I AM Presence of every person to open their 5th-Dimensional Heart Chakra to new breadths. The Beings of Light said the increased Light that had been flowing through every person's Heart Chakra since August 8th had gently softened and prepared our hearts for the next phase of our Divine Mission.

Our Father-Mother God reiterated to us the greatest need of the hour. They affirmed that since the July 12th New Moon Solar Eclipse that began the rare triple Eclipse Series we had just experienced, they had been sounding a Cosmic Tone within the silence of every person's Heart Flame. The Divine Intent of that Cosmic Tone was to awaken within each of us the knowing that we are One and that there is no separation. We were told that our Divine Mission for August 13th was to be the Open Door for a greatly intensified activity of Light that would exponentially expand that holy endeavor.

The Company of Heaven guided us through an activity of Light that was designed to Love ALL Life free and to assist every person on Earth, even the most recalcitrant and asleep Sons and Daughters of God, to hear the Cosmic Tone that was reverberating within their Heart Flame.

Within an Invincible Forcefield of God's Infinite Love, we took our sisters and brothers into the Kingdom of Heaven within our heart. We embraced them in our arms of Light as we would an injured child. They could not overwhelm us or control us in any way, nor did we need to fear them or shun them. We simply held them and Loved them until they surrendered to the Love of God, desiring on their own to enter the Kingdom of Heaven within the Divinity of their own Heart Flames.

The Beings of Light said that rather than feeling rejected and thus perpetuating their negative behavior patterns, our sisters and brothers felt accepted and Loved as the innate Sons and Daughters of God they are.

Through their multidimensional superconscious minds these precious Ones then voluntarily released themselves into the Light. As they did, they began to remember that they are One with ALL Life and that there is no separation. Within the deepest recesses of their hearts they realized that Love is ALL there is.

As this occurred, our Father-Mother God asked us to focus on the words they shared with us 15 years ago when our Mother God was finally able to return to Earth and reclaim her position within the Divinity of every person's Heart Flame.

Please go within to the Divinity of your heart and contemplate these words describing the Love of our Mother God.

"So much has been written about Love that it has almost become a platitude, but the Transfiguring Divine Love of our Mother God is the mightiest force in the Universe. It is the vibration from which we were born out of the Heart of God and it is the vibration through which we must now evolve and Ascend back into the Heart of God. The Love of our Mother God has no bonds, nor barriers or conditions. Within the infinite power of our Mother God's Love there is no pain or sorrow, no lack or limitation. Her Love contains within its essence the full potential to rise above all human conditions, all self-inflicted suffering, and all manner of chaos, confusion, hopelessness and despair.

"Our Mother God's Love heals the illusion of separation. It rejuvenates, revitalizes and makes whole all that it embraces. It is the single greatest source of Forgiveness,

and it reverberates with the full gathered momentum of our Eternal Freedom in the Light. Our Mother's Love is the foundation of ALL Creation. It is the indivisible, unchanging ecstasy that allows us to know Love in all things. When we experience the Love of our Mother God, we understand that we are all One. We KNOW that every particle and wave of Life is interconnected, interdependent and interrelated. Whether we are a magnificent Sun, a person or a blade of grass, we are united in the Body of our Father-Mother God by the all encompassing cohesive Light of our Mother God's Transfiguring Divine Love.

"As our Mother God reclaims this Earth and once again anoints Humanity with her Infinite Love, we are beginning to experience a deep Reverence for ALL Life. Our Mother's Love is now pulsating within the core of our Beings; it is not outside of us. We no longer need to seek the Divine Feminine from afar. We need to merely accept that our Mother God has returned, and that she is now abiding within every person's Heart Flame. Her Love is pulsating within the silent rhythm of every heartbeat, every breath. It is the universal language now speaking to all Humanity through our Gift of Life. As we take the time to listen in the silence of our heart, we hear the tones and whisperings of our Mother's Love inspired by the wonders of Nature and the Music of the Spheres.

"Our Mother God is now reestablishing her Covenant of Divine Love with the Children of Earth, which will enhance our ability to once and for all accept the Gifts of Eternal Peace and God's Infinite Abundance. Through this Covenant, the supply of all good things will forever and ever flood into the hands and use of the Sons and Daughters of God. The glory of God's Eternal Peace and Infinite Abundance

*will be a manifest reality not only in this moment, but far
beyond the Earth and time into Eternity."*

With the completion of those words, our Father-Mother
God's Cosmic Tone exponentially expanded within every
person's Heart Flame. As it built in momentum throughout the day, the I AM Presence of every person assisted in
awakening within their Heart Flame the knowing that *"We
are One."*

81

AN UNPRECEDENTED HEALING
FROM MOTHER MARY AND
PALLAS ATHENA

As I continue sharing information about the various events that took place in August during the 32nd Annual World Congress on Illumination, the Company of Heaven wants to remind us that through the focus of our attention we are empowering these activities of Light. This is assisting the I AM Presence of every person on Earth to integrate these miracles into our hearts and conscious minds.

On August 14, 2018 we all participated in the activity of Light that was shared around the world that morning on our Weekly Vlog 75. In order to intensify that activity of Light in monumental ways, our Father-Mother God asked the Angel of Resurrection to intervene. In response to our God Parent's request, the Angel of Resurrection descended into the atmosphere of Earth and expanded his luminous Presence until the Earth and all her Life were cradled within the Divinity of his Heart.

The Angel of Resurrection then breathed the most intensified frequencies of the Mother of Pearl

Resurrection Flame that we were capable of receiving into the Core of Purity in every atomic and subatomic particle and wave of Life on Earth. This Gift of the Resurrection Flame greatly enhanced the activity of Light we were guided through on Vlog 75. As One unified Heart Flame, thousands of people around the world participated with us consciously. Together, we accelerated the Divine Alchemy taking place within the Earthly Bodies of every man, woman and child completing the next level of our physical preparation.

After that activity of Light in the morning, the attendees at the conference had a free day. They were guided to listen to their heart and to go wherever they were inspired to go on the island. Everywhere these dedicated Lightworkers went, they spread their Light and expanded the Portal of Light at Diamond Head in preparation for the events that would take place on August 15th and 16th.

August 15th is celebrated around the world as Mother Mary's Ascension Day. The exquisite Light associated with this exponent of our Mother God and the Divine Feminine began bathing the Earth the moment the Sun crossed the International Date Line in the Pacific Ocean. This was actually August 14th in Honolulu, Hawaii. On August 14th Mother Mary projected her luminous Presence into the auras of the attendees at the World Congress as they traversed the island. In preparation for the next day, Mother Mary anchored her Healing Light wherever these dedicated Lightworkers were called to be.

On August 15th, as Mother Mary's Healing Light continued to infuse our Planetary Grid of Transfiguring Divine Love, she asked her Beloved Sister Pallas Athena to join her for an unprecedented activity of Healing. Pallas Athena is known through all Creation as the Goddess of Truth and the Keeper of the Flame of Illumined Truth. She joyfully accepted Mother Mary's invitation.

As the luminous Presence of Mother Mary and Pallas Athena pulsated in the atmosphere of Earth, Mother Mary breathed the Madonna Blue and Crystalline White Flame of the Immaculate Concept into the Heart Flame of every person on Earth. This Sacred Fire contains within its frequencies the matrix for the Divine Potential within every Son and Daughter of God.

Once the Flame of the Immaculate Concept was secured within every Heart Flame, Pallas Athena breathed the Emerald Green and Sunshine Yellow Flame of Illumined Truth into the Heart Flame of every person. The Divine Intent of that Gift from Pallas Athena was to illuminate and to awaken within every person the profound Truth of who we are and why we are on Earth during this auspicious Cosmic Moment.

When all was in readiness Mother Mary and Pallas Athena assisted the I AM Presence of every person on Earth to anchor the Immaculate Concept of our Divine Potential and the Illumined Truth of who we are and why we are here within the Core of Purity in every electron of our physical, etheric, mental and emotional bodies.

When that was complete, those of us gathered within the Portal of Light at Diamond Head were asked to serve as surrogates on behalf of the Millennials and the children for an activation of their 5th-Dimensional Crystalline Solar Light Bodies. As we were guided through this powerful activation, we also held the sacred space for the activation of the 5th-Dimensional Crystalline Solar Light Bodies of both awakened and unawakened Humanity.

After that activity of Light was complete, Mother Mary sent forth her Legions of 5th-Dimensional Archangels to gather from all time frames and dimensions the indigenous Grandmothers and Grandfathers who have tenaciously held the sacred space and the Divine Intention that one day Mother Earth would be restored to her original beauty and glorious expression of Heaven on Earth.

In response to the Clarion Call of Mother Mary's Archangels, our precious ancestors in the Family of Humanity, from all indigenous traditions, descended into the atmosphere of Earth from the far reaches of the Cosmos. These selfless Ones traversed the Earth north, south, east and west and took their strategic positions within Mother Earth's Crystal Grid System to serve as acupuncture needles along the meridians of this planet.

The Mighty Elohim and the Directors of the Elements then took their strategic positions around the Earth in order to assist with the final step of preparation for the most intensified Healing that Humanity and Mother Earth had ever received.

When all was in readiness, Mother Mary sounded a Cosmic Tone and the Mighty Elohim began Inbreathing from the Core of Creation the most intensified frequencies of the Emerald Green and Violet Flame of Healing Through the Power of Transmutation that Cosmic Law would allow.

Then on the Outbreath, these Mighty Builders of Form breathed this unfathomable Healing Flame into our Planetary Grid of Transfiguring Divine Love. Once this Healing Light was infused into our Grid of Divine Love, it was anchored within the Heart Flames of the indigenous Grandmothers and Grandfathers stationed along the acupuncture meridians in Mother Earth's Crystal Grid System.

Once the Healing Flame was secured within the Heart Flames of our ancestors, on the Outbreath they breathed these powerful new frequencies of the Emerald

Green and Violet Flame of Healing Through the Power of Transmutation through their Heart Chakras and secured it in the physical world of form.

With the assistance of every person's I AM Presence, this powerful Healing Light was encoded within the Core of Purity in every atomic and subatomic particle and wave of Humanity's physical, etheric, mental and emotional bodies. This miraculous activity of Light, blessed this sweet Earth and all her Life with the most effective and intensified Healing we had ever received.

That afternoon our Father-Mother God revealed to us that the activities of Light that had been God Victoriously accomplished during the first days of the World Congress had created a rare opportunity for the recalcitrant souls who were still resisting Earth's Ascension in the Light to reclaim their path of Divine Love. The Company of Heaven said the possibility of that miracle occurring during the 32nd WCI was actually beyond their greatest expectations

82

A RARE OPPORTUNITY FOR THE RECALCITRANT SOULS

As we continue sharing information about the various miracles that took place in August 2018 to assist with activating the *consciousness codes* of the Millennial's and the children, the Company of Heaven wants to remind us that through the focus of our attention on these events we are empowering the results of these activities of Light. This is assisting the I AM Presence of every person on Earth to integrate the outer-world affects of these miracles into their heart and conscious mind much more quickly.

During the afternoon of August 15th, our Father-Mother God revealed to us that the activities of Light that had been God Victoriously accomplished during the first days of the *32nd Annual World Congress on Illumination* had created a rare opportunity for the recalcitrant souls, who were still resisting Earth's Ascension in the Light, to reclaim their path of Divine Love.

These recalcitrant souls are our sisters and brothers who were in danger of being left behind during the Shift of the Ages but who, through an act of Divine Grace, eventually made the decision to do what was necessary in order to transmute their karmic liabilities in time. After the New Earth was birthed in the Realms of Cause and the Shift of the Ages was victoriously accomplished on December 21–22, 2012, our wayward sisters and brothers began to tangibly experience what it meant for them to give up their power and greed in order to function from a place of Oneness and Reverence for all Life. This terrified them and caused them to revert to the old behavior patterns they have used for centuries to control and manipulate the masses of Humanity.

Tragically when that occurred, our recalcitrant sisters and brothers began to renege on their commitment to transmute their karmic liabilities. Instead, they began doing whatever they could to block Humanity's forward progress in the Light. Their actions are what caused our Father-Mother God to initiate the New Divine Plan in 2018. The Divine Intent of that plan was to greatly empower every person's Lightwork and to inspire awakening Humanity to assist with the activation the *consciousness codes* within the DNA of the Millennials and the children.

On August 15th, in a powerful activity of Light involving their I AM Presence and their multidimensional consciousness, these fallen Sons and Daughters of God were called Home and escorted by Mother Mary and Pallas Athena into the very Heart of our Father-Mother God. In the Realms of Illumined Truth, they were once again shown who they truly are as Beloved Sons and Daughters of God.

While the Lightworkers gathered in Honolulu, Hawaii and those tuning in from around the world held the sacred space, our Father-Mother God gave our sisters and brothers another chance to commit to their agreement of transmuting their karmic liabilities and of reclaiming the Path of Divine Love they will need to follow on their journey to the 5th-Dimensional New Earth.

When that activity of Light was complete, the Company of Heaven said that a critical mass of these resistant souls had made the choice to renew their commitment to transmute their karmic liabilities and to return to the Path of Divine Love. This positive decision by a critical mass of our resistant sisters and brothers created an unstoppable shift that lifted the remaining recalcitrant souls, who had refused this opportunity, into a Higher Order of Being. This will hopefully give their I AM Presence and the Company of Heaven a better chance of still reaching them before the completion of the final stages of Earth's Ascension into the 5th-Dimensional Crystalline Solar frequencies of the New Earth.

The Company of Heaven asked us to contemplate that event, and to take time to try and fathom the magnitude of that demonstration of our Father-Mother God's Infinite Grace.

83

ACTIVATION OF THE CONSCIOUSNESS CODES WITHIN THE MILLENNIALS AND THE CHILDREN

As you read this final chapter, know that the focus of your attention is empowering these miraculous activities of Light. Our Father-Mother God said this is assisting the I AM Presence of every person on Earth to assimilate these wondrous events into our hearts and conscious minds.

August 16, 2018 was the final day of the *32nd Annual World Congress on Illumination.* As Beloved Pallas Athena embraces us all in the Flame of Illumined Truth, I will share with you step by step the wonders that unfolded that glorious day.

Our Father-Mother God revealed to us that since July 12th, which was the New Moon Solar Eclipse that initiated the triple Eclipse Series we had just experienced, the Millennials and the children had been escorted into the Temples of the Central Sun of Alpha and Omega in their finer bodies as they slept at night.

Through their I AM Presence and within their multidimensional consciousness, these Holy Innocents were given refresher courses to remind them of the sacred knowledge they have encoded within their *consciousness codes.* This knowledge contains viable solutions to the maladies on Earth and new information that they will use to assist Humanity and all Life on this planet to cocreate the patterns of perfection for the New Earth. The Company of Heaven said that this sacred knowledge would surface into their conscious minds in Divine Timing once these codes were activated within their DNA.

During the night time hours of August 15th-16th, within the Eternal Moment of Now, a glorious graduation ceremony took place for the Millennials and the children. That celebration occurred within the Temples of our Great, Great Central Sun. The Solar Logos for that Sun are El and Ela. Attending the ceremony were the I AM Presences of the Sons and Daughters of God evolving on Earth who have been holding the sacred space for the awakening of the Millennials and the children. The guests also included the I AM Presences of our asleep and recalcitrant sisters and brothers who had just renewed their commitment to return to the Path of Divine Love. That sacred and holy night these previously resistant souls were given permission to enter the Temples of El and Ela for the very first time.

The morning of August 16th began with a glorious procession through the Portals of the Suns in our system of worlds. El and Ela led the procession involving the Millennials, the children and all of us who were celebrating with them through the Portal of the Great, Great Central Sun. Then El and Ela were joined by Elohae and Eloha as the procession passed through the Portal of the Great Central Sun. Next El and Ela and Elohae and Eloha were joined by Alpha and

Omega as the procession passed through the Portal of the Central Sun. And finally Helios and Vesta joined the procession as we all passed through the Portal of our physical Sun.

As this glorious procession descended into the atmosphere of Earth, the Holy Innocents and the rest of the Family of Humanity embodied on Earth traversed the planet taking our places within our specific locations around the world. When this was complete, all was in readiness for the activation of the *consciousness codes* within the DNA of the Millennials and the children.

The first activity of Light was conducted by Beloved Kwan Yin. This Feminine Being of Light represents our Mother God in the Buddhist tradition. Kwan Yin is known through all Creation as the Goddess of Divine Family Life. In a sacred initiation, Kwan Yin guided the I AM Presences of the Mothers and Fathers and the Grandmothers and Grandfathers of the Millennials and the children through an activity of Light that awakened within them the highest possible frequencies of Christ Consciousness. This initiation will help them remember that they have been preparing for lifetimes to be the most nurturing and enlightening support systems possible for the awakening Holy Innocents. At the conclusion of the initiation, Kwan Yin blessed Mother Earth and the entire Family of Humanity with her Celestial Song.

Next, the Mighty Elohim took their strategic positions equal distance around the equator of the Earth. All twelve masculine and feminine Elohim brought to Earth within the Divinity of their Heart Flames powerful new frequencies of the Twelve 5th-Dimensional Crystalline Solar Aspects of Deity. It is this 5th-Dimensional Crystalline Solar Light substance that the Holy Innocents and the rest of Humanity will use to cocreate the patterns of perfection for the New Earth.

The Elohim were followed by Serapis Bey and his Angelic Legions of the Ascension Flame. These Mighty Angels traversed the Earth and took their positions in, through and around every facet of Life on this planet. When they were in their designated positions, these magnificent Ascension Angels Inbreathed the Crystalline White Ascension Flame from the Heart of God, and projected it on the Outbreath into the Core of Purity within every electron of precious Life energy on Earth. With the Ascension Flame blazing through every particle and wave of Life in the body of Mother Earth and all Life evolving upon her, the activation of the *consciousness codes* within the DNA of the Holy Innocents began.

Our Father-Mother God sounded a Cosmic Tone and the Mighty Elohim began their descent into the center of the Earth carrying within their Heart Flames the highest frequencies of the Twelve Solar Aspects of Deity the Earth had ever experienced. As they entered the Sun of Even Pressure in the Heart of Mother Earth, they knelt before the mighty pillar of Light that forms the axis of the Earth.

One by one, the Elohim breathed the specific Aspect of Deity they were responsible for into the Twelve 5th-Dimensional Solar Chakras aligned along the axis of Mother Earth. When the Elohim were finished, Mother Earth's Twelve Solar Chakras were pulsating with the highest frequencies of the Twelve 5th-Dimensional Solar Aspects of Deity that this planet had ever experienced. Within each Chakra, all Twelve Solar Aspects of Deity formed the *Circle of the Sacred Twelve.*

When that phase of the Divine Ceremony was complete, the exquisite Light anchored in Mother Earth's Chakras began radiating through her Crystal Grid System. As it did, the Grandmothers and the Grandfathers from all indigenous traditions who were selflessly serving as acupuncture needles within Mother Earth's Crystal Grid System, breathed this Light into their Heart Flames and permanently secured it in the physical, etheric, mental and emotional strata of Mother Earth.

With that activity of Light complete, the frequency of Light from the Heart of our Father-Mother God that would allow the I AM Presences of the Millennials and the children to activate the *consciousness code* within their DNA began flowing into our Planetary Grid of Transfiguring Divine Love. As that unfathomable Light flowed through the Portal at Diamond Head, it descended into the Heart of Mother Earth and was transmitted through her Crystal Grid System into the newly balanced and recalibrated Heart Flames of awakening Humanity.

Through the dedication and the Divine Intentions of Lightworkers around the world, our Father-Mother God's Light was amplified one thousand fold as it entered the Twelve 5th-Dimensional Solar Strands of DNA within the Holy Innocents. As this occurred, the I AM Presence of every child and every Millennial gently activated the *consciousness codes* that were placed in their DNA prior to this embodiment.

Once this miraculous event was God Victoriously accomplished in perfect Divine Order, our Father-Mother God revealed to us that this blessed planet was now pulsating with a frequency of Light that would allow her to Ascend up the Spiral of Evolution and, at long last, reclaim her rightful place in our Solar System. This is something that Mother Earth had not been able to accomplish since our fall from Grace aeons ago.

As all Creation watched in breathless awe, our Father-Mother God Inbreathed Mother Earth and all Life evolving upon her up the Spiral of Evolution where she was able to reclaim her rightful place in the Solar Systems of Helios and Vesta, Alpha and Omega, Elohae and Eloha and El and Ela.

Our Father-Mother God then revealed that with the success of that awesome event the old Earth was absorbed into the Light of the New Earth. **This means that the old Earth no longer exists.** Our God Parents said that only a small amount of the negative residue from Humanity's miscreations remains to be transmuted into the Light.

Now, through our deliberate and heart-based efforts, the Millennials, the children and the rest of Humanity will be able to cocreate the patterns of perfection for the New Earth in ways that we have not even dreamed about.

Our Father-Mother God and the Company of Heaven are asking all of us to stay focused on the Light, to listen to our hearts, and to BE the Open Door for the Light of God that no one can shut.

We are the cocreators of the New Earth. And with the God Victorious accomplishment of this miraculous facet of our Father-Mother God's Divine Plan, our purpose and reason for being has moved a quantum leap forward in the Light.

Whether we are in or out of embodiment, we now have the responsibility of holding the Immaculate Concept for the successful fulfillment of the Divine Plans for the Millennials and the children. This includes those embodied now and those yet to come.

Our Father-Mother God, the Company of Heaven, Mother Earth and the I AM Presence of every person on this planet are Eternally Grateful for you, and your willingness to BE the Instrument of God you have been preparing to be for lifetimes.

God Bless you Dear One. Know that Victory is Ours!

ABOUT THE AUTHOR
PATRICIA COTA-ROBLES

Patricia is cofounder and president of the nonprofit, educational organization New Age Study of Humanity's Purpose, which is now doing business as Era of Peace. Era of Peace sponsors Patricia's work and the *Annual World Congress on Illumination.*

Patricia was a marriage and family counselor for 20 years. She now spends her time freely sharing the information she is receiving from our Father-Mother God and the Company of Heaven. This is accomplished through her website **www.eraofpeace.org,** her weekly vlogs, online webinars, teleconferences, monthly email articles, YouTube videos, Facebook sharings, online radio shows, and the Free Seminars titled *"It is Time to Take the Next Step"* that she offers throughout the United States. She also distributes the information she is receiving from On High through her many books, E-books, CDs, MP3s and DVDs.

This sacred knowledge clearly reveals the Bigger Picture of the events unfolding on Earth at this time. This heart-based perspective is designed to enlighten Humanity by giving all of us greater insight, encouragement, clarity and understanding as we progress through these wondrous but often challenging times on Earth.

Patricia is an internationally known teacher and has taught workshops in the former Soviet Union, Ireland, England, South Africa, the Dominican Republic, Venezuela, Brazil, Bolivia, Mexico, Canada, Greece, Italy, Australia, New Zealand, Thailand, France, Bali, Turkey, Japan, and throughout the United States of America. She participated in the *Soviet-American Citizens' Summit* in Moscow, and represented the United States in the category of Holistic Models in Health, Psychology, and Healing. Patricia also participated in the *First Global Earth Summit* held in Rio de Janeiro, Brazil. Patricia had the honor of being a presenter at the *"Call to World Peace from the Universal Brotherhood"* gathering in Istanbul, Turkey, and the *"Symphony of Peace Prayers,"* which was a gathering of over 10,000 people that took place at sacred Mt. Fuji in Japan.

Patricia's philosophy is: Every person is precious and Divine, regardless of how far his or her behavior patterns and life experiences may be from reflecting that Truth. We are not the victims of our lives. We are the cocreators of our lives. We have a choice, and we have the ability to transform our lives into what we want them to be. The time for us to do so is now!

Printed in Great Britain
by Amazon

46216102R00271